THE FUTURE OF EDUCATION FROM 14+

Apprenticeship

Towards a New Paradigm of Learning

**Edited by
Patrick Ainley and
Helen Rainbird**

**KOGAN
PAGE**

First published 1999

Kogan Page Limited
120 Pentonville Road
London N1 9JN

British Library Cataloguing in Publication Data

A CIP record for this book is available from the British Library.

ISBN 0 7494 2728 0

Typeset by Kogan Page Limited
Printed and bound in Great Britain by Biddles Ltd, Guildford and King's Lynn

Contents

Contents

Contributors

Patrick Ainley is Reader in Learning Policy at the University of Greenwich School of Post-compulsory Education and Training. His latest book is *Learning Policy: Towards the certified society* (Macmillan, 1999).

Richard Aldrich is Professor of History of Education at the Institute of Education, University of London, Head of the History and Philosophy Group, and a former President of the International Standing Conference for the History of Education and of the British History of Education Society.

Stephanie Bunn is an anthropologist currently undertaking fieldwork in Kyrghizia. She is also an artist and weaver whose hedges can be seen in the New Botanical Gardens on the Wirral.

Dr Linda Clarke is Reader in the Westminster Business School, University of Westminster, researching and teaching on training and employee relations in Europe. Her publications include *Building Capitalism* (Routledge, 1992) and, with Christine Wall, *A Blueprint for Change: Construction skills training in Britain* (Policy Press, 1998).

Phil Cohen is Reader in Cultural Studies at the University of East London, where he directs the Centre for New Ethnicities Research. His most recent book is *Rethinking the Youth Question – Education, labour and cultural studies* (Macmillan, 1997).

Karen Evans is Director of the University of Surrey's Postgraduate Centre for Professional and Adult Education. She is a Professor in Post-compulsory Education and Training, a field of study she has pioneered and developed in the University of Surrey. She has directed numerous research studies on aspects of learning and the world of work.

Michael A Forrester is Senior Lecturer in Psychology at the University of Kent, Canterbury. His research interests include conversation skills, critical developmental psychology and communication. Forthcoming publications include *Psychology of the Image* to be published by Routledge.

Alison Fuller is an associate member of the Centre for Research into Post-compulsory Education and Training at the University of Sheffield and a freelance researcher. She founded and co-ordinates the national Work and Learning Network with Lorna Unwin.

David Guile is Research Officer at the Post-16 Education Centre, Institute of Education, University of London. His current interests are learning in work-based contexts. He is undertaking a comparative study of work experience funded through the EU TSER 4th Framework. His most recent publications include *Information and Communication Technologies and Education* (Institute of Education, 1999).

Phil Hodkinson is Professor of Education in the Crewe School of Education of the Manchester Metropolitan University. He has written and researched widely on vocational education and training policy and practice. He has a particular interest in the progression of young people through post-compulsory education and in their career decision-making.

Prue Huddleston is Principal Research Fellow and Director of the Centre for Education and Industry, University of Warwick. She has a particular interest in the post-16 curriculum focusing on vocational qualifications. She is involved in postgraduate teacher training, in addition to which she has been involved in assignments for the DfEE, DTI, European Commission, companies, colleges, schools and local authorities.

Ewart Keep was a member of the CBI's Education and Training Directorate between 1985 and 1998. He worked at the Industrial Relations Research Unit at the University of Warwick. In 1998 he became the Deputy Director of the ESRC's Research Centre on Skills, Knowledge and Organizational Performance (SKOPE) at the University of Warwick. He has written extensively on UK vocational education and training policy, youth training, the learning society and personnel management in the education sector.

Malcolm Maguire is Principal Research Fellow at the Institute for Employment Research, University of Warwick. He has been undertaking research into aspects of employment, training and the labour market since 1975. Recent topics include: national targets for education and training; Modern Apprenticeships; lifetime learning; employee development schemes; the youth labour market; and the development of labour market indicators.

David Raffe is Professor of Sociology of Education at the University of Edinburgh, where he directs the Centre for Education Sociology and co-directs the Institute for the Study of Education and Society. He has worked on secondary, further and higher education, vocational training and the labour market transitions of young people. He has studied post-16 developments in Scotland, England and other European countries.

Helen Rainbird is Professor of Industrial Relations at University College Northampton and an Associate Fellow at the Industrial Relations Research Unit at the University of Warwick. Her research interests lie in the relationship between industrial relations and vocational training. She is the author of *Training Matters: Industrial restructuring and training* (Blackwell, 1990) and co-editor with Annette Jobert, Catherine Marry and Lucie Tanguy of *Education and Work in Great Britain, Germany and Italy* (Routledge, 1997).

Glenn Rikowski is Research Fellow in Post-compulsory Education and Training in the University of Birmingham School of Education. He has written widely on Marxist educational theory, labour power theory and Nietzschean perspectives on education. He is currently working on a critique of the notion of 'employability' and editing a book on post-modern excess in educational theory, to be published by the Tufnell Press.

Paul Ryan is Lecturer in the Faculty of Economics and Politics and Fellow of King's College at the University of Cambridge. His publications include *The Problem of Youth: The regulation of youth employment and training in advanced economies,* co-edited with Paolo Garonna and Richard Edwards (Macmillan, 1992) and *International Comparisons of VET for Intermediate Skills* (Falmer Press, 1992).

Peter Senker is Chairman of IPRA and Visiting Professor in the department of Innovation Studies, University of East London. He has had 25 years of research and consultancy experience related mainly to training in the engineering and construction industries in IPRA and in the Science Policy Research Unit and Institute of Education at the University of Sussex.

Lorna Unwin is Senior Lecturer and Director of the Centre for Research in Post-compulsory Education and Training at the University of Sheffield. She is currently carrying out research on the Modern Apprenticeship and, with Alison Fuller, on the workplace as a site for learning.

Edwin Webb has worked in secondary schools and a technical college. He is Reader in English and Education in the School of Post-compulsory Education and Training, the University of Greenwich, London. His writings cover a diverse range of literary and critical subjects as well as educational matters.

Michael Young is Professor and Director of the Post-16 Centre at the Institute of Education, University of London. His research interests include curriculum issues in secondary and post-secondary education and their links to changes in world economies and in the organization of work. He recently published *The Curriculum of the Future: From the 'new sociology of education' to a critical theory of learning* (Falmer Press, 1998).

Series Editors' Preface

We have included this volume in the *Future of Education from 14+* series both because of its theoretical strengths and also because we feel there is a need to counteract the tendency in the UK to marginalize the role of work-based education and training.

A book on apprenticeship and the role of workplace learning is a timely addition to the current literature on education and training in the UK. At the end of the 20th century, the UK is firmly stuck in a 'medium participation/low achievement' education and training system. After dramatic rises in participation and achievement rates from the late 1980s to the mid-1990s, the percentage of 16-year-olds now staying on in full-time education has begun to decline and the increase in achievement rates at GCSE, A level and Advanced Level GNVQ has significantly slowed.

In this changing context, there is a renewed interest in the potential role of work-based learning, particularly in relation to motivating young people to continue in education and training and to gain further qualifications and skills. This interest has also been stimulated by the introduction of Modern Apprenticeships in 1995 and National Traineeships in 1997. These programmes are attempting to overcome the legacy of poor quality training in this country and the association of the work-based route with second class education. However, several of the authors in this volume highlight the limitations of the current apprenticeship frameworks.

The growing interest in work-based learning is not simply confined to the UK. Even those countries that have strong patterns of full-time participation in the 16–19 age range (for example, the Scandinavian countries), are exploring the potential of apprenticeships and work-based learning for the development of higher level skills. Moreover, in those countries which have traditionally had strong apprenticeship systems (such as Germany and Austria), experimentation is taking place with new models of learning in the workplace to respond to changing patterns of production and work.

This book attempts to define the specific contribution of apprenticeship to the education and training of young people. It explores the historical roots of apprenticeship as well as its more contemporary forms. The main focus of the book, however, is a discussion of one of the major strengths of the apprenticeship system; that is, the idea of a 'community of learners'. This concept is then applied more widely as a way of exploring different contexts for learning and, in doing so, challenges some of the prevailing pedagogical orthodoxies. In particular, the concept of a community of learners raises questions about the current preoccupation with the individualization of learning.

One of the underlying messages of the book is that the social context for learning should be seen as a major factor in any learning situation. The way in which the book broadens its focus to combine a study of apprenticeship with discussion around new theories of learning ensures it a place in future debates about changes in economic life, pedagogy and lifelong learning.

Ann Hodgson and Ken Spours
Institute of Education
University of London

Acknowledgements

This book draws on a collection of papers presented at an ESRC seminar series on 'Apprenticeship in Education and Work' held at University College Northampton between 1996 and 1997. It represented a collaboration with the University of Greenwich's School of Post-compulsory Education and Training. The editors are grateful to the ESRC for funding the seminar series, to colleagues at University College Northampton for their support and hospitality, and to all the participants in the four workshops who made it such an interesting and challenging series. We would like to thank, in particular, Charlotte Knight and Michelle Webster at the Nene Centre for Research for their professionalism in preparing the manuscript for publication. Helen would also like to thank Francisco Salazar for his support and understanding throughout the project, and Patrick thanks Beulah and Adam as usual.

Introduction

Patrick Ainley and Helen Rainbird

Towards a new paradigm of learning

After a period of decline in the 1970s and its official denigration in the 1980s as 'mere time-serving', the concept of apprenticeship is now exciting interest not only for academic research and in professional disciplines but as an active policy issue. Whether it concerns day release in further education colleges, training for professional employment in higher education or the Department for Education and Employment's Modern Apprenticeships associated with work-based learning, this form of skill acquisition and learning is enjoying a renaissance both in Britain and elsewhere. (See for example, the special edition of the *Journal of Vocational Education and Training*, 1998, or the international comparative perspective presented by Finlay *et al,* 1998). However, it is as a model for thinking about all learning that apprenticeship affords a focus for what can be described as a new paradigm for learning about learning. This book aims to introduce readers to this new way of thinking about what learning is and how it occurs, through its examination of apprenticeships of many different types from a variety of perspectives.

New ways of thinking about learning are prompted by 'changing divisions of knowledge and labour' (Ainley, 1993) that are reintegrating manual and mental labour in many areas of employment. These changes are driven by incrementally rapid technological transformations and accompanying reorganizations of work. Even where manual and mental labour are not being so integrated, the new information and communications technology (ICT) provides the potential for doing so. This has led to a reconceptualization of 'knowledge' and 'skill'. From being for so long considered separately, they are also now being reintegrated theoretically, though still thought of in terms of an obdurate individualism that mistakes the social nature of knowledge/skill. As a consequence, different academic disciplines – themselves becoming accessible to one another through new forms of inter-communication that represent information and knowledge across traditional subject boundaries – are approaching the central subject of learning from different directions. As this collection shows, they are building towards a new paradigm for understanding learning. Such a new paradigm would place, as Ranson wrote (1993: 177):

> a theoretically informed education discipline at the centre of the social sciences whose task is to understand the conditions for creating a learning society. This would [he continues] move the field of education from its perceived position at the periphery to the centre of analysis and purpose within the social sciences as much as within the study of society.

It was the recognition that such a new paradigm was in formation that stimulated the seminar series on which this book is based. The Economic and Social Research Council-funded seminars brought together academics working in various traditional disciplines to focus via the lens of apprenticeship on the common issue of learning. They revisited the institution and conception of apprenticeship from across disciplinary boundaries. They shared a concern – as Guile and Young say in Chapter 8 in this book – 'to reconceptualize apprenticeship as the basis for a social theory of learning'. Complementary to this 'social theory of learning', the seminars also sought to build what Pierre Bourdieu has called a new 'sociology of learning' (in Robbins, 1991: 46), one that examines the opportunities (and obstacles) to learning that contemporary society offers to individuals, together with the use that they make of them in the process of 'becoming a person with a distinctive agency in the world' (Ranson, 1998: 21).

Modern Apprenticeships have been developed to inject content and status into work-based learning by drawing on the continuing resonance and appeal of apprenticeship amongst employers, trade unions, young people and their families. It is therefore apposite to focus perspectives from a range of different disciplines upon apprenticeships as they were historically constituted and as they have survived in craft work and in further and higher education. This is especially relevant as many of the objections that have been raised to the framework of National Vocational Qualifications point to the lack of time (which was integral to traditional apprenticeships) in which to acquire the underlying skills and knowledge that are seen as necessary to move beyond competence. It is also vital to consider what sort of apprenticeship in the widest sense of Lave and Wenger's 'legitimate peripheral participation' can contribute to individuals' membership of communities of practice (1991). This conceptualization is as significant to the analysis of participation in a 'learning society', where training and retraining and indeed 'lifelong learning' are seen as prerequisites for adapting to changes in employment and technology, as it is to the risks of social exclusion. Before moving to such considerations in conclusion, the book begins by examining the history of apprenticeship from feudal times.

Historical approaches to apprenticeship

There are two basic interpretations of the historical experience of craft apprenticeship: one, that they were wasteful exercises in time-serving, oppressing youth labour and excluding others from employment in trades that sought to protect themselves through union rules and restrictive practices in collusion with management (Turner, 1962). Alternatively, they are seen as a valuable legacy of the past in nurturing knowledge and skills in entrants to the labour market on which they continued to build for the rest of their lives.[1] The historical truth lies between these two extreme positions – some traditional craft apprenticeships in British industry were very good and some were appalling.[2]

Although studenthood and apprenticeship have often been conflated and the notion of student as apprentice has been revisited recently (for example by Ainley, 1994 and Barnett, 1994), apprenticeship is here presented historically in its conventional form of 'diligent and faithful service' (Lane, 1996). So in the first section of this book, Aldrich traces the history of apprenticeship from medieval England through to the impact of the world's first industrial revolution up until the end of the 19th century.

This story is taken up by Clarke through her analysis of apprenticeship in the construction industry or 'building trades'. As she points out, the formalized roles of apprentice, journeyman and master were well established in medieval Europe where they contributed to the unique flowering of cathedral building on which so much time and effort was expended across the continent (Gimpel, 1983). The meanings of these terms changed as apprenticeship developed from the guild to the artisan system and then, with industrialization, into apprenticeships that at their best regulated the acquisition of knowledge for entry to skilled crafts and at their worst grossly exploited child labour. The Construction Industry Training Board survives today with the Engineering Training Board as the two last statutory bodies in the UK integrating formal vocational training with learning at work in their sectors of employment.

Looking at the history of apprenticeship in another industry in the third chapter of this section, Ryan examines engineering apprenticeship during the period of classic heavy, or 'Fordist', industry in Britain. He begins before the Great Depression and continues into recovery in World War II and then describes the development of engineering apprenticeship during the anomalous post-war period of '30 glorious years' of sustained economic growth and expansion. From the General Strike of 1926 up to the engineering strikes of the 1960s and 1970s, including notably the engineering apprentices' strikes in Coventry and elsewhere, the regulation of apprenticeship by employers and unions bound up this institutionalized form of learning at work with industrial relations in general and the conflicts this involved. Questions concerning the recognition of unions to bargain on apprentice pay were to the fore, resulting in price-oriented rather than skill-oriented union strategies. Indeed, institutional structures were not present to facilitate the development of a joint approach to the regulation of training quality. Consequently, as Ryan suggests, this influenced academic consideration of apprenticeship in the UK to the extent that it was treated as part of industrial relations rather than education.

Theoretical approaches to apprenticeship

The second section of this book opens up this historically familiar idea of apprenticeship to a variety of different disciplinary perspectives. Rikowski, for instance, begins by looking at apprenticeship from the viewpoint of philosophy to explain what Nietzsche meant by mastery – the neglected polar term to apprenticeship. Mastery of a craft, as well as the mastery enjoyed by the enigmatic 'superman', was a key term for Nietzsche who urged his readers to self-mastery through daring to 'Become what you are'. Rikowski grounds this philosophy with reference also to Marx's equally materialist theory of labour power. From this perspective he outlines a critique of the 'ideology of learning' that disguises the new reality of a society and an economy in which technology is developing so fast no one can catch up with it. This is not only because the nature of expertise or 'mastery' is transformed by the application of 'expert' (sic) systems of information technology (Collins, 1989); it is also because all members of 'the learning society' are relegated to the position of perpetual (sorcerer's) apprentices as final 'mastery' becomes unattainable.

A completely contrasted social order is described in Bunn's chapter on nomads in Central Asia. The Kyrgyz are not only a traditional society whose history is embodied in their still-growing oral epic poetry but one in which – typically of nomadic pastoralists and also hunter-gatherers – division of labour is limited (Gellner, 1983). It is, however, also a 'learning society' in the sense that for the society to survive, as Sir Geoffrey Vickers wrote, 'the revolution of the generations' makes it necessary for 'the whole expanding corpus of human knowledge' to be 'relearnt about three times in each century' (1965: 108). In Kyrgyz society, every individual, save a few specialists – such as the Hunter-with-Eagles or the Epic Poet, shares all the skills and knowledge of the collectivity so as to become what would in our type of 'Learning Society' be called 'flexibly multiskilled'. Even the division between manual and mental labour is limited under conditions that require all members of society to undertake physical work, so that the mental work of directing the labour of others and that of instructing the young falls to the old, whose wisdom is universally revered. The most rudimentary division of labour is then that between men and women (Douglas, 1986: 76), accounting for the different types of 'apprenticeship' which Bunn describes among the Kyrgyz.

Because they have mainly studied societies without formally institutionalized specialist education and training, anthropologists have contributed most to the new reconceptualization of learning which does not confuse education with schooling, or what is learnt with what is taught, or knowledge with what can be assessed. In place of these habitually accepted understandings, the new paradigmatic conception of learning is indicated by Lave and Wenger's 1991 notion of apprenticeship as a form of 'legitimate peripheral participation'. Apprenticeship so conceived is a participation in activity and in learning that is legitimate because it is socially recognized but is as yet only peripheral – not the right to full participation in the practice. Legitimate peripheral participation, or LPP, provides an operationalizable concept going beyond imprecise pedagogic metaphors of 'structuration' and 'levels' of learning. Or rather, LPP links these metaphors to the social 'structures' and 'levels' within social hierarchies of power and control in which particular types of apprenticeship are institutionalized and to the variously valued roles for which such legitimated learning prepares its peripheral participants. LPP thus allows considerations of individual identity or character 'formation' (what the Germans call *bildung*) to be brought into cross-cultural comparisons of apprentices and students. It also puts in question many of the psychological assumptions – such as the supposed 'transfer' (see Lave, 1988) of so-called 'personal and transferable skills' – upon which currently dominant regimes of learning at nearly all levels of both education and training in the UK are based.

While deriving most obviously from cultural anthropology, Lave and Wenger's theory of 'situated cognition' owes much also to Vygotskian perspectives in psychology. These have been reinvigorated recently by what Claxton (1997: 3–4) called 'The newly formed hybrid discipline of "cognitive science"', which he described as 'an alliance of neuro-science, philosophy, artificial intelligence and experimental psychology'. The motto of this approach might be that 'The knowledge is out there' for it raises the paradoxical suggestion that learning does not fundamentally and primarily occur within the heads of individuals but is to be located in the process of their shared practice. What exist within the heads of the individuals involved in the practice are the neural networks to support learned activities. This does not mean that you do not have to learn to perform those activities by participation in the social practice within which their meanings are culturally embedded but it does mean that you do not do so by some sort of 'information' or 'skill' 'transfer'. What happens is, as Gee explained, 'Once you are a member of the group, once your behaviours count as meaningful within the social practice, you get the "meanings" free' (1992: 10). So, instead of seeking the somehow physically corresponding 'structures' of learning inside the black box of individual minds, this apparently paradoxical perspective on learning directs attention to the linguistic and technical supports for learning within particular social ecologies upon which participants may draw in their various social practices.

The integration of mind and body with the social and natural environment in this new paradigm abandons the traditional Cartesian privileging of thinking over doing and feeling. It reintegrates the 'affective' with the 'cognitive' and 'physical' domains which orthodox psychology convention-ally treats separately but which every teacher knows cannot be separated in practice as they are integral to learning at all levels. The new perspective or paradigm also opposes previous mistakings of the analysis for the actuality of learning in accounts based upon either behaviourist psychology or the computational modelling involved in many cognitivist approaches.

Forrester's chapter borrows the metaphor of affordances from Gibson's perceptual psychology where objects in its environment afford an animal vari-ous opportunities or obstacles to the pursuit of its ends. Forrester translates this notion from an animal's natural environment into the artificial environ-ment of language and technology with which human beings are surrounded and suffused. Here he finds 'affordances for learning' offered in pedagogic conversations and demonstrations by masters, teachers, or others whose au-thoritative knowledge of and skill in some particular practice is legitimately recognized. So Forrester takes us inside Vygotsky's 'zone of proximal develop-ment' which exists between the unaided efforts and understandings of the learner, be he or she apprentice, child, or student, and the abilities and un-derstandings of the Master, adult, or teacher. Using the exacting techniques of conversational analysis, Forrester reveals in the verbal interactions be-tween primary pupil and teacher or researcher how the former makes use of the affordances in language that are provided by the latter to understand how to join in the mathematical exercise of estimation. The child's excited cry of 'a-ha!' registers a real recognition of new ability, understanding and thus em-powerment when she masters a task that previously she could not complete unaided. 'Now I can go on', as Wittgenstein said (1968: 73e).

Apprenticeship as a model of learning

Whatever instructional methods are employed in whatever sort and level of education and training is undertaken, language will feature as a fundamen-tal means by which learning is communicated, implemented and assessed. However, because, as Allen (1990: 40) pointed out, 'All knowing... always involves skilful performances', even the most apparently abstract and lin-guistically formalized knowledge (of algebraic formulae, for instance) 'can never be rendered wholly explicit and removed entirely from its tacit roots'. This is because, as Polanyi argued 'we remain ever unable to say all we know... [and] we can never quite know all that is implied in what we say' (1958: 95), so that 'The inarticulate always has the last word' (1958: 71). Nevertheless, language is intimately involved even with those pedagogic projects concerned with developing their own musical, visual or otherwise tactile languages. 'To shade and knit anew the patch of words/Left by the dead', as Dylan Thomas put it (1978: 19), is especially central to current efforts to raise 'standards' of literacy in Britain's schools as part of the 'foundation' for subsequent 'lifelong learning'. So it is the dominance of standard literary English over the compulsory school National Curriculum that is the focus of Webb's contribution. He draws attention to the prime purpose of communicating meaning and values in the 'language for learning' and criticizes the technicization of learning within schools that has occurred as the result of the imposition of a narrowly academic National Curriculum. Webb thus takes the discussion into the main institutions of formal learning in contemporary society – schools, colleges and universities.

What is actually learnt in formal learning environments is the theme developed by the next two chapters in the third section of the book. Both apply and elaborate the concept of legitimate peripheral participation to answer this 'million dollar' question. As Lave and Wenger have indicated, it has been a long-term problem of traditional (academic) school and higher education that:

> the didactic use of language, not itself the discourse of practice, creates a new linguistic practice, which has an existence of its own. Legitimate peripheral participation in such linguistic practice is a form of learning, but does not imply that newcomers learn the actual practice the language is supposed to be about.
>
> (1991: 108)

Moreover, they argue:

> When the process of increasing participation is not the primary motivation for learning... the focus of attention shifts from co-participation in practice to acting upon the person-to-be-changed. Such a shift is typical of situations, such as schooling, in which pedagogically structured content organizes learning activities [so that] the identity of learners becomes an explicit object of change [and] where there is no cultural identity encompassing the activity in which the newcomers participate and no field of mature practice for what is being learned, exchange value replaces the use value of increasing participation. The commoditization of learning engenders a fundamental contradiction between the use and exchange values of the outcome of learning, which manifests itself in conflicts between learning to know and learning to display knowledge for evaluation. Test taking then becomes a new parasitic practice, the goal of which is to increase the exchange value of learning independently of its use value.
>
> (1991: 112)

Guile and Young do not go so far with Lave and Wenger's critique of the increasingly commodified didacticism of all levels of institutional learning. However, they also critique transmission models, including the attempted transmission of so-called 'transferable', 'core' or 'key skills' that would be better treated as the generic apprehension of the essential identity underlying a range of superficially dissimilar appearances. Guile and Young also show similarities between classroom and work-based learning and therefore also the similarities between the institutions of schooling and apprenticeship. To achieve this they apply the concept of LPP to formal learning in schools, colleges and universities, agreeing as they do so with other commentators who have seen Lave and Wenger's conception as too critical of such institutions – witness Jean Lave's comment during the second seminar of the series that 'If you want to study learning, the last place to look is in school!' Guile and Young thus escape from what Hoyles and Noss (1996: 33) call 'the cul de sac of situated learning' into which they see Lave and Wenger's approach leading. At the same time, like Hoyles and Noss, Guile and Young also recognize the potential for facilitating learning by using ICT. They give examples from the work of Engestrom (1987) in Finland of ICTs that reflexively 'informate' (as Zuboff put it in 1988) the work environments in which they are applied. This 'transformative' – rather than conventionally 'informative' – view of learning again follows Vygotsky by integrating scientific and other generalized (or abstracted) knowledge with everyday concepts to solve problems in particular practical situations. It deepens Lave and Wenger's concept of apprenticeship as LPP to again invite consideration of the affective and emotional dimensions of learning, which Bunn also implies are underdeveloped in Lave and Wenger's account.

Cohen's chapter, which approaches apprenticeship from the perspective of cultural studies, also emphasizes the 'psychodynamic dimension'. This, he says, is too often missing from accounts of apprenticeship to a master or to learning from an authority or a source, for example by discovery or experimentation, or just by trial and error. As Polanyi recorded:

> By watching the master and emulating his efforts in the presence of his example, the apprentice unconsciously picks up the rules of the art, including those which are not explicitly known to the master himself. These hidden rules can be assimilated only by a person who surrenders himself to that extent uncritically to the imitation of another.
>
> (1958: 53)

This is not to confuse authority with power (Winch, 1998: 55), but it does draw attention to the importance of structures of feeling and fantasy that can influence learning outcomes. Cohen explains how these psychic structures are culturally embedded and narrativized as 'codes' which provide 'templates' for the distinctive trajectories of the 'identity work' that he points out is involved in all learning (not just in the superficial 'presentation of self' featured in the commodified approaches Lave and Wenger criticize above) and in 'learning to learn' – as well as in 'learning not to learn'.

As summarized here, Cohen's previous work relates this 'identity work' integral to all learning to the subcultural styles assumed by different factions of post-war working- and middle-class youth. They informally 'apprenticed' themselves to various shifting combinations of codes of what Cohen called 'apprenticeship, vocation, career or inheritance'. With processes of class reformation still continuing in contemporary society, another (or is it the same?) question is, as Cohen put it in 1988, 'how the decline in the political cultures of the manual working class, and the rise of structural youth unemployment have affected the formation and outlook of youth'. The fact that there are still groups of socially excluded youth who try to deal with their lack of real participation in learning and society by adopting magical solutions associated with subcultural styles, makes his search for a general theory of learning regeneration all the more pressing. It also links this third section of the book to the last by connecting the theoretical considerations above with the latest avatars of apprenticeship in government social and economic policies.

Modern Apprenticeship: a renaissance of work-based learning?

Contemporary policy debates on work-based learning and, in particular, the analysis of Modern Apprenticeship make up the concluding section of the book. Modern Apprenticeships were launched in 1994 and have gradually extended from the pilots to a range of occupational sectors, consciously drawing on the status of an institution that was known and understood in different communities of practice. Their expansion is recommended in the latest Report of the National Skills Task Force (1998: 35). The numbers of apprentices have already tripled but nevertheless this route is still only chosen by 10 per cent of the relevant age group, having many more people who are over 18, including those with A levels and degrees, than 16–18-year-olds. In this respect, Modern Apprenticeships represent a break with the practice of age limitations, which was a feature of traditional apprenticeship. Yet in the report, *Apprenticeship: A strategy for growth,* the Centre for Economic Performance at the London School of Economics recommends an expansion to 30 per cent of those eligible as an alternative route to higher education, reducing wage levels from a half to a third of the average skilled worker's wage to provide more places (Steedman *et al,* 1988: 26). This emphasis on wage rates is a powerful reminder of apprenticeship's roots in the world of work and the association of industrial relations with questions of learning.

In an analysis of the relationship between communities of practice and Modern Apprenticeships, Fuller and Unwin point to the need to actively build learning and support structures to reconstruct the communities of practice that apprentices benefited from in the past. They point to the importance of regulatory structures in legitimating routes into occupational communities, identifying four aspects of community: the pedagogical; the occupational; the locational; and the social. They argue that one of the problems with the Youth Training Scheme in its various incarnations was the way in which it fractured the relationship between communities and their training traditions. The incorporation of further education colleges following the 1993 Further and Higher Education Act, alongside revisions to funding formulae, have contributed to the fracturing of links with their local communities and their ability to meet local labour market needs (see Ainley and Bailey, 1997). Fuller and Unwin argue that while some sectors, such as engineering and electrical contracting are able to build on their inheritance of apprenticeship, including its forms of institutional regulation, those sectors that have no such tradition have yet to provide the institutional underpinning necessary to establish a community of practice. In an overview of the development of Modern Apprenticeships, Maguire documents the ways in which they are linked to the changing structure of the youth labour market, reflecting shifts in the occupational structure on the one hand, and increased staying-on rates in post-compulsory education on the other. He argues that Modern Apprenticeships explicitly drew on the nostalgia which traditional apprenticeship still held for employers and were aimed at addressing weaknesses in vocational training at intermediate and technician level. However, their success may be undermined by competing policy priorities: the objective of increasing educational achievements through increasing participation rates which must be set against the declining pool of early school-leavers entering the work-based route. As a consequence, employers recruiting young people onto Modern Apprenticeships claim that there are issues concerning the quality of recruits into the work-based route, while the Training and Enterprise Councils' promotion of the scheme as the quality route has the effect of devaluing other forms of youth training.

Further education colleges have traditionally constituted the link between off-the-job provision and work-based learning, articulated through their relationships with local employers. In a chapter focusing on apprentices in college, Huddleston examines the shifts in this relationship over time. She identifies the significance of the context of learning: the integration of learning by doing and from experienced practitioners in the workplace which is set against classroom learning and the transfer of knowledge in the college environment. She emphasizes the apprentices' identification with their companies, along with the opportunity this confers to become a part of the local social structure. She also points to the capacity of large companies to organize bespoke courses for their apprentices and to contribute to the quality of facilities through the provision of up-to-date equipment. Even here, links between learning sites need to be forged because the training and development needs of apprentices' supervisors and line managers need to be addressed if they are to act as effective masters and mentors in the workplace. Where apprentices from smaller companies 'infill' on college-run courses there are greater problems of integration between on- and off-the-job provision.

The final contribution to this volume engages more directly with contemporary policy debate. Senker and his colleagues draw on the arguments of the proposals put forward in *Working to Learn* (Evans *et al,* 1997) to argue that more than a piecemeal approach is required to develop a coherent strategy towards the reform of work-based learning. They argue that government policy, under Conservative and Labour governments alike, has been bedevilled by conflicting visions of economic development which are fundamentally incompatible. The first of these is the high-skill, high-productivity model, which is at odds with the second, based on the pursuit of flexible labour markets, deregulation and a casualized labour force. The authors argue that voluntarism has failed and that a holistic approach is required in order to address the question of companies' product market strategies and their demand for skills. While the authors do not use the term 'apprenticeship' explicitly, they argue for statutory intervention and the need to involve a range of stakeholders, including trade unions and professional trainers as well as employers in the regulation of the system. They argue for an emphasis on learning process, as opposed to outputs narrowly conceived in terms of NVQs, and for breadth both in educational content and in the range of work experiences. In sum, they are arguing for Guile and Young's 'institution of apprenticeship' for work-based learning and for a context in which the workplace can provide real opportunities for skill enhancement.

This concluding chapter opens for consideration what sort of an apprenticeship in the widest sense of Lave and Wenger's 'legitimate peripheral participation' might now be served for citizenship of a 'learning society' in which training and retraining for constantly and increasingly rapidly revolutionized technology is the norm but in which the uses of that technology and the aims and purposes of that society are democratically determined by its citizens. As a contribution to this debate, apprenticeship is presented in this book as an affordance, tool, metaphor, model or paradigm for thinking about all learning. This takes discussion beyond any of the specific historical forms which apprenticeship has taken, the full range of which is only hinted at in this collection.

With acknowledgement to Sherry Hallmond of Woolwich College and Greenwich University for her comments on the draft for this introduction.

Notes

1. Mike Cooley, personal communication.
2. Sarah Vickerstaff, personal communication.

References

Ainley, P (1993) *Class and Skill: Changing divisions of knowledge and labour*, Cassell, London

Ainley, P (1994) *Degrees of Difference: Higher education in the 1990s*, Lawrence and Wishart, London

Ainley, P and Bailey, B (1997) *The Business of Learning: Staff and student experiences of further education in the 1990s*, Cassell, London

Allen, R (1990) *Polanyi*, Claridge Press, London

Barnett, R (1994) *The Limits of Competence*, Open University Press, Buckingham

Claxton, G (1997) *Hare Brain, Tortoise Mind: Why intelligence increases when you think less*, Fourth Estate, London

Cohen, P (1988) *Rethinking the Youth Question*, occasional monograph, London University Institute of Education Post-16 Centre, London

Collins, H (1989) *Artificial Experts, Social Knowledge and Intelligent Machines*, MIT Press, Cambridge, MA

Douglas, M (1986) *Risk Acceptability According to the Social Sciences*, Routledge, London

Engestrom, Y (1987) *Learning by Expanding: An activity-theoretical approach to developmental research*, Orienta-Konsultit, Helsinki

Evans, K, Hodkinson, P, Keep, E, Maguire, M, Raffe, D, Rainbird, H, Senker, P and Unwin, L (1997) *Working to Learn: A work-based route to learning for young people*, Institute of Personnel Management, London

Finlay, I, Niven, S and Young, S (eds) (1998) *Changing Vocational Education and Training: An international comparative perspective*, Routledge, London

Gee, J (1992) *The Social Mind, Language, Ideology and Social Practice*, Bergin and Garvey, New York

Gellner, E (1983) *Nations and Nationalism*, Blackwell, Oxford

Gimpel, J (1983) *The Cathedral Builders*, tr T Waugh, Michael Russell, London

Hoyles, R and Noss, C (1996) *Windows on Mathematical Meanings, Learning Cultures and Computers*, Kluwer, Dordrecht

Journal of Vocational Education and Training (1998) Special edition: 'Contemporary apprenticeships: perspectives on learning, teaching, policy and design', **50** (2)

Lane, J (1996) *Apprenticeship in England 1600–1914*, UCL Press, London

Lave, J (1988) *Cognition in Practice: Mind, mathematics and culture in everyday life*, Cambridge University Press, Cambridge

Lave, J and Wenger, E (1991) *Situated Learning: Legitimate peripheral participation*, Cambridge University Press, Cambridge

National Skills Task Force (1998) *Towards a National Skills Agenda*, first report of the National Skills Task Force, Department for Education and Employment, London

Polanyi, M (1958) *Personal Knowledge: Towards a post-critical philosophy*, Routledge, London

Ranson, S (1993) The management and organization of educational research, research papers in *Education, Policy and Practice*, ed T Wragg, **8** (2), Routledge, London

Ranson, S (1998) Lineages of the learning society, in *Inside the Learning Society*, ed S Ranson, Cassell, London

Robbins, D (1991) *The Work of Pierre Bourdieu: Recognizing society*, Open University Press, Buckingham

Steedman, H, Gospel, H and Ryan, P (1998) *Apprenticeship: A strategy for growth*, London School of Economics Centre for Economic Performance, London

Thomas, D (1978) *Collected Poems 1934–52*, Everyman, London

Turner, H (1962) *Trade Union Growth, Structure and Policy*, Allen and Unwin, London

Vickers, G (1965) *The Art of Judgement: A study of policy making*, Chapman and Hall, London

Winch, C (1998) *The Philosophy of Human Learning*, Routledge, London

Wittgenstein, L (1968) *Philosophical Investigations*, tr G Anscombe, Blackwell, Oxford

Zuboff, S (1988) *In the Age of the Smart Machine: The future of work and power*, Heinemann, Oxford

Part 1
Historical Approaches
to Apprenticeship

1

The Apprentice in History

Richard Aldrich

Introduction

Apprenticeship is one of those institutions, in common with the university and parliament, that has a history stretching back at least to medieval times. Such longevity immediately suggests a host of basic questions to the historian. Why has apprenticeship lasted so long? What basic human need or needs does it fulfil? Has it fulfilled the same function across the centuries or been subject to considerable changes? Has it, indeed, been a catch-all term to describe a variety of practices which have been, and remain, essentially different? These and other issues are considered in this chapter, which begins with a basic identification of the key elements of apprenticeship in medieval and early modern England. It then proceeds to review the impact upon apprenticeship of the first industrial revolution, and highlights the pupil-teacher apprenticeship scheme of the second half of the 19th century. The 20th century and the recent revival of (modern) apprenticeships are dealt with in other chapters in this book. Finally, some conclusions are drawn.

Such periodization, with its emphases upon the last two centuries, is somewhat at variance with traditional historical divisions. As a recent article has rightly suggested:

> When historians consider 'apprenticeship', they often generalize in terms of three extended periods. These may broadly be characterized as that of 'guild apprenticeship', let us say from about the 12th century to 1563, with the state underpinning much practice; the period of statutory apprenticeship, from 1563 to 1814 (with guilds slowly attenuating); and finally a great diversity of forms which might be summarized as 'voluntary' apprenticeship, often agreements between employers and unions, from 1814 to the present day.

> (Snell, 1996: 303)

Medieval and early modern

It would appear that the essential elements of apprenticeship in medieval England were consistent with those that existed in other European countries. Apprentices (who were usually male) were bound by indentures to a master for a term of years, commonly seven, and invariably between five and nine, while they were initiated into the theory and practice and other mysteries associated with a particular occupation. Parents (or other guardians) of the apprentice paid a premium and signed a contract of articles with the employer which specified the conditions of service. While premiums varied considerably, those for entry to prestigious occupations might be very high indeed. Apprentices were provided with food, clothing, shelter and instruction by the master, and in return worked for him during the term of their apprenticeships. The system, which was enforced both by custom and by law, was certainly flourishing by the 14th century and was applied to a range of occupations. These included both manual and professional pursuits. Although the main emphasis, both historically and conceptually, has been upon the former, it is important to note here that many of the principles and practices of apprenticeship as applied to the university (with its master's degree), to medicine and to the law, were to continue into the modern period. In the England of the 20th century the training of doctors and lawyers, and the status and roles of partially and newly qualified staff in these professions, have continued to exhibit apprenticeship characteristics.

Two pieces of legislation from the Elizabethan period, the Statute of Artificers of 1563 and the Poor Law Act of 1601, indicate the two main species of apprenticeship which had emerged by that time. On the one hand was the classic system inherited from the guilds of the medieval period, which indeed provided much of the administrative machinery for the Act. The Statute of Artificers prescribed that written indentures were to be drawn up for each apprentice, and that no person should exercise a craft or trade until at least a seven-year apprenticeship had been served and the age of 24 attained. Even entry to apprenticeship in certain occupations was to be denied to those who could not boast parents of the appropriate condition and status. This requirement was not necessarily as restrictive as might first appear, because in certain crafts the habit had grown up of apprenticeships being restricted to the sons or other relatives of masters. Such restrictions in respect of family membership, though enforced by custom rather than by law, continued in some occupations, for example those of dockers and printers, until the 20th century. A ratio was also established between the numbers of apprentices and journeymen, for example each master with three apprentices was compelled to keep one journeyman. This stipulation was introduced both to guard against the possibility of apprentices simply being used as cheap labour and to furnish some role models and guidance in addition to that provided by the master. Justices of the Peace (JPs), who also had the authority to determine wages in many occupations, were required to ensure that the statute was being obeyed. These provisions of 1563 reflected the recognition by central government of the importance of apprenticeship and of the need to regulate it both in the general interest of social, economic and political stability, and in the particular interests of consumers, producers and the very apprentices themselves.

The 1563 Act, however, also contained other clauses which were to be extended in 1597 and finally consolidated in the Poor Law Act of 1601. These set out a different model – that of parish apprenticeship. Parish apprenticeship was designed to transfer immediate responsibility for illegitimate and orphaned children, and those of vagrants, paupers or criminals, from the parish and local justices to local employers and residents. Thus the Act of 1601 empowered 'Churchwardens and Overseers... by the assent of any Two Justices of the Peace... to bind any such children... to be Apprentices, where they shall see convenient' (quoted in Lane, 1996: 3). When, from 1662, apprenticeship also afforded the right of settlement, it was sometimes in the interests of parish authorities to send their young charges as far away as possible.

In the medieval and early modern periods, therefore, apprenticeship was widely used. But while skilled crafts and trades, for example those of cabinet makers and grocers, recruited almost entirely through indentures freely entered into by both parties, occupations of low status or danger – farm labourers, brickmakers, chimney sweeps, menial household servants – were supplied from parish apprentices.

Industrial revolution

During the 17th and 18th centuries social and geographical mobility, population increases and the development of new occupations, made serious inroads into both the concept and the practice of apprenticeship. The details of 18th-century legislation have been well summarized by Lane who has shown how parliamentary Statutes of 1709, 1747, 1757, 1766, 1768, 1780, 1788, 1792 and 1793 reflected the continuing regulatory concerns of successive governments (Lane, 1996: 4–5). The purposes of this legislation ranged from the raising of governmental revenue by a tax on premiums, to combating some of the more common abuses of the system, both by masters and by apprentices themselves.

The Act of 1563 was finally repealed in 1814, and in her seminal study Dunlop (1912) saw this event as marking the end of the true period and nature of apprenticeship. It is difficult to determine precisely what was lost at this point, for apprenticeship continued both in name and in a variety of practices throughout the 19th and 20th centuries. Five elements may be suggested:

1. the loss of a continuity with the medieval tradition provided by the legislation of 1563;
2. the abandonment of the mutually binding nature of the indentures;
3. a diminution in the breadth of the master's responsibilities, which had formerly extended both to occupational instruction and moral supervision, as well as to board and lodging in his own premises;
4. an increase in the scale of operations which led to the withdrawal of the master from immediate supervision of the workshop and its trainees;
5. an increase in the numbers of occupations for which little skill or training was required.

It is clear that the changes that took place in England at the turn of the 18th and 19th centuries, changes characterized by industrialization, urbanization and population explosion, were accompanied by considerable changes in apprenticeship. Nevertheless, the name and many of the original concepts and practices (albeit in modified context and form) survived into the new era. Traditional apprenticeships continued in many occupations and were added to and redefined in others. For example, More has suggested that 'in the second half of the century, what I will call new-style apprenticeship was associated in particular with five growing industries: engineering, iron-shipbuilding, building, woodworking and printing' (More, 1980: 43). The complexity of the situation is shown by the fact that in some trades apprenticeships were still necessary for some sectors of the operation, for example to ensure the production of good quality furniture and clothing, while goods for the mass market might be produced by unskilled labour by means of modern machinery.

The fate of parish, pauper or factory apprentices under the impact of the industrial revolution excited considerable, though belated, contemporary attention. The factories, mills, mines and workshops of early 19th-century England had an apparently insatiable appetite for child labour. Accordingly, cartloads of children were despatched from various parts of England to the industrial areas. There they were maintained, as apprentices had always been – fed, clothed and housed – but frequently worked very hard indeed and without either training or hope of advancement. Three features of this type of apprenticeship which proliferated during the early years of the industrial revolution may be noted. First, children were sent to industrial occupations by parishes whose principal motive was to be rid of them so that they would no longer be a charge on the rates. Second, although a premium might be paid by the parish, on occasion apprentices were virtually bought by employers who had no interest in teaching them skills and mastery of a trade, but simply wanted to use them as cheap labour. Third, there was no intention that these apprentices would become masters themselves. When their apprenticeships were ended, the young people, far from being equipped to find a job, found themselves supplanted by the next batch of juveniles.

In 1802 the seriousness of this situation was recognized when an 'Act for the Preservation of the Health and Morals of Apprentices and Others Employed in Cotton and other Mills and Cotton and other Factories' was placed on the Statute Book. This legislation, which applied to cotton and wool mills with three or more apprentices stated that:

> Every apprentice shall be instructed in some part of every working day for the first four years at least of his or her apprenticeship... in the usual hours of work in reading, writing and arithmetic or either of them according to the age and abilities of the apprentice, by some discreet and proper person to be provided and paid for by the master or mistress of such apprentice....

(Quoted in Sanderson, 1967: 267)

Three elements in this legislation may be noted here. First, it placed the responsibility for instruction upon the mill owner; second, the instruction was to be of a general kind, rather than specifically devoted to the occupation; third, these provisions were rendered largely ineffective by the absence of any proper inspectorate. Not until 1833 were the first government factory inspectors appointed; not until the 1870s was legislation extended to cover all occupations; not until 1880 was compulsory schooling introduced in England. Compulsory schooling, indeed, was to be another crucial factor in redefining the nature of apprenticeship.

Nevertheless, one important new link between the worlds of schooling and apprenticeship was created on the initiative of central government. This was the pupil-teacher system begun in 1846, under which boys and girls aged 13 were bound to a five-year apprenticeship. These apprentices received a basic payment of some £10 per year, rising by increments of £2.10 shillings per year to a maximum of £20. During their five years of apprenticeship pupil-teachers taught in schools, and received extra instruction from the master or mistress of the school at the end of the school day. On completion of their apprenticeships pupil-teachers would either leave teaching altogether, proceed to a teaching post in a school, or go on to a training college to acquire a teaching certificate.

In the second half of the 19th century pupil-teachers, who were annually inspected by one of Her Majesty's Inspectors (HMI), were essential to the staffing of elementary schools in England. At times, indeed, they constituted about a quarter of the whole teaching force. In the last 20 years of the 19th century the system underwent significant modification as the larger school boards established centres in which pupil-teachers could receive structured education and training in groups rather than at the hands of individual headteachers in separate schools. These pupil-teacher centres proved to be very effective means of instruction, as measured by the performance of their students in the highly competitive Queen's scholarship examinations.

From the beginning of the 20th century, however, the numbers of pupil-teachers rapidly declined. Several reasons may be adduced for this change.

First, there was a growing belief that the education of a large percentage of the children of the country should not be directed by those who were little more than children themselves. Second, since from 1902 there were maintained secondary grammar schools which offered free secondary education to able pupils, there was no need for the pupil-teacher apprenticeship to serve as a substitute for secondary schooling. Third, the decline in the birth rate reduced the numerical pressures on schools. Fourth, the development of teachers' unions and professional associations from 1870 and the establishment of Local Education Authorities (LEAs) as employers from 1902, helped to make teaching a more stable career and one in which increasing numbers of people, both men and women, would be prepared to spend their whole lives.

Technical education provided a further extension of, and challenge to, apprenticeship. Pupil-teacher centres indicated that some elements in the apprenticeship of prospective teachers could be more effectively supplied outside the schools themselves. Similarly it became apparent that some elements, for example basic scientific and technical knowledge necessary for other forms of apprenticeship, could be supplied more efficiently in the classroom than in the workplace. In England, however, provision of technical education was and remained poor. Writing of the situation in the second half of the 19th century, Green has drawn attention to the failures of English apprentices, and shown how a commentator such as Silvanus Thompson, in his study, *The Apprentice Schools in France* (1878), contrasted the repetitive and unimaginative drudgery of an English apprenticeship with the combination of theoretical and practical training provided in the French trade schools. As Green has rightly maintained, in England 'apprenticeship was often of dubious efficacy and rarely sought to train beyond the level of basic practical skills' (Green, 1994: 69). By contrast, students in French trade schools, as Thompson argued:

> are more methodical and intelligent in their work, steadier in general conduct, have a far better grasp of the whole subjects, and are pronounced to be more competent than the average workman at executing repairs, since they have learned the principles and have not been kept doing the same thing... all through the years of their apprenticeship.

(Thompson, 1878: 44, quoted in Green, 1994: 87)

Explanations of this failure either to adapt the old apprenticeship system or to replace it with something superior, have been many and various. Some have blamed the general anti-industrial ethos exemplified in the rural, classical ethos of the landed elites and many of the intelligentsia. Others have placed the responsibility at the door of those industrial and commercial entrepreneurs whose successes in the first industrial revolution were secured without any scientific and technical training themselves or recourse to a highly skilled workforce. The triumphs of the Great Exhibition of 1851 produced a mood of confidence in British industrial and commercial might which stood firm against the warnings of such commentators as Thomas Huxley, Lyon Playfair and Bernhard Samuelson. In the third quarter of the 19th century there were neither the incentives nor the mechanisms in place for employers to develop substantial technical and scientific schemes of training at local, regional or national levels. Others, again, would emphasize the reluctance of central governments to intervene in this sphere. Such reluctance stemmed from a general anxiety about interfering in economic matters for fear of upsetting the free operation of the market, an anxiety which affected not only the area of general economics but also that of education itself. In consequence, the Department of Science and Art, established in 1853 at South Kensington in the wake of the Great Exhibition, remained separate from the Education Department until 1899, and had to proceed by a haphazard and supplementary system of examinations and grants.

The last 20 years of the 19th century have been identified, in relative terms, as a 'golden age' for vocational education in England. This was manifested in a relaxation in hostility towards central intervention, the authorization of local authority expenditure on technical studies, and the development of institutes and polytechnics. In this situation apprenticeship was strengthened and sustained: in *Skill and the English Working Class 1870–1914,* More calculated that in any single year in the early 20th century there were some 350–400,000 apprentices in the United Kingdom (More, 1980: 64). Apprenticeship still dominated recruitment to engineering fitting, and to many areas of building, shipbuilding and printing. In 1906 the largest groups of apprentices were in building (100,200) and engineering (94,100), and More suggests that in this year 21 per cent of all working males between the ages of 15 and 19 were serving apprenticeships (More, 1980: 99, 103).

Nevertheless, it was generally perceived, and the perception was to be heightened during two world wars, that in comparison with many of their European counterparts, British workers, including those who had undergone apprenticeships, were still less competent both in general theoretical and in the more specifically practical elements of their work. Although a national system of awards, the ordinary and higher national certificates and diplomas, backed both by government and professional bodies, was introduced in the 1920s, a part-time, evening approach still prevailed in the technical field. Product standards were frequently inferior to those of goods produced in other countries. Some luxury items apart, the label 'Made in Britain' began to acquire a negative connotation. The most important point to note is that in the second half of the 20th century the criticisms of, and explanations for, the failure of apprenticeship in England current in the third quarter of the 19th century were still being repeated.

Conclusion

A number of points may be made in conclusion. The first, in answer to those questions raised in the opening paragraph, is that apprenticeship has survived in some form or forms across the centuries because it was originally composed of many elements that lay at the centre of human existence. Changes across the centuries have led to a concentration upon some of those original elements to the neglect of others. Apprenticeship as it existed as an ideal (though not always as a reality) from the 12th to the 17th centuries was a most substantial phenomenon indeed, encompassing social, occupational, educational, religious, familial, group and legal dimensions. It was a central core, both formal and informal, which impinged in a variety of ways upon individuals, males and females, young and old alike, and upon communities large and small. Centrality and variety were exemplified by the parish apprentices, whose lives were lived under similar but more stringent structures to those experienced by their more fortunate contemporaries. Informal apprenticeships seem to have operated particularly in respect of girls, for example in the case of handywomen. Informal apprenticeship in this area was ended by the Midwives Act of 1936, which restricted the right to deliver babies to qualified midwives. Even less formal and more secretive were the apprenticeships of those who trained to be abortionists.

The early years of the 19th century saw the legislation of 1563 finally overturned, the replacement or re-designation of many traditional occupations, and a new and even more stringent set of structures within which many parish or factory apprentices were located. Such legal and economic changes, however, were accompanied by social changes, including changes in traditional arrangements for social welfare which, in the long run, were to prove equally damaging to the traditional elements of apprenticeship. The relationship between apprenticeship and the right of settlement, that is to say the right to receive welfare at the hands of the parish, was particularly important in the period between 1662 and the introduction of the new Poor Law in 1834. Discussion of this topic has often focused upon the desire of parish authorities to offload their potential claimants (the parish apprentices) upon another area. But equally important was the positive side of that relationship. As Snell has argued:

> A parish... operated in the security that time expended in training young people within its parochial boundaries was likely to be of future benefit to itself. The close dependency between apprenticeship, settlement, employment, poor relief, rate-paying, access to local raw materials and means of production guaranteed this.
>
> (1996: 311)

Another point concerns a relatively neglected cause of the decline of apprenticeship in the 19th and 20th centuries – that of a fundamental change in the nature and location of education. The integrated nature of education as expressed through apprenticeship, whereby the master was responsible for the total well-being of the apprentice's health, morals, religious observance, literacy, occupational skills, etc was replaced by a division of labour. The 19th century witnessed industrialization, urbanization and population explosion, but it also saw the decline of the educative family and occupation and the rise of the schooled society. Education itself was subjected to a division of labour, so that it became accepted that some skills would be learnt at home, others at school, and others again in employment. Considerable benefits accrued from these developments, and universal schooling provided some guarantees against the evils of widespread ignorance and premature employment. In contrast apprenticeship, linked through settlement to the notion of small self-sufficient enclaves and the maintenance of the social, economic and political status quo – a system that required young people to reside in a master's household, and in that further enclosed environment to acquire all manner of skills – might well appear anachronistic and outdated. Not surprisingly those arch advocates of national and social efficiency, Sidney and Beatrice Webb, opposed it in the strongest terms, arguing in 1919 that:

> undemocratic in its scope, unscientific in its educational methods, and fundamentally unsound in its financial aspects, the apprenticeship system, in spite of all the practical arguments in its favour, is not likely to be deliberately revived by a modern democracy.

(Quoted in Snell, 1996: 318)

Whereas the all-embracing nature of apprenticeship had its disadvantages, the major current problem in respect of education and employment in England appears to be that of fragmentation, coupled with poor standards of provision and performance. Evidence on this point is readily available. Modern Apprenticeships may represent a significant advance upon the Youth Opportunities Programme (YOP) and the Youth Training Scheme (YTS), yet such a development is both long overdue and must be located within European and global perspectives. There are some 7 million people in the UK without any qualifications at all. The UK ranks 24th in the World Economic Forum league of workforce skills, while the overall performance of its education system is placed only 35th out of 48 countries (Kinnock, 1996: 15). The 1994 World Competitiveness Report on the availability of skilled labour put the UK only 18th out of 23 countries, while a recent IMF Competitiveness Report placed the UK 19th out of 22 countries for in-company training (Kinnock, 1996: 25). In consequence, although ambitious targets have been set to ensure that by 2000, 60 per cent of 21-year-olds gain at least two A levels or their vocational equivalents, it has to be acknowledged both that such targets may be unattainable within this space of time, and that France, Germany and Japan have already surpassed them.

The causes of such low standards of performance are many and complex, and these figures themselves, which are quoted from one side of the political spectrum, must be balanced by other perceptions that unemployment rates and economic prospects are currently better in the United Kingdom than in many other countries. Nevertheless, it is not difficult to point to uncoordinated and unfulfilled government policies in the areas of apprenticeship and broader vocational training. Indeed the reluctance of central governments to intervene in these areas, as opposed to frequent interventions in respect of mainstream schooling, is most noticeable. After 1945 there was an acute failure either to develop technical and vocational schools (the third element in a supposedly tripartite system) or to implement radical changes in respect of apprenticeship of the type which took place in West Germany. Even those clauses in the 1944 Education Act which required the establishment of county colleges and the implementation of compulsory continuation education to 18, were never put into effect. In consequence, while some major employers managed to continue, create or develop their own apprenticeship schemes, as in the aeronautical and motor industries, in other areas sustained provision at the craft level was and remained poor.

While the pupil-teacher system rapidly declined in the first decade of the 20th century, in the last decade apprenticeship methods of training – learning by doing on the job under the control of skilled practitioners – have seen a remarkable resurgence. In contrast to changes in other occupations such as nursing where the apprenticeship model has continued to decline, central government directives and initiatives have strengthened the practice. The term 'teacher training' has supplanted that of 'teacher education' and is enshrined in the very names of such bodies as the Teacher Training Agency. Students on one-year courses must spend two-thirds of their time in schools rather than in institutions of higher education. Indeed, those students enrolled under a School Centred Initial Teacher Training scheme may spend all of their time in schools.

One of the major themes of this chapter has been that apprenticeship, though currently principally conceived as employment training for a particular range of occupations, has embraced many dimensions and appeared in many forms. The future of apprenticeship may well be determined not only by specific initiatives such as the Modern Apprenticeship scheme, but also by broader changes within the fields of education, employment and society at large, of which two may be noted here. The first is that in 1995 the two separate Departments of Education and Employment were merged into a single Department for Education and Employment. It is certainly too early yet to determine what effect this may have, but statements as to the aims and objectives of education have been recast in competitive and employment terms, and attempts made to secure a greater coherence between academic and vocational routes and qualifications, particularly in the 16–19 age range. The second is that the massive change in higher education participation rates over the last 10 years, from some 12 per cent to more than 30 per cent, may mean that in future learning and qualifications will occupy a more central place in all elements in British life, including the industrial and commercial worlds, than hitherto.

Finally, the potential of apprenticeship to reach and inspire across the ages must be acknowledged. In a speech to a conference entitled 'Modern Apprenticeships in Action', held in London in April 1994, Valerie Bayliss stated that:

> In Penzance in 1459 an apprenticeship was reckoned to last for eight years. We have made a great deal of progress since then, and time-serving will not be an element in Modern Apprenticeships. But, to aim (in the words of the 15th century) to 'teach, train and inform' strikes me as not a bad watchword for what we are now trying to do in not a 20th century but, I hope, a 21st century way.

> (*Insight*, 1994: 13)

Note

This chapter is a revised version of a paper first published in Heikkinen, A and Sultana, R (eds) (1997) *Vocational Education and Apprenticeships in Europe – Challenges for practice and research,* Tampereen Yliopisto, Tampere. I am most grateful to Anja Heikkinen for her courtesy in allowing me to draw on this earlier work and to Pat Ainley, David Crook, Andy Green and Susan Williams for their comments.

References

Dunlop, O J (1912) *English Apprenticeship and Child Labour: A history*, T Fisher Unwin, London

Green, A (1994) Technical education and state formation in 19th century England and France, in *Vocational Education and Culture: European prospects from history and life-history*, ed A Heikkinen, Tampereen Yliopisto, Hämeenlinna

Insight (1994) Modern apprenticeships: a conference report, **30**, pp 10–13

Kinnock, G (1996) *Could Do Better – Where is Britain in the European education league tables?* National Union of Teachers, London

Lane, J (1996) *Apprenticeship in England, 1600–1914*, UCL Press, London

More, C (1980) *Skill and the English Working Class, 1870–1914*, Croom Helm, Beckenham

Sanderson, M (1967) Education and the factory in industrial Lancashire, 1780–1840, *Economic History Review*, **XX**, pp 266–79

Snell, K (1996) The apprenticeship system in British history: the fragmentation of a cultural institution, *History of Education*, **25** (4), pp 303–21

2

The Changing Structure and Significance of Apprenticeship with Special Reference to Construction

Linda Clarke

Introduction

It is often assumed that apprenticeship is timeless, that it has existed for ever and a day in the same form. The aim here is to show its very different stages of development in Britain, each associated with specific characteristics with respect to: its regulation; its scope, length, form and skill basis; the status of the apprentice; and the conditions of employment permitting its survival. The chapter provides a sweep through the centuries that is intended to raise the question as to whether apprenticeship is the most appropriate form for vocational training today.

The examples given refer almost exclusively to the construction industry, though many characteristics identified apply also to other sectors. Construction, or rather 'building', is a particularly good example, being the first sector where wage labour developed on a significant scale, one of the prime targets of the 1562/3 Statute of Artificers or Apprentices and the only remaining sector to have statutory training boards – that is, the Construction Industry and Engineering Construction Industry Training Boards (CITB and ECITB).

Though changing, apprenticeship does nevertheless have abiding features. In the first place, it is part of the development of wage labour, the apprentice being classified even in the 14th century as a landless category. Secondly, it is based on the acquisition of skills through work experience, embedding it in the workplace and making it highly dependent on the individual master or firm. Thirdly, it serves as a means of entry into a trade or industry. Fourthly, the apprentice is destined to be a crafts- or tradesman (only rarely a tradeswoman) and distinguished from the labourer. And, finally, apprenticeship is formulated, regulated and divided at a higher social level than just the master, the workshop, the firm or the single unit of production, whether through the guilds or trade companies, the state or the social partners. Consequently skill divisions, such as between carpenters and bricklayers, are defined at this level and the maintenance of apprenticeship depends as much on labour and industrial organization in general as on specific employment and working conditions.

Apart from these general defining features, the characteristics of apprenticeship have varied according to changes in the form of production. Four stages can be identified, the first two under feudal and the last two under capitalist relations of production: the late medieval trade company apprenticeship (sometimes termed the guild apprenticeship) regulated by charter that began to flourish from the 14th century; statutory apprenticeship regulated by Justices of the Peace (JPs) and introduced through the Statute of Artificers; collectively bargained apprenticeship under the social partners (sometimes known as the 'laissez-faire' system) emerging in the early 19th century; and apprenticeship with an element of formal vocational training, regulated through the state and the social partners, and first introduced in 1964 through the Industrial Training Boards (see Table 2.1).

Stage 1: The trade company apprenticeship

The trade company apprenticeship existed from the 14th century in chartered cities and towns, above all London, and was essential to ensuring that citizenship was synonymous with craft membership. The apprentice was controlled by the individual master who registered with the respective craft company for a fee. The companies in turn issued ordinances limiting the length of the apprenticeship to seven years, the age of the apprentice to under 21, and the number of apprentices employed to a maximum of three according to the status and experience of the freemen master. Anyone found breaking the ordinances was liable to a fine.

The apprentice was apprenticed to be a master and embedded in a clearly defined hierarchy of master/apprentice/servant or labourer. Legally, his status was one of 'working for wages' and, therefore, indirectly regulated through the 1349 Statute of Labourers. This referred only to agricultural and building wages and provided for payment by the day, the apprentice receiving 40 per cent of the fixed rate (Janssen, 1985a). In this respect and in issuing of charters of recognition to towns and companies, the feudal state played a regulatory role.

Apprenticeships were divided along the same lines as the companies themselves, according to trades. These in turn related primarily to different materials – whether carpenters to wood, plumbers to lead, bricklayers and tilers to clay, or masons to stone – that companies had the royal privilege to sell. One of the conditions of each company was that members were not allowed to undertake the work of other trades, providing an important means of defining skill boundaries.

Table 2.1 Stages in the development of apprenticeship in the building industry in Britain

	Regulation	Scope/coverage	Duration/structure	Status/division of labour	Reasons for demise
Trade company apprenticeship 1349–1562	- by trade companies to whom fee paid by individual masters; - indirectly through the 1349 Statute of Labourers	- trades, covered by craft companies and bound to particular materials	- seven years - limited in numbers (eg, masters and wardens: three; livery men: two; ordinary freemen: one)	- bound to individual master; part of wage labour, apprenticed to be master, hierarchy – master/apprentice/ servant or labourer	- rise of 'forrens', failure to control numbers, binding of apprentices with other companies, loss of allegiance of master to craft
Statutory apprenticeship 1562–1814	- by Justices of the Peace under Statute of Artificers but subject to local prescription/ ordinance	- throughout realm, including a range of trades/occupations but excluding those regarded as 'labourers'	- seven years under 21 (24) years of age; three apprentices to one journeyman; varied whether with parish, town trade/ corporation or country master	- part of wage labour; apprenticed with individual master or parish to become journeyman, who could then take apprentices	- use of piecework; rise of large capitalist establishments with apprentice as cheap labour; masters having no competence in particular trade
Collectively-bargained apprenticeship 1824–1964	- by agreement between social partners, but especially through trade and/or local-based trade union rule books	- confined to traditional crafts/trades	- restrictions of age and length (five to seven years); limitations in numbers (eg, three apprentices to seven journeymen); 1940s National Standard Apprenticeship scheme	- *employee* of individual employer but training by skilled workers; often just cheap labour; foreman/ skilled/semi-skilled/ labourer	- use of piecework/ 'lump' and 'competitive contracting'; Smithian fragmentation of work process; replacement of indentures by verbal agreements
Apprenticeship with formal vocational training 1964–	- originally tripartite CITB based on statutory levy on employers but increasingly employer-led	- industry-wide but still craft/trade-based and only covering 45% of construction work	- including ever more important formal college training; change from time-serving to achieving standards	- apprentice as *trainee* attached to 'craft', as distinct from 'labourer'	- weakening in union involvement; rise in self-employment; dependence on individual employer

A good example of the trade company apprenticeship is the Carpenters' Company. Not until 1487 did ordinances deal systematically with trade issues, stipulating that all apprentices were to be presented to the masters and wardens before being bound and signalling the control of the company over the individual master. A large source of income throughout the 15th and 16th centuries was from the operation of apprenticeship, whether the fee paid by masters for presenting the apprentice, the fines payable for setting apprentices to work before seven years, the payment for obtaining freedom of the city on completion, or fines for enforcing control of the crafts (Alford and Barker, 1968: 47–48). Throughout this period though, complaints increased that master carpenters employed 'forrens', that is those not bound to a company or free of the City, and more apprentices than the company ordinances allowed. As a result, in 1569 greater limitations were imposed, including that no freeman could take on apprentices until free of the company for three years. And in 1607 numbers were strictly limited: three for masters and wardens; two for livery members; one for ordinary freemen who had not yet practised for three years, and two for those already practising three to seven years. By the mid-17th century, however, numerous suits were brought to the Court for Apprentices and reports made that members were binding and assigning apprentices to 'other company'. At the end of the century, as the system declined, the Carpenters Court of Assistants enacted that free carpenters could take as many apprentices as they wished provided these were bound to the company and a fee paid (Alford and Barker, 1968: 22, 30, 70). By the early 18th century, the company had ceased to regulate the crafts, apprentices were frequently found bound to other companies and, as with other companies, the operative element had vanished.

As illustrated in the carpenters' case, therefore, the trade company system, though not actively dismantled, no longer played a determinant role in the regulation of labour, even by the 16th century. The companies themselves lost control over individual trades as the enrolment of apprentices ceased to be a condition for securing privileges and their own members employed 'forrens', took on more apprentices than laid down and became members of other trade companies to which apprentices were then bound (Derry, 1931: 67–68; Welch, 1909: 64–65).

Stage 2: Statutory apprenticeship

The trade company system was progressively undermined by the new system of apprenticeship introduced through the 1562/3 Statute of Artificers, 'An Acte containing divers Orders for Artificers, Labourers, Servants of Husbandry and Apprentices'. This served to transform local (or, rather, City Corporation) law to national statutory law (that is, to the kingdom) and in so doing weakened municipal and trade company control over entry into the trades and crafts (Perry, 1976: xxiii). Implementation of the Statute was controlled through JPs and had a three-fold purpose: regulation of a contract of services for all hired labour, wage assessment, and apprenticeship regulation. Apprenticeship was to be for seven years, not to be completed before 21 years of age, uniformly applied without distinction of place, and with a limitation on the proportion of apprentices to journeymen of 3:1, any additional apprentices requiring a further journeyman (5 Elizabeth I, c. 4, §XXVII).[1] Enforcement occurred if evasion of regulations was prosecuted, but the authorities were relatively indifferent either to evasion or to the exclusion of unapprenticed workers, being more concerned to resolve master/apprentice disputes and discharge contracts of apprenticeship (Davies, 1956: 164, 172, 223, 259).

The aim of the Statute was both to integrate and stabilize the growing class of wage labour – the 'poor labourer and hired man' – into feudal relations and at the same time encourage its further development (§I). It was simultaneously intended to stem vagrancy and 'banish Idleness', particularly through the system of parish apprentices whereby parish officers bound out as apprentices those unable to support themselves (Deakin, 1991). There was no right of qualified craftsmen to ply their craft where they pleased; they were subject to the prescriptions of the borough, corporate custom or local ordinance (§XXXIX). The Statute thereby acted as a means to bind the wage earner to the locality (Clarke, 1992a: 44–47). Apprentices continued to be regarded as a landless category, using and exercising any 'Art, Mystery or Manual Occupation... albeit the Father or Mother of any Apprentice have no lands, Tenements or Hereditaments' – whether with respect to carpenters, roughmasons, plasterers, sawyers, limeburners, brickmakers, tilers, slaters and thatchers (5 Eliz. I c. 4, §XXIII).

The Statute predominantly related to the agricultural and building sectors, regulated through a rate for the day. However, apprenticeship was extended to cover many occupations not associated or attached to companies, in particular husbandry, as well as trades attached to unchartered companies such as plumbers, joiners, paviors and painters (§XVIII). Most important were those previously excluded, such as brickmaking and quarrying, regarded as 'labourers' work'.

The Statute appears to have been so successful that apprenticeship became the rule rather than the exception, solidly established for village and town crafts. It facilitated the creation of a specialized building force in the countryside instrumental to the great building activity in the last third of the 16th century (Hoskins, 1953).

The demise of the feudal apprenticeship system

Apprenticeship was the key to the artisan system of production: a master was defined as someone who took on apprentices, that is employed others, and who had gained residence or settlement in an area through having served an apprenticeship. By the 17th century, however, it was apparent that most apprentices, having served their time, just because of the difficulties of becoming masters, worked as journeymen. Even then they could still themselves take on apprentices and labourers. As a result, a master became generally distinguished as someone who employed journeymen at day rates, that is a master of work over others, while a 'workman' was a person qualified to work at gross and therefore have journeymen because he had served a seven-year apprenticeship (Clarke, 1992a: 73–76).

The situation continued to be different in chartered towns like London where the old trade company system survived, though not in the outskirts, over which it was constantly disputed how far the companies had control. The congregation of wage labour termed 'forrens' around London and its employment even by members of the trade companies very much reflected the widespread application of the statutory system. The final demise of the trade company system through this influx of 'forrens' in the mid-17th century marked, therefore, at the same time, the successful impact of the Elizabethan Statute (Unwin, 1908: 329–43).

The crunch came through the Great Fire of London, with the Rebuilding Act giving to non-freemen the same liberties as freemen of the city, so that henceforth 'forrens' were allowed, if they had served an apprenticeship, the status of master, not just journeyman, eligible to take on apprentices, hire labour and take on work in the city. In consequence the number of masters soared, as all journeymen who had the resources could employ a mate, work at gross and employ other journeymen, and the city companies relaxed their apprentice regulations (Bell, 1938: 39–40; Clarke, 1992a: 46; Janssen, 1986: 167; Reddaway, 1940: 115–16). By the end of the 17th century, too, large establishments employing many journeymen were emerging, covering all the different building trades and taking on apprentices as cheap labour. As Dobb described:

> The road of advancement to the journeyman or even the small master was all but blocked without any deliberate restriction on freedom to a trade, simply by the size of capital required to initiate production.
>
> (1963: 236)

By the end of the 18th century, however, the political apparatus conserving the legal institution of apprenticeship had become ineffective as JPs ceased to control it. Conflicts again came to a head in and around London with an unprecedented level of building activity, accomplished through a dramatic migration from all counties of England and Wales into Middlesex and London (Deane and Cole, 1967: 103–09). No other force could have so effectively dislodged the statutory system or undermined conditions of settlement laid down in the 17th century Poor Law (Clarke, 1992a: 118–20). Under these, JPs were empowered to remove any new inhabitant to the parish where they were last settled unless sufficient security was given, one important means of gaining settlement being through serving an apprenticeship (13 and 14 Charles II, c. 12, 1662).

As the system declined, so opposition to it mounted (Derry, 1931: 70–74). Adam Smith, for example, saw apprenticeship as part of the 'Policy of Europe', claiming that: it represented the exclusive privileges of corporations, established to prevent any reduction in prices; its length and the limitations in numbers restricted competition; it offered no guarantee of quality; and those on piecework were likely to be more 'industrious' and to 'practise with more diligence and attention'. There were also many occupations to which it did not apply: those exercised after the Statute; those governed by privileges in incorporated towns; and country labour where no apprenticeship was deemed necessary (Smith, 1910: 90–91, 107–14, 117–18). The committee of manufacturers further argued in their campaigning for the repeal that the old system made for a rigid differentiation of trades that encouraged combinations and the subservience of industry to agriculture, being appropriate rather 'to feudal governance and the tyranny of ancient barons' (Derry, 1931: 82).

The campaign for extension of the Statute, which reached a peak in 1812, was composed of 'mechanics, handicraftsmen and artificers', rarely journeymen, and led by the city companies and corporation, who complained of 'price undercutting' by 'illegal men' and defended the legal benefits of apprenticeship as preserving quality and preventing 'vagabonds and blackguards'. Appeal was made to Parliament 'to prevent masters from employing those persons who have not served apprenticeships or to prevent regular journeymen from working where such persons are employed'. A petition, urging the Statute's extension to cover new trades and branches, ran to hundreds of thousands of signatures nationally (Clarke, 1992a: 220; Derry, 1931: 74–81). With the formal abolition of the wage-fixing clauses of the Statute in 1813, the master and the journeyman status ceased to exist as legal categories and shortly afterwards, in 1814, the apprenticeship clauses were repealed. Henceforth the two systems of apprenticeship prevailing under feudalism – the trade company followed by the statutory system – no longer applied.

Collectively bargained apprenticeship

The repeal of the Statute of Artificers was one of the most significant events in the history of vocational training because of the failure to redefine or reconstitute any system in its place. It did not mean, however, that apprenticeship ceased to exist. Indeed, the campaign was not against apprenticeship as such but its legal form, regarded as restrictive and irrelevant (Derry, 1931: 82–86). Even after the repeal, therefore, apprenticeship continued and was enforced in most trades (Lane, 1996).

Nevertheless, though continuing, apprenticeship took a different form, as explained by Howell:

> There are no longer any statutory or legal formularies or instructions binding upon masters or journeymen in the matter of apprentices, either as to the number which may be employed or as to the terms for which they serve; it is now simply a question of free contract or agreement between the master on the one hand, and the apprentice, his parents or representatives, on the other.
>
> (1877: 842)

Given the lack of obligation on the part of the employer, the system was rather maintained by trade unions whose:

> whole history is one long record of persistent and sometimes not very wise efforts to maintain and enforce the apprenticeship system as the only means in their opinion for securing good and capable workmen in every branch of labour.
>
> (1877: 851)

The history of apprenticeship in any regulated form in the 19th century is, therefore, inextricably bound up with the development and strength of the trade unions and collective bargaining.

Labour organization in the building industry was relatively well established even from the end of the 18th century, though trade union organization was prohibited until 1824 under the terms of the Combination Acts (Postgate, 1923). Shortly after this, in 1827, the first trade union was formed, the General Union of Carpenters and Joiners, followed by the Friendly Society of Bricklayers in 1829 and the Operative Stonemasons in 1831. Two of the main demands of the Operative Building Union, formed in 1832 as a national union of the separate trade unions, was for a limitation in the number of apprentices and a prohibition of piecework.

Even though these early trade unions were often 'non-exclusive' unions of 'non-society' men, the structure of apprenticeship they attempted to preserve tended to refer to the old statutory system, including the seven-year term, age restrictions, limitations on numbers and the occupations covered. In practice, such conditions were impossible to maintain and apprenticeship was extremely variable, being anything from three to seven years. Indeed, the new unions of the 1860s such as the Amalgamated Society of Carpenters and Joiners and the London Order of Operative Bricklayers judged apprentice rules as illiberal. In the last third of the 19th century, painters had no restrictions; the bricklayers practically none; while the plasterers, masons and plumbers had some. However, attempts to maintain a fixed proportion of apprentices to journeymen met with some success, especially in the north of England where there were strikes to fix a proportion of three apprentices to seven journeymen (Howell, 1877: 842–49; Postgate, 1923).

One of the main problems was that apprenticeship remained bound to the traditional trades; anyone outside these was classified as a labourer and labourers themselves were not accepted into trade unions and did not begin to organize separately in the building industry until towards the end of the

19th century. Traditional trades were assimilated to capitalism to become sections of wage labour with abilities and privileges to work with tools related to particular materials, but it was difficult to accommodate to changes in the labour process within what remained a craft system (Clarke, 1992a: 72; Janssen, 1985b: 2–11). The only method was for new processes to be 'claimed' by a craft union as within the potential remit of apprenticeship, such as cement floors and breeze-block partitions variously disputed between plasterers and bricklayers (Hilton, 1963: 180, 199). Rather than accommodation, protectionism tended to prevail as trade unions maintained their own sectional interests, as reflected in craft inter-union disputes, such as the plumbers against the gas fitters (Postgate, 1923: 245–50). By the end of the 19th century, there were 13 labour federations for the building industry alone and 72 different unions, local and national, each attempting to regulate apprenticeship.

Another difficulty in maintaining apprenticeship was the different division of labour. Under capitalist relations the master was transformed into a contractor who was no longer tied to the workshop or exercised a trade himself. The apprentice had to pick it up as best he could. Much of the responsibility for teaching a trade fell upon journeymen who often resented training boy workers, this not being part of their contract and only a means to replace themselves, hence the interest in restricting apprenticeships (Howell, 1877: 836). In effect, the old artisan hierarchy of master/journeyman/apprentice/labourer or servant gradually broke down to be replaced by a new hierarchy of foreman/skilled worker/semi-skilled worker/labourer into which it was unclear where the apprentice was to be inserted.

Another specificity of collectively bargained apprenticeship was the lack of any formal skill requirement; there was no exam at the end of the period and the tendency was to train for the needs of yesterday, for specific firms or work processes, or to use apprentices as a form of cheap labour. This impaired the 'efficiency of a workman in being able to undertake a complete branch of any one trade, though greater skill is attained in the special parts assigned to each worker' (Howell, 1877: 838). As criticized in the Report of the Royal Commission on Technical Instruction (the Samuelson Commission) of 1884: 'at the best all that is learned in the workshop is manual dexterity and how to do things by "rule of thumb", "wrinkles", and "dodges"'. Trade unions that continued to try to maintain standards tended to be associated with those occupations or trades where apprentices were taught, as opposed to being simply exploited (More, 1980: 42).

Even by the 1870s Howell was reporting that the 'almost universal rule of apprenticeship is now very nearly abolished in all the more important trades' as employers were concerned only to obtain cheap labour. Complaints about lack of skills mounted as these were only picked up rather than learned (1877: 836–37). In 1884 the Secretary of the Amalgamated Society of House Decorators and Painters, the Trade Guild of Learning and the London Trades Council reported to the Samuelson Commission that 'the apprenticeship system has broken down', as a result of the 'method of work by competitive contract with the division and subdivision of labour under capitalistic employers who have failed to take proper precaution for the production of industrial skill' (Minutes: 3858). This picture was underlined in the 1890s by Charles Booth, who complained that large builders 'won't be bothered' about training, preferring 'improvers', making it impossible to restrict admission to a trade to those apprenticed (1895: 100, 104). By 1909 Bray attributed the 'passing away of the old system of indentured apprenticeship in London' to: the small percentage of boys following their fathers; 'the master is no longer bound to train the apprentice'; the apprentice can usually leave at a week's notice; and the lack of opportunity for a boy 'to become an all round craftsman' (1909: 404, 411, 413).

Nationally, however, the ratio of apprentices remained relatively high. The 1925 Enquiry into Apprenticeship and Training found the ratio of building craftsmen to trainees (many of whom were apprentices) was 3.6:1, though 7.1:1 in London. The nature of apprenticeship was, however, increasingly informal as the use of indentures declined in favour of a simple written or verbal contract. Only 37 per cent of apprentices had written indentures, 53 per cent verbal, and 18 per cent were classed as improvers. Furthermore 30 per cent were required to serve as improvers after their apprenticeship (HMSO, 1927–28: 17, 180). Apprentices were also concentrated in small firms, the ratio being 1:23 male workers in firms of 500 or more and 1:2.4 in firms with under five employees (Williams, 1957: 13). Only 36 per cent of building employers were estimated to employ any apprentices.

Apprenticeship also underwent a subtle change associated with improvements in the position of building labour, as piecework was gradually brought under control, wages became predominantly time-based and employment more stable. It became less a means of employing cheap labour and more a means of reproducing craft skills, so that restricting numbers ceased to be an issue for trade unions. In the lock-out of 1899, employers' demands for no limitation of apprenticeship were agreed to, though not until after World War II did unions erase fixed ratios of apprentices to craftsmen from their rule books. Instead of restrictions, employers and unions became concerned about threats to standards (More, 1980: 14). In 1899 the National Federation of Building Trade Employers (NFBTE) was formed, partly in order to encourage and promote education and training. This was followed during World War I by the formation of the National Federation of Building Trade Operatives (NFBTO), a federation of existing trade unions. With the formation of the Industrial Council for the Building Industry in 1918 and the National Wages and Conditions Council for the Building Industry in 1921, the institutional basis was set for National Apprenticeship Agreements aimed at joint regulation of industrial training at national and local level through collectively agreed standards.

Employers continued, nevertheless, to object to trade unions influencing apprenticeship conditions, to the commitment involved in written indentures and to government involvement (Cole, 1945: 23). The last had been argued for since the 1870s, partly as a result of Gladstone's call to the surviving London companies to help develop the crafts based on the German model of a combination of theoretical and practical training (Bray, 1909: 411; Howell, 1877: 857). The City and Guilds of London Institute for the Advancement of Technical Education was founded, followed from the early 1900s by local trade schools as local authorities gradually took over the role formerly assumed by the Mechanics Institutes (Lang, 1979). Trade unions also actively encouraged the technical education of apprentices and some system of practical examination (Booth, 1895: 103). So did the minority report on the Poor Law Commission and the supplementary report on apprenticeship of the Education Committee of the London County Council, in which it was argued that 15–18-year-olds should have education half-time (Bray, 1909: 114). There was, however, no pressure from industry before the 1930s for an extension of technical education (Cotgrove, 1958: 80).

By the 1930s and 1940s union proposals for reform included: joint regulation, the attachment of the apprentice to industry rather than the individual employer, the involvement of education authorities, and day release as a right (Lee, 1979: 39). In the event, the main difference between these and the new National Standard Apprenticeship Scheme, agreed during World War II by the NFBTO and the NFBTE, related to the role of the state. The scheme, which represented the culmination of the collectively agreed system, was mainly for bricklayers and carpenters, extended for five years or a minimum of four, involved day release, no overtime, national and local regulation in the form of the National Joint Apprenticeship Board and a trust fund should the apprenticeship break down. The continued decline in apprenticeships in spite of this more co-ordinated effort only demonstrated the inadequacy of any system based on voluntarism with no statutory basis.

Stage 4: 'Statutory' apprenticeship with formal vocational training

The refusal of government to take any responsibility for apprenticeship continued even as apprentice numbers fell (Cotgrove, 1958: 61). As reasserted in a Command of 1943 on Training for the Building Industry:

> Apart from the State's responsibility for supervising or grant-aiding technical instruction, apprenticeship unlike special adult training will not be provided and paid by the state... these are traditionally settled by the industry itself.
>
> (Command 6428)

By this insistence, the division between education and practical knowledge, between knowledge acquired outside the workshop and within, a division established in the days of the Mechanics Institutes, was reaffirmed (Cotgrove, 1958: 33). It was even sharpened as technical instruction rapidly expanded following the 1944 Education Act, which contained provisions for local authorities to provide further education, and the setting up of the National Joint Apprenticeship Boards, which meant that apprentices were educated in the employer's time at technical colleges, combined with firms' own work schools and apprentice training centres.

After World War II there was increased concern about leaving training to industry, as expressed by Harold Clay, Assistant General Secretary of the TGWU, to the British Association for Commercial and Industrial Training in 1947:

> There has got to be consideration of issues beyond the individual, beyond the firm, even beyond the industry... we have to get away from the idea that schemes of education and training represent something that a benevolent employer provides for his worker.
>
> (Lee, 1979: 40)

As a result of the continuing decline in employers' training commitment, the 1956 White Paper on Technical Education outlined plans for a massive injection of public funds into further education and for major reorganization (Command 0903). Under the Industrial Training Act, representing 'the first attempt to formulate a modern industrial manpower policy', tripartite statutory Industrial Training Boards for Construction, Shipbuilding and Engineering were set up in 1964 and by 1969 there were over 27 different boards (Perry, 1976: xix). The remit of these was to: establish policy with respect to training, including its length, the registration of trainees and their attendance at further education college; set standards of training and syllabuses; provide advice and assistance about training; devise tests to be taken by apprentices and instructors; run training courses in training centres; pay grants to reimburse firms and allowances to trainees not taken on by firms; collect levies; and borrow (Perry, 1976: 101). The levy-grant mechanism, whereby all firms except those below a certain size paid a levy and those providing training received grants, was central to the operation of the boards.

A revolutionary aspect of the new system was the integration of formal vocational training. A course of further education approved by the National Joint Council for the Building Industry (NJCBI) and not less than one day per week became a necessary part of a CITB apprenticeship. Under the Standard Scheme of Training introduced in the 1970s, concentrated block release was the preferred method and allowed the length of apprenticeship to be reduced from the five years of 1945, to four years in 1964, to three years by 1973.

In theory the CITB represented a means to implement industry-wide training, administered jointly by trade unions and employers. It was an important complement to union structure, which became increasingly industry- rather than trade-based, culminating in the formation of the Union of Construction Allied Trades and Technicians in 1971. In practice, however, the CITB, instead of adopting an industry-wide approach to the division of construction skills, remained locked in the well-established trade divisions, in the main those classified as 'craft' trades within the National Working Rule Agreement (NWRA) for the Building Industry with its continued distinction between 'craftsmen' and 'labourers' (Clarke, 1992b; Clarke and Wall, 1998). Though initially tripartite, too, with trade unions and government well represented on the Board, from 1979 the CITB underwent a gradual metamorphosis into an employer-led body, catering for employers' specific and often temporary needs, rather than looking after the long-term needs of the industry as a whole. Employers reasserted their managerial prerogatives and the right to train, and in so doing 'scotched' the link between unions and the craft tradition of apprenticeship (Gospel, 1995; Lee, 1979: 40–46). The recruitment of trainees or apprentices continued to rest with the individual employer, so that without a job it was difficult to obtain training except on government-sponsored training schemes for the unemployed, and without training it was difficult to get a job.

This dependence of training for the building industry on the individual 'benevolent' employer was all the more ironic, given that employers, large and small alike, increasingly throughout the 1970s and 1980s gave up the direct employment of labour, and with this their responsibility for training (Austrin, 1977: 187). With increased use of labour-only subcontracting and recognition of the self-employed construction worker as a particular tax category in 1974, the proportion of those classified as 'self-employed' increased steadily to reach officially over 60 per cent of construction workers in the private sector by 1996 and unofficially very many more. This provided open access into the industry, contributing to unpredictable skill levels, a high apprentice drop-out rate, a decline in union membership and an undermining of the training infrastructure.

All the weaknesses in the new system of apprenticeship – its trade rather than industry structure, its division according to specific occupations rather than broad-based skill areas, its increasingly employer-led regulation, the dependence of intake on individual employers, the lack of union involvement, and the widespread use of self-employment and labour-only subcontracting – were reflected in the numbers actually trained. The number of apprentices in the construction industry fell from 112,000 in 1966 to 75,000 in 1970, that is immediately after the inception of the CITB. Between 1970 and 1984, there was a 43 per cent decline in the number of trainees, in spite of the success of the CITB in channelling government funding for the Youth Training (YT) Scheme into apprentice training. By 1985, the number of CITB YT entrants stood at 16,400, a figure that was reduced by more than half by 1995, with under 8,000 entering training (CITB, 1996). The fall in the number of registered apprentices was even greater, as registration ceased to have any advantage for the employer: in 1985 8,700 were registered and by 1992 this figure was only 2,500 (CITB, 1994). This did not, however, represent the sum total of trainees, as the further education colleges increasingly came to train the unemployed and self-employed; by 1995/6 there were more adult trainees on construction training courses than CITB YT (Clarke and Wall, 1998).

Conclusions

From this sweep through the centuries, several general factors have emerged that have been vital to the maintenance and decline of apprenticeship. With respect to its maintenance, employment conditions have been vital, in particular the wage structure, through which skills are socially recognized and negotiated. Another important issue is with respect to regulation. Both the Elizabethan statutory system and the early CITB tripartite system involved state regulation, and to this is attributable much of their success. It is ironic that in Britain, with its greater reliance on an element of state-provided formal college-based vocational training, the apprenticeship system has become increasingly employer-led and decreasingly state regulated.

It is arguable that the system for the construction industry has been undermined in Britain precisely because, rather than becoming more integrated into the education system, it has become less so. In effect, it continues to be based on the will of individual employers to take on trainees, that is, on a form of voluntarism – as was the collectively bargained system. Unlike the collectively bargained system, however, training has become less and less a trade union issue for collective agreements (though this may change with the Labour government's 'Fairness at Work' proposals). Indeed, the trade union role in training has been marginalized, especially through the introduction of Modern Apprenticeships. It is, however, impossible to envisage the high-level vocational training required for today's labour process through a system regulated effectively by the individual employer, without real social partner and state involvement (Clarke and Wall, 1996). It needs to become industry-based, as has occurred in Germany and Denmark, with an integrated educational component, a tripartite structure and a clear means of incorporating the trainee into the workplace, or vocational training will lose its work basis altogether and become largely based on formal vocational training, as occurred in France.

A final important issue is the scope and status of apprenticeship. Only under the Elizabethan system was the scope of apprenticeship significantly extended to cover areas and occupations previously regarded as 'labouring' work. Though attempts have been made to incorporate new areas and occupations, success has been limited and apprenticeship has remained essentially craft-based, largely reflecting collective agreements. This is at odds with a labour process that is more and more industry-wide, integrated, mechanized and skilled, where all occupations involve a considerable degree of skill and traditional divisions between craft and labourer have become anachronistic. The logic of such an industry-based construction process is a graded system, rather than one resting on divisions between the tradesman, the labourer and the apprentice. It is, therefore, no accident that in many other European countries, including Germany, the term 'apprentice' has been discarded, to be replaced by 'trainee' and embedded within a system of skill grades rather than a craft system.

Note

1. This denotes the year the Statute was issued, under which monarch, and relevant chapter and paragraphs.

References

Alford, B W E and Barker, T C (1968) *A History of the Carpenters Company*, George Allen and Unwin, London

Austrin, T (1977) Industrial relations in the construction industry: some sociological considerations on wage contracts and trade unionism (1919–1973), PhD thesis, University of Bristol

Bell, W G (1938) *A Short History of the Worshipful Company of Tylers and Bricklayers of the City of London*, H G Montgomery, London

Booth, C (1895) *Life and Labour of the People in London, Vol V: Population, classified by trades*, Macmillan, Basingstoke

Bray, R A (1909) The apprenticeship question, *Economic Journal*, **19**, pp 404–15

CITB (Construction Industry Training Board) (1994) *Proposals for the Construction Industry Training Scheme for Craft and Operative New Entrants*, Joint Action Group on New Entrant Training, CITB, Bircham Newton, Norfolk

CITB (1996) The CITB College Survey, annual (unpublished)

Clarke, L (1992a) *Building Capitalism: Historical change and the labour process in the production of the built environment*, Routledge, London

Clarke, L (1992b) *The Building Labour Process: Problems of skills, training and employment in the British construction industry in the 1980s*, Occasional Paper 50, Chartered Institute of Building, Ascot

Clarke, L and Wall, C (1996) *Skills and the Construction Process: A comparative study of vocational training and quality in social housebuilding*, The Policy Press, Bristol

Clarke, L and Wall, C (1998) *A Blueprint for Change: Construction skills training in Britain*, The Policy Press, Bristol

Cole, G D H (1945) *Building and Planning*, Cassell, London

Cotgrove, S F (1958) *Technical Education and Social Change*, George Allen and Unwin, London

Davies, M G (1956) *The Enforcement of English Apprenticeship – A study in applied mercantilism 1563–1642*, Harvard University Press, Cambridge, MA

Deakin, S (1991) The legal origins of wage labour: industrialization and labour market institutions in historical perspective, paper presented to the 13th Annual

Conference of the International Working Party on Labour Market Segmentation, July, Bremen

Deane, P and Cole, W A (1967) *British Economic Growth 1688–1959: Trends and structures*, Cambridge University Press, Cambridge

Derry, T K (1931) The repeal of the apprenticeship clauses of the Statute of Apprentices, *Economic History Review*, **3**, pp 67–87

Dobb, M (1963) *Studies in the Development of Capitalism*, Routledge, London

Gospel, H F (1995) The decline of apprenticeship training in Britain, *Industrial Relations Journal*, **26** (1), pp 32–44

Hilton, W S (1963) *Foes to Tyranny: A history of the AUBTW*, AUBTW, London

HMSO (1927–28) *Report of Enquiry into Apprenticeship and Training 1925–26, Vols II and VIII*, HMSO, London

Hoskins, W G (1953) The rebuilding of rural England 1570–1640, *Past and Present*, **4**, pp 44–59

Howell, G (1877) Trade unions, apprentices and technical education, *Contemporary Review*, **30**, pp 833–57

Janssen, J (1985a) *Building Labour – Labour Legislation at the Eve of Capitalism: Labour under the Statute of Artificers, Labourers, Servants of Husbandry and Apprentices in England*, proceedings of Bartlett International Summer School: The Production of the Built Environment, University College London, September 1994, **6**, pp 3.1–3.17

Janssen, J (1985b) *Three Theses on the Division of Labour in Building Production*, proceedings of Bartlett International Summer School: The Production of the Built Environment, University College London, September 1994, **6**, pp 2.8–2.13

Janssen, J (1986) *Disparities Constituting the Dynamics Modes of Production: Middlesex and London Building Production in the Transition to Capitalism*, proceedings of Bartlett International Summer School: The Production of the Built Environment, University College London, September 1994, **7**, pp 165–81

Lane, J (1996) *Apprenticeship in England, 1600–1914*, UCL Press, London

Lang, J (1979) *City & Guilds of London Institute, 1878–1978 Centenary*, City & Guilds of London Institute, London

Lee, D (1979) Craft union and the force of tradition: the case, *British Journal of Industrial Relations*, **17** (1), pp 34–49

More, C (1980) *Skill and the English Working Class*, Croom Helm, Beckenham

Perry, P J C (1976) *The Evolution of British Manpower Policy: From the Statute of Artificers 1563 to the Industrial Training Act 1964*, Grosvenor Press, Portsmouth

Postgate, R (1923) *The Builders' History*, The National Federation of Building Trade Operatives, London

Reddaway, T F (1940) *The Rebuilding of London after the Great Fire*, Cape, London

Samuelson Commission (1884) *Report of the Royal Commission on Technical Instruction*, No 2096, HMSO, London

Smith, A (1910) *The Wealth of Nations, Vol 1*, J M Dent, London

Unwin, G (1908) *The Guilds and Companies of London*, Methuen, London

Welch, C (1909) *A History of Worshipful Company of Paviors*, Paviors' Company, London

Williams, G (1957) *Recruitment to the Skilled Trades*, Routledge and Kegan Paul, London

3

The Embedding of Apprenticeship in Industrial Relations: British Engineering, 1925–65

Paul Ryan

Introduction: the place of British apprenticeship

Apprenticeship tends to be viewed either as part of vocational education or as part of labour market training (Ryan, 1998a). The former conception predominates in continental Europe, the latter in Britain, where apprenticeship has traditionally been viewed in labour market terms, as vocational training for intermediate skills. Part-time vocational schooling has certainly featured in British apprenticeship, but its role has been belated and partial. Indeed, apprenticeship has traditionally been treated in the UK as part of industrial relations rather than education. The paradigm of learning embedded in traditional British apprenticeship has been one of job training and work experience, geared to acquiring a trade. The wider educational and personal development implied by apprenticeship as a route to a *Beruf* in Germany or a *profession* in France has been largely absent in the UK (Lemaire, 1993; Ryan, 1998).

The historical orientation of industrial apprenticeship in the UK to job training and industrial relations reflects a range of social and economic factors, including feeble public support for technical education, weak employer associations, marked social class divisions and low status for manual skill. More specifically, apprenticeship was until the 1960s left to 'collective *laissez-faire*', ie, the fluctuating mix of market forces, collective organization and industrial conflict which regulated employment issues in general.

When the regulation of apprenticeship is left to the labour market, the policies of employers and trade unions become crucial to its evolution. This chapter considers the labour market attributes of apprenticeship in its largest field of operation, the engineering industry, from the slump of the early 1920s to the inception of statutory regulation in the mid-1960s, a period which saw the consolidation of the links between apprenticeship and industrial relations. The chapter points up those aspects of employer and trade union policies which encouraged that consolidation.

The key issues are:

1. the uses to which employers put apprenticeship, particularly during the inter-war period, when they fought to retain unilateral control over it;
2. the threats posed thereby to trade union interests; and
3. the regulatory policies pursued by trade unions when they gained the power to force employers to negotiate their demands.

The material offers a potentially valuable case study concerning trade union policies towards youth employment and training (Garonna and Ryan, 1991; Green *et al,* 1997; Rainbird, 1990; Ryan, 1987, 1994, 1995).

The chapter is confined to an outline of both the main developments and some promising lines of explanation. Evidence is drawn primarily from the archives of the Engineering Employers' Federation (EEF), which pursued throughout the employment-related interests of member firms (Marsh, 1965; Wigham, 1973; Zeitlin, 1989).[1]

Engineering apprenticeship: methods and content

Apprenticeship comprises some blend of vocational schooling, workplace-based formal training, informal training and work experience. The traditional mix in the UK engineering industry was slanted towards the informal training and work experience end of the spectrum.

In the mid-1920s, an engineering apprenticeship was a fixed-term contract which typically ran for five to seven years, from 14–16 to 21 years of age. The employer undertook during that period to teach the relevant trade and offer continuous employment, the apprentice to serve the employer faithfully, protect trade secrets, etc. In that regard, however, reality and principle were poorly aligned. Most apprenticeship contracts were highly informal. In the mid-1920s, three-quarters of engineering apprentices (and 'learners') had no written agreement or formal indenture, serving only under a verbal agreement or no agreement at all. Concerning being taught the trade, most apprentices picked up what they could from informal training and work experience, receiving little formal training and no vocational schooling (Ministry of Labour, 1927). As for continuous employment, apprentices became vulnerable to lay-off in the post-war slump. The EEF facilitated both derogations from formal duty by encouraging firms that still used written agreements to adopt its Model Form 'B' of 1922, in which the employer's obligations to teach the trade and keep the apprentice on the books throughout an apprenticeship were so circumscribed as to be unenforceable at law.[2]

Moreover, although collective bargaining was by the 1920s the norm for regulating labour issues in the industry, when it came to apprenticeship the

EEF insisted upon unilateral regulation.[3] Claiming that the apprentice – who dominated the junior male category numerically[4] – was a minor for whom they alone were responsible, employers insisted on the right to manage apprenticeship without reference to trade unions. The pay of apprentices in federated firms during most of the inter-war period was consequently governed by the maximum pay scales that were adopted locally by EEF member associations in order to prevent competition for apprentices from driving up pay. Under those scales, the pay of an apprentice increased in yearly steps, roughly from one-fifth of the adult rate at age 16 to one-half at age 20 (see Table 3.1) – a set of relative prices at which the potentially lower productivity of an apprentice in many tasks was more than offset by his lower pay.

Table 3.1   Age–wage scales in engineering apprenticeships, 1935 and 1965. *Apprentice wage rates as percentages of adult craft (minimum district fitter) rate in EEF firms*

Age	1935[a]	1965[b]
16	21	35
17	25	42.5
18	33	57.5
19	40	67.5
20	48	80
21	100[c]	100

Notes
a. Average of (maximum) rates recommended by the five largest EEF member associations, accounting for half of federated apprentice employment in 1935.
b. After that year's increase in age–wage scales.
c. Often reduced under 'improver' rates, paid for up to two years to 21–23-year-old ex-apprentices.

Sources: Ministry of Labour and National Service/Department of Employment, *Time Rates of Wages and Hours of Labour*, various issues; EEF, file, 'Wages of Apprentices, Boys and Youths', and national wage agreements with AEU.

The result was widespread use of apprentices by employers as 'cheap labour', ie, as substitutes for journeymen and other adults in a range of tasks. That policy dovetailed with wider employer strategies. Influenced by mass production and scientific management, engineering firms preferred mechanization, the deskilling of work and piecework incentives to the upgrading of product design and employee skills as the means to increase competitiveness in depressed inter-war product markets. In that context, apprenticeship was valued as a means more to lower wage costs than to higher labour quality (Lee, 1982; Zeitlin, 1983, 1990, 1994).

A variety of evidence suggests that production dominated learning in much engineering apprenticeship during the period. The first is the sheer number of apprentices taken on. In the late 1920s, there was one apprentice for every three craft workers in federated employment as a whole. In some smaller EEF associations, including Aberdeen, Kilmarnock, Northern Ireland, Chester and Border Counties, where apprentice pay was particularly low, apprentices actually outnumbered craft workers during the 1920s. Even in the large industrial centres of the Clyde and Tyne-Tees, apprentices were more than half as numerous as journeymen.[5]

Apprentice:journeyman ratios that were much greater than needed to reproduce the craft labour force had long been interpreted by unions as evidence of the substitution of apprentice for adult labour, encouraged by low apprentice pay (More, 1980). A factory in which apprentices were numerous could of course be functioning principally as a major training facility, but even employer representatives proved reluctant to make such an inference.

Secondly, there was the extensive involvement of apprentices in piecework. Through the early 1960s, apprentices working under payment-by-results amounted to more than two-fifths of all apprentices in EEF member firms – and more than one-third of 16–17-year-olds.[6] The implications for training quality were hardly favourable. For piecework payment to be feasible, output must be easily measurable, which requires task specialization within a subdivision of labour. Moreover, piecework payment attunes the economic interests of both employer and apprentice to keeping the rotation of apprentice tasks to a minimum, in order to avoid losses of both output for the employer and earnings for the worker, thereby weakening an important ingredient of a craft training. Moreover, as such apprentices received only a fraction (the age-scale rate) of the adult bonus rate for producing an identical type of output, they constituted an attractive source of piece-working labour.

Thirdly, there is the slowness with which part-time technical education ('day release') for apprentices spread during the period. Although the EEF agreed as part of the 1947 Recruitment and Training of Juveniles in Engineering (RTJE) agreement to recommend that member firms provide it to all apprentices aged under 18, they refused to do the same for 18–20-year-olds. Moreover, many employers, particularly smaller ones in smaller districts, declined to follow that advice, claiming that they could not afford the loss of apprentice services during working time.[7]

The training picture was far from uniformly bleak. Some employers, particularly larger ones, offered high quality training, including company training facilities and time off for evening classes (Ministry of Labour, 1927). Moreover, the overall picture changed rapidly after the end of the period, as the Engineering Industry Training Board (EITB) raised training standards in apprenticeship. Partly as a result, the incidence of piecework among apprentices declined sharply during the 1960s, particularly among 16–17-year-olds.[8] The 1968–70 reform of wage structures reduced the scope for using older apprentices as cheap labour by shortening contract durations to three to four years.[9] The extension of day release for technical education during the 1970s achieved for EITB-approved apprenticeships a first year spent entirely 'off-the-job', in vocational education and formal training (Jones, 1986; Senker, 1993). To some extent, therefore, production was subsequently replaced by training as the primary function of engineering apprenticeship. During the period in hand, however, the management of apprenticeship in engineering as a whole emphasized specialized production rather than craft preparation.[10]

Apprenticeship as a threat to trade union interests

Trade unions had long complained, in engineering and elsewhere, that employers were abusing apprenticeship by substituting apprentice for adult labour, at the expense of the apprentices' own training (More, 1980). As an electrical crafts (ETU) representative put it in 1927, 'it is an economic value to you to put the married man on the street... the father and sometimes the grandfather is unemployed and it is only the boy, the apprentice, who is kept on'.[11] Similarly, the AEU reported in 1936 that:

> the evidence which we have in some districts is rather startling, where employers, in their desire to cheapen production, have introduced large numbers of boys without any regard at all to the number of men which are employed. They have introduced these boys onto automatic and semi-automatic machines and in by far the big number of cases the machines the boys have been introduced onto are machines previously manned by men and, in many cases, fully skilled men. [12]

The criticism was typically rejected by employer representatives, concerned as they were to protect their economic interests. The substance of the allegations was however conceded occasionally in private, as by a marine engineering employer in 1933:

> owing to the great volume of unemployment which has prevailed in recent years, some employers have traded upon apprenticeship to the extent of using them to do current work and, when their apprenticeship has ceased, discharged them and taken on new apprentices... many employers are using apprentices as a form of cheap labour at the present time, evading all responsibility in respect of the boys' training.[13]

Such practices involved four detailed threats to union interests. The first was the overstocking of the trade: flooding the occupational markets in question with fresh labour, thereby reducing employment opportunities for adult members. The AEU had gone on record as 'not anxious that their trade should be overburdened with a large number of workpeople when there is no reasonable hope of their being adequately employed throughout the remainder of their lives'.[14] The second threat involved craft standards. Low quality training in factories which employed many apprentices reduced the skills possessed by the next generation of craft workers, which in turn promised to weaken union opposition to the mechanization-related deskilling of the largest crafts (fitting and turning). The AEU stated bluntly to the employers in 1937: 'you have given an undertaking to train the lads. We are prepared to admit that you give that undertaking; we are not prepared to admit that you implement that undertaking'.[15] Thirdly, extensive use of apprentices in production reduced union bargaining power. Employers not only refused to allow unions to negotiate on behalf of junior males, they also expected young workers to remain at work during trade disputes. The services of apprentices could then cushion the damage done to production by any dispute with adult workers. The benefit to employers had been noted in various conflicts, notably the 1922 national lockout, when apprentices were widely used to do the work of adults. Their services, along with those of supervisors, not only helped the employers to win the dispute but in some cases revealed scope for intensifying work after the adults had returned.[16] Finally, the interests of apprentices themselves were ill-served by substitution. Most faced several years of low pay, hard work and inadequate training before qualifying for craft rates. Some were made redundant at age 21 in favour of fresh intakes of apprentice labour. The only consolation was a buoyant supply of apprenticeships.

The relative importance to unions of the four threats is not easily determined. Several factors suggest that the first and third threats (flooding the trade, reducing bargaining power), which primarily affected existing adult workers, counted for more than the final one (low apprentice pay), which concerned apprentices themselves, or the second one (future skill supplies), which concerned future craft workers. Firstly, there is the numerical and organizational importance of adult craft workers within the relevant trade unions, particularly given low rates of membership and involvement among junior males; secondly, the craft basis of many of the leading trade unions involved, led by the AEU; thirdly, the strength of paternalist values, according to which junior workers were expected to defer to adult authority within trade unions. On the other side of the coin, there was the intensity of the youth threat to adult interests; the status of youth as potential lifetime members if only they could be recruited; and, in some cases, union competition for members. Those considerations increased the influence of youth interests upon union policies (Ryan, 1987, 1995). In any case, as potential union responses to all four threats ran largely along similar lines, the relative importance of the latter need not be pursued further here.

The threats associated with substitution were by no means universal. As noted above, some larger employers provided high quality training to their apprentices. The severity of the threat declined somewhat during the 1930s, as apprentice intakes declined, followed by the fall in adult unemployment induced by rearmament and economic recovery. In 1936 a union representative was prepared to concede that substitution was a problem in particular districts rather than to the country as a whole.[17] Full employment during the next three decades turned surplus into shortage in craft labour markets, improving the job security of adult workers.

Those developments did not however dispose of union concerns over the matter. Fears that mass unemployment would return – together with a desire to reduce union vulnerability were that to happen – persisted into the post-war period, as did the importance of apprentices to piecework production and the low quality of much training. The spread of day release proved slow and partial. Overtime and night-work continued to be extensive among apprentices during the 1950s. As late as 1963 union representatives alleged that employer use of apprentices on night-work was damaging their technical training.[18]

Trade union policy

Further evidence of the threats posed by apprenticeship is provided by trade union efforts to counter them. As noted above, at the start of the period, employers reserved the right to manage apprenticeship as they chose. In reaction, trade unions adopted goals, both procedural and substantive, that promised to alleviate the problems associated with apprenticeship. The procedural requirement was to secure the right to represent apprentices and establish the joint regulation of apprenticeship; the substantive one was to regulate apprentices' terms and conditions so as to remove the threats posed by youth-adult substitution in production. The former was logically prior to the latter.

The engineering unions in question were dominated by the Amalgamated Engineering Union (AEU), which evolved during the period into an all-grades industrial union. The various small craft unions, the general unions and, eventually, the AEU combined into successive federations (FEST, CSEU) in order to negotiate with the EEF (Marsh, 1965).

Evidence on the negotiating objectives of engineering unions is derived from verbatim records of the sector-wide special conferences that were held during the period between the EEF and recognized unions. The number of conferences at which an issue was discussed provides an index of union interest, using four categories of objective (see Figure 3.1).

The merits of this 'conference count' index are enhanced by trade unions' rights to request the EEF to convene a special conference on claims of their choosing, and by the formal obligation on unions to do so before launching any industrial action in support of those claims.[19] At the same time, the index has some manifest limitations. The number of conferences held on any particular union claim depended on the strength of employer resistance as well as union interest. Secondly, during 1925–37 the EEF occasionally

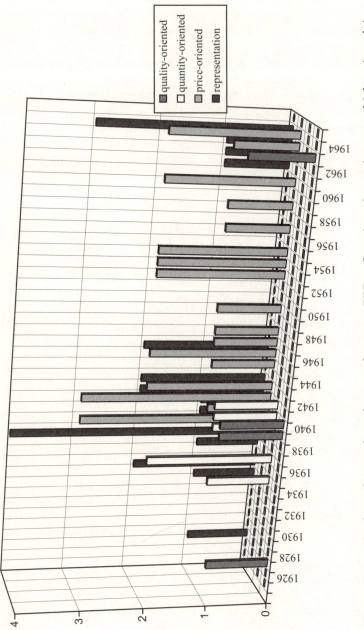

Figure 3.1 Number of special conferences between EEF and engineering unions at which union claims concerning apprenticeship were discussed, by category of claim, 1925–65

Source: EEF, records of proceedings of Central and Special Conferences.
Note: all claims were submitted either by union confederations (FEST, CSEU) or by the AEU acting separately.

rejected union requests to discuss apprenticeship as inconsistent with uni-lateral regulation by employers. Finally, union submission of a claim to con-ference did not necessarily indicate willingness to act in support of it, particularly where apprenticeship was concerned. Indeed, trade unions mounted only one official dispute over apprenticeship-related claims during the period: a one-day sympathy strike during the apprentice strike wave in the spring of 1937.[20] The paucity of official strike activity need not however indicate low union interest: to some extent unions could rely on the unoffi-cial apprentice strikes that periodically induced the EEF to increase age–wage scales (Ryan, 1999).

Procedural goals: representation rights

The immediate objective of engineering unions at the start of the period was to extend existing collective regulation to cover apprenticeship. The EEF was called upon to recognize trade union rights to represent and negotiate for apprentices, and to bring apprentices under existing sectoral procedures for regulating disputes. In doing so, rather than seeking a regulation of appren-ticeship separate from that of regular employment, unions helped reduce further an already narrow gap between apprenticeship and employment.

During the period, nine separate claims for rights to represent appren-tices and other junior males were discussed at 23 different conferences (Fig-ure 3.1). Pressure on employers to accept trade union representation was concentrated in three sub-periods: 1933–37, 1939–45 and 1961–64. Representation claims remained therefore a major, if intermittent, feature of the negotiating landscape throughout the period.

During 1933–37, representation rights dominated apprentice-ship-oriented claims. Introducing the claim in 1936 for the fourth time in three years, Jack Little remarked that 'we have had so many conferences that it almost a difficult matter to find new reasons in order to back up this very persistent claim'.[21] The EEF acknowledged the importance of the claim to unions – 'since the war there have been more than 20 conferences with the trade unions, individually and collectively, when they have pressed to the Federation their demand for recognition in respect of apprentices, boys and youths'[22] – but rejected it repeatedly, relying on the inability of unions to force its hand during the inter-war slump. The employers' arguments were moral and paternalistic, rejecting what they termed interference by third parties – or by fourth parties, when the role of the guardian was remembered – in their relationships with junior male workers in general and apprentices in particular: 'apprentices are the particular charge of the employer, who is responsible for their efficient training and welfare'.[23] The details of the argument varied with the audience. Craft unions, including the AEU, were rebuffed by emphasizing the training aspect of the employer's responsibilities to young people; general unions, including the TGWU, which represented non-apprenticed youths, by stressing the employer's role *in loco parentis,* as a guiding influence over the immature 'high spirits' of young males.

The stalemate was broken in 1937 by a combination of economic recovery and apprentice strikes (Ryan, 1999). The second strike wave of the year convinced a majority of employers of the unavoidability of concessions – and even of their desirability, in the hope that unions would help to discipline juvenile unrest (Croucher, 1982; McKinlay 1985). The procedure agreement of December 1937 recognized nationally for the first time the right of unions to represent junior male workers and broadly brought apprentices under the existing national machinery for settlement of disputes.

The procedural issue was however only partially resolved in the unions' favour in 1937. The EEF had insisted on two variances relative to adult procedure. Apprentices serving under written agreements (here, 'indentured') were excluded, although the EEF recommended to members that such apprentices should function under conditions no less favourable than those of other junior male employees. Secondly, junior male grievances were to be taken either direct to management by the juvenile involved or to be handled by unions' district official without any role for workplace representatives (shop stewards).

The two exclusions reflected continuing employer concern to retain a privileged 'domestic' relationship with juvenile employees in general and apprentices in particular. They also kept the issue of representation rights alive until the end of the period. Between 1939 and 1945, engineering unions lodged four separate claims for the inclusion of indentured apprentices and/or the inclusion of shop stewards in junior male procedure. The EEF continued to justify its refusals of those claims in terms of the sanctity of the apprenticeship contract and the 'special domestic relationship' with its 'sense of responsibility on the one hand and... sense of discipline on the other...'.[24] The employers' argument might have been expected to have carried greater weight after 1937, once a formal apprenticeship contract had become necessary to perpetuate the exclusion of youths from disputes procedures. As, however, the EEF advised its members that an exchange of letters with a boy's parent constituted a written agreement, the argument remained hollow and the continuing pressure from unions is not surprising.

The representation claim was however allowed to lapse in 1945, as part of the wider discussions which led to the 1947 RTJE agreement. That agreement potentially intensified the problems posed to unions by employer control of apprenticeship, as it recommended that all apprentices serve henceforth under written agreements – which, had it been observed, would have removed all apprentices, not just a modest minority, from the scope of the 1937 procedure agreement.

The claim to represent all junior males was raised again in 1961 and discussed regularly until the signing of the 1965 Procedure Agreement for Apprentices, Boys and Youths, which moved the status of junior males still closer to that of other employees.[25] In terms of industrial conflict, the agreement removed a long-standing bone of contention by effectively demilitarizing apprenticeship: the AEU undertook to discipline apprentices who went on strike, the employers neither to lock out apprentices nor to use them during a dispute to do the work of strikers. Taken with the better known Industrial Training Act of 1964, the 1965 procedure agreement represents a watershed in the history of engineering apprenticeship, particularly from the standpoint of industrial relations and industrial conflict.

Substantive goals: principles

Having largely won in 1937 the right to negotiate on behalf of apprentices and other junior males, trade unions had to decide what to do with their new powers. What changes would remove the threats posed to union interests by the use to which many employers put apprenticeship?

In principle three regulatory options face the union under such conditions (Ryan, 1994). The first focuses on the quality of training (here, the 'quality-oriented' option). The incentive to substitute apprentices for adult employees is removed by raising the quality of training. A high quality training programme, involving, for example, mandatory day release, and sufficient instruction and task rotation on the job, reduces the net productivity of an apprentice, by reducing both the time available for productive work during training and the relative proficiency of apprentices on productive work. The incentive to substitute apprentice for adult labour is then removed, even at low apprentice wages.

A second regulatory option is price-oriented. The relative pay of apprentices is increased until the substitution of their labour for that of adults becomes unprofitable. Even if training quality remains low, with apprentices heavily involved in routine production work, the incentive to substitute is removed as long as the gap between apprentice and adult pay is less than that in productivity.

Finally, there is a quantity-oriented option. The employment of apprentices is restricted by quota. Maximum apprentice:journeymen ratios are applied, whether at department, plant, district or sectoral level. If those ratios are set sufficiently low, employers' ability to substitute apprentice for adult labour can be held down to acceptable levels even though the underlying incentive to do so remains unchanged.

The appeal of the three strategies to a union differs in three respects. The first is their intrinsic contribution, ie, how much they can contribute to union goals if successfully negotiated and enforced. Secondly, there is their negotiability: the prospect of successfully negotiating them, which depends on the lengths to which employers will go to avoid conceding them. Finally, there is their enforceability: the prospects for their successful implementation once negotiated. The *a priori* merits of the strategies in terms of these criteria are now discussed in turn. The results are summarized in Table 3.2.

Table 3.2 Union strategy options ranked by their prospective
contributions to union goals

Strategy	Intrinsic contribution	Negotiability	Enforceability
Quality-oriented	1	3	3
Price-oriented	2	2	1
Quantity-oriented	3	1	2

It is assumed initially that union interests centre upon the current pay and employment of adult members, particularly craft workers. In terms of the first criterion – the potential contribution to union goals – the quality-oriented and price-oriented strategies are equivalent. Both, if carried far enough, remove the incentive to employers to substitute apprentice for adult labour. The quantity-oriented option offers less: it constrains, but does not remove, the incentive to substitution. At the same time, if kept sufficiently low, a quota on apprentice numbers can also effectively neuter the threat posed by substitution.

The merits of the quality-oriented and price-oriented strategies diverge, however, if it is assumed that the union cares also about the dilution of future skills, the second threat associated with traditional apprenticeship. The quality-oriented strategy is then superior to the price-oriented one, as the latter, unlike the former, accepts – and even encourages – low training quality.

On the second criterion – the willingness of employers to concede to union demands – the ranking of union regulatory options is the reverse. Assuming initially that employers seek only to maximize profits, as the effect of quotas on profits is again less than that of price-oriented and quality-oriented rules, firms are expected to oppose quotas less strongly. Quotas limit the employer's ability to profit from substitution, whereas the other two strategies in principle eliminate it entirely.

The equivalence on the negotiability criterion of the price-oriented and quality-oriented strategies dissolves in turn under a wider view of employer objectives. If employers value hierarchical control for itself, not solely for greater profit, their opposition to price-oriented claims is weaker than that to quality-oriented and quantity-oriented ones. A price-oriented strategy avoids the overt and everyday incursions into 'managerial prerogative' associated with employment quotas and rules on training methods.

The strategies differ also on the third criterion – enforceability. The employer benefits in principle from evading agreements that embody any of the three union strategies. The question is therefore how well the union can monitor employer compliance. On this criterion, the quality-oriented strategy is the least attractive to the union. The quality of work-based training is intrinsically difficult to measure – as reflected in the difficulty of establishing, for example, how much, if anything, an employer invests in an employee's skills (Jones, 1986; Ryan, 1991). Secondly, the employer enjoys informational advantages over union representatives, particularly national officials, as a result of greater proximity to, and managerial powers over, workplace-based training. Finally, while apprentices themselves have incentives to facilitate monitoring by reporting substandard training to the union, they may not know how well they are being trained, at least until their training has been completed.

The results of a price-oriented strategy are by contrast relatively easy to monitor. Apprentices are as well informed as employers about their own pay, and they have strong incentives to report any underpayment to the union for corrective action. A quantity-oriented strategy occupies an intermediate position. Apprentice employment is probably easier for a union to measure than is training quality, but less easy than trainee pay. Individual apprentices hold only limited information and have little incentive to convey even that to the union; as employers control the flow of such information, they may choose to delay and modify its presentation to suit.

The enforceability of price-oriented strategies is therefore markedly greater than that of quality-oriented or quantity-oriented ones. The imbalance is reduced, potentially to zero, when a public authority bears the costs of monitoring employment (rarely the case, at plant and company levels at least) or training quality (as to some extent under the EITB after 1964). In the largely non-interventionist climate of the UK during the period, however, public monitoring of training quality in particular was absent, making a quality-oriented strategy difficult for a union to enforce.

There is therefore no unambiguous ranking across the three criteria of the contribution of the three regulatory options to union goals (Table 3.2). The union's preference depends then on the relative importance of the three criteria. Here a ranking is visible, in which under particular circumstances enforceability becomes the crucial criterion. Negotiability may be seen as a gateway condition. When a union lacks bargaining power, negotiability is low and it matters little which strategy the union favours: the employer can reject them all. When a union enjoys a strong bargaining advantage, negotiability is high: all three strategies become negotiable in principle. Then, given that differences in 'intrinsic contribution' are trivial when low apprentice:journeyman ratios are allowed, the key criterion becomes enforceability, and a price-oriented strategy is chosen rather than the quality-oriented and quantity-oriented alternatives.

In sum, when apprenticeship is regulated by the labour market, uninfluenced by public intervention, unions are expected to respond to apprenticeship-related threats by demanding higher relative pay for apprentices rather than better training or fewer apprentices, primarily because such an approach has a better chance of being enforced.

Substantive demands: practice

The preceding analysis can be used to analyse the behaviour of engineering unions after the acquisition of representation rights in 1937. All three types of claim cropped up in practice (Figure 3.1). Price-oriented claims concentrated initially on achieving uniform national age–wage scales for junior males, including apprentices. After the achievement of national age–wage scales in 1941, price-oriented demands involved increases in national scale rates – ie, increases in apprentice relative pay separate from and in addition to general wage increases. The only exception was an October 1963 claim for four weeks' annual paid holiday and exclusion from night-work. Quality-oriented claims involved improved training quality for apprentices, primarily through guaranteed access to day release. Quantity-oriented demands took the form of maximum apprentice:journeyman ratios, excepting only the August 1941 claim for the limitation of the normal age of apprenticeship to 16–21 years.

The presence of all three types of claim, sometimes in the same package, indicates therefore, much as one might expect, that unions did not view the three strategies as mutually exclusive. At the same time, the bulk of negotiations subsequent to 1937 were pay-oriented, ie, demands for increased age–wage scales (Figure 3.1). Thirteen distinct pay-related claims were lodged, and considered at 28 different conferences, specifically on behalf of junior males and apprentices, between 1938 and 1965. In most years engineering unions either made a new effort or continued an existing one, to raise the relative pay of apprentices. EEF representatives expressed particular frustration when the unions (CSEU) demanded a further increase in age–wage scale rates in January 1953, only nine months after an earlier increase had been conceded. By contrast, training methods and apprentice numbers attracted only two and three claims, involving only three and six conferences, respectively. Higher apprentice relative pay therefore joined representation rights as the predominant negotiating demands on behalf of junior males during the period; quality-oriented and quantity-oriented demands both trailed behind.

Figure 3.1 shows also that the predominance of price-oriented claims over quality-oriented and quantity-oriented ones increased during the period. No claim subsequent to 1941 concerned apprentice numbers; only one related to training methods – a 1963 demand for day release for all apprentices aged under 18. Although demands for apprentice:journeyman ratios had been commonplace historically, after the 1937 watershed no further demand for a specific maximum was lodged. The issue was raised again only as a general principle, as part of the wide-ranging reform proposals of the early months of the war.

The paucity of quality-oriented and quantity-oriented claims after the war may reflect to some extent the success of pay-oriented claims in raising apprentices' relative pay, making alternative regulatory approaches potentially redundant. This interpretation is however weakened by evidence that relative apprentice hourly earnings (as opposed to wage rates) increased strongly only after 1965. The increases in age–wage scales negotiated during the 1950s appear to have been more than offset by piecework-based 'wage drift' in favour of adults (Ryan, 1993). The same timing applies to apprentice numbers, whose downward trend began only in the late 1960s following their broad stability in the post-war period (Gospel, 1995; Stevens, 1994).

The incidence and timing of quality-oriented claims is however potentially deceptive. Much of the 1940s and early 1950s was taken up with negotiating and implementing the sector-wide RTJE agreement of 1947, under which voluntary joint bodies – Local Training Committees and a National Joint Body – were to improve youth recruitment and training. The unions attached considerable importance to the RTJE agreement, pressing the EEF to recommend that all apprentices, irrespective of age, should receive access to day release, and subsequently complaining frequently about uneven employer implementation of the agreement. To that extent, it is not possible to conclude that unions opted only for a price-oriented regulation of apprenticeship.

The way in which unions pursued training quality is however broadly consistent with the interpretation offered here. As anticipated, union efforts to improve training quality through collective bargaining proved limited in both frequency and content. The two claims lodged during the period both called for compulsory day release for all apprentices (in 1963, for all apprentices aged under 18). As the visibility to apprentices and unions of day release is greater than that of training practices within the workplace (eg, task rotation), the prospects for monitoring the implementation of such provisions were relatively favourable. Unions therefore confined their negotiating demands to a relatively easily monitored aspect of training quality: day release. Even that proved difficult to enforce. Some employers, notably in Aberdeen and Dundee, refused to accord day release to their 16–17-year-old apprentices, as expected of them under the 1947 RTJE agreement.[26]

A further attribute of training quality whose monitoring was potentially easy was the use of apprentices for piecework, which was widely interpreted as evidence of excessive specialization, to the detriment of training quality, even if it did teach the skills required subsequently for fast work as an adult. While the craft unions sometimes criticized piecework as inimical to training quality, particularly for 16 and 17-year-olds,[27] they did not demand the exclusion of apprentices from it. This reluctance may also have reflected an anticipation of enforcement difficulties, but a more immediate consideration was the potential implications for apprentice incomes, which regularly led the AEU's Youth Conference to vote down abolitionist motions.

Other attributes of apprenticeship training were prospectively harder for unions to regulate effectively. The claim of October 1939 did indeed call for 'proper workshop training', but a single instance of so unenforceable a demand is taken here as evidence of early wartime reforming zeal rather its adoption as a regulatory strategy. The issue was raised frequently in conference thereafter, but as a stick with which to beat employers rather than as part of negotiating demands.

The fact that trade unions pursued their quality-related goals more through joint regulation than through collective bargaining during the 1940s and 1950s is also interpreted as evidence of the regulatory weakness of collective bargaining. The prospects for improving quality through the joint bodies whose formation was encouraged at the time by government appeared promising under the political conditions of the 1940s, only to dwindle in the 1950s, leading unions to join the subsequent groundswell in favour of statutory regulation. Again, union choices suggest not so much indifference to training quality as awareness of the difficulties of achieving it through collective bargaining.

In sum, the evidence indicates that trade unions sought to counter the threat of substitution posed by traditional apprenticeship, particularly during the inter-war years, by negotiating, first, for the right to represent apprentices and, when that had been largely established, for higher age–wage rates for apprentices, rather than for better training or restrictions on apprentice numbers. Improvements in training quality were also seen as important, but they were pursued primarily through joint regulation. (The potential incompatibility of simultaneous demands for higher pay and better quality with the continued existence of apprenticeship was largely ignored by all parties.) The unions' approach is interpreted as evidence of the greater enforceability of collective agreements on trainee pay than of those on training quality or apprentice numbers.[28]

Conclusions

This chapter has considered a period during which engineering apprenticeship, which had traditionally been treated primarily as a labour market phenomenon, became firmly ensconced in industrial relations. The failure of government to develop the educational potential of apprenticeship was reflected notoriously in the non-implementation of the pledge made during both world wars of compulsory day release for all workers aged under 18. Given that lacuna, it was left to employers and trade unions – and to some extent apprentices themselves – to make what they could out of apprenticeship.

At the start of the period, employers combined the widespread use of apprentices as production labour with a rearguard defence of unilateral regulation. The two policies sat poorly together. The privileged 'domestic' relationship with the apprentice that employers cited in rejecting any role for trade unions conflicted vividly with their widespread neglect of the training – let alone the education – of apprentices. The *de facto* treatment of apprentices by many employers as another category of labour contributed in turn to the erosion of prior distinctions – economic, social and legal – between apprenticeship and employment.

Trade union reactions reinforced the tendency. Insofar as the notion of a 'strategy' is appropriate to union policy, it emphasized two components: first, the inclusion of apprentices within regular industry-wide collective bargaining; secondly, increases in their relative pay. In the account offered here, engineering unions were not indifferent to training quality, but could reasonably expect, in the absence of effective public support, a pay-oriented approach to prove more effective than a quality-oriented one. Both policies were successfully realized during the period, though the full effects of higher age–wage scale rates on apprentice earnings appear to have come through only in the 1970s. Both reinforced the positioning of apprenticeship within industrial relations and the reduction of status differentiation between apprenticeship and employment. Apprentices were encouraged in turn to perceive themselves as production workers and to act accordingly, in pursuit of their immediate economic interests, providing crucial impetus to the unions' pay-oriented approach (Ryan, 1999).

A more attractive alternative can be discerned within the policy agendas of employers and trade unions. The efforts of employers to keep apprenticeship, particularly indentured apprenticeship, formally segregated from regular employment, might have linked with union interest in improved training, fostering the reorientation of apprenticeship from industrial relations towards vocational education and the stabilization of training costs that has broadly characterized metalworking apprenticeship in post-war Germany. Effective public action would undoubtedly have been necessary – though perhaps not sufficient – to realize that alternative.

A move towards such an alternative was indeed made subsequently, under EITB auspices (Senker, 1993). The developments considered here arguably undermined that attempt. Increases in relative apprentice pay rates bit as employers switched from piecework to time-work. Given the high training quality promoted by the EITB, apprenticeship changed rapidly from a source of low-priced production labour into a major financial burden on employers, leading to a sharp reduction in the supply of places (Gospel, 1995; Marsden and Ryan, 1991; Stevens, 1994).

Acknowledgement

Support provided by the Centre for History and Economics and King's College, Cambridge, the Nuffield Foundation, and the Laboratoire d'Economie et de Sociologie du Travail (LEST-CNRS), Aix-en-Provence, is gratefully acknowledged, as is EEF permission to use its archives. I would like to thank William Brown, Tsuneo Ishikawa, Martine Möbus, Roger Penn, Helen Rainbird, Alistair Reid, Keith Snell, George Strauss, Lloyd Ulman, Eric

Verdier, Jonathan Zeitlin, and participants in seminars in Cambridge (the 1994 Colloquium on Skills and Training of the Centre for History and Economics, King's College), Tokyo, Northampton and Aix-en- Provence for comments and suggestions.

Notes

1. The EEF archive is held at the Modern Record Centre, University of Warwick. Archival references below refer to microfilm records.
2. 'The legal position', internal memorandum to Special Committee in Regard to the Supply, Selection and Training of Apprentices, 1927–29; EEF A 7 (91).
3. The EEF had offered in 1920 to recognize union representation of junior males, but withdrew the offer in 1923; the EEF Management Board decided in 1926 to offer negotiating rights to general unions on behalf of non-apprenticed juveniles, but the decision was not implemented (Conferences of 17 November 1920 and 31 July 1923).
4. Apprentices accounted for 80 per cent of junior male employees in the EEF in 1930 (EEF file, 'Proportion of apprentices to journeymen, 1902–38'). Training for female employment did not involve apprenticeship during the period.
5. EEF: file, 'Proportion of apprentices to journeymen', undated; A 7 (91).
6. EEF: A 7 (330), A 12 (36), Z67.590.
7. EEF: A 7 (265), A 7 (305).
8. Internal surveys found that the share of piece-working apprentices declined after 1960, falling from 42 to 21 per cent between 1960 and 1968 (note 6, above).
9. EEF: Z67.590.
10. Further evidence of low average training quality is provided by the role of unofficial apprentice strikes in obtaining concessions from employers, which would have been minimal had apprenticeship been dominated by training rather than production (Ryan, 1999).
11. Conference of 24 March 1927; EEF: A 12 (1).
12. Conference, 5 May 1936.
13. EEF subcommittee on Apprentices and Young Persons, transcript of meeting of 7 December 1933, p 4; A 7 (111).
14. Conference of May 1919; EEF internal memorandum, 'Rights of unions to negotiate on behalf of apprentices, boys and youths; proposals which have passed between the Federation and the AEU', c.1922.
15. Remarks of Jack Little, AEU; Special Conference, 1 July 1937. The problem had long been recognized as endemic to industrial apprenticeship: 'the scores of apprentices in a modern shipyard are necessarily left to learn their business for themselves, by watching workmen who are indifferent or even unfriendly to their progress, with possibly some occasional hints from a benevolent foreman' (Webb and Webb, 1920: 480).
16. Two-thirds of the apprentices functioning in EEF firms remained at work during the 1922 lockout (EEF, M 19, Appendix 12). An example of the benefits which one employer subsequently derived from re-timing work is provided in EEF: A 7 (111).
17. Conference of 5 May 1936.

18. Conference of 31 October 1963.
19. Conference procedures involved the submission by one or more trade unions of one or (typically) more issues, often including specific claims, for consideration by a panel of EEF and trade union representatives, chaired by an employer. Typically, after discussion, the EEF representatives would withdraw and, on their return, either make an offer, reject the claim outright ('failure to agree'), or suggest that it be carried over, as for several apprenticeship-related claims during the 1940s and 1950s.
20. The threat that unions might back apprenticeship-related claims with official industrial action was apparently discounted by the EEF, which carried over repeatedly a 1946 claim for increased age–wage scale rates until faced with an unofficial apprentice strike in 1952.
21. Conference of 5 May 1936.
22. EEF: Circular Letter 116, 21 October 1937.
23. Conference of 23 August 1923.
24. Conferences of 26 January 1940, 2 May 1941 and 15 October 1962.
25. Wigham (1973: 241–42). The 1965 agreement partially relaxed the restriction on shop steward representation of apprentices, by permitting their involvement should the apprentice opt to process a dispute within the plant rather than through the local union official, but only after the apprentice had taken it first to the supervisor and thereafter without any further involvement by the apprentice complainant himself. As before, there was to be no initial works conference stage in the handling of apprentice disputes.
26. EEF, A 7 (265).
27. For example, conference of 21 March 1963.
28. The conclusions may not apply to other times and places. In particular, craft unions in the printing industry apparently preferred quotas to high relative pay in regulating apprenticeship (Child, 1967).

References

Child, J (1967) *Industrial Relations in the British Printing Industry*, George Allen and Unwin, London

Croucher, R (1982) *Engineers at War*, Merlin, London

Garonna, P and Ryan, P (1991) The regulation and deregulation of youth activity, in *The Problem of Youth*, ed P Ryan, P Garonna and R C Edwards, Macmillan, Basingstoke

Gospel, H (1995) The decline of apprenticeship in Britain, *Industrial Relations Journal*, **26** (1), pp 32–44

Green, F, Machin, S and Wilkinson, D (1997) Trade unions and training practices in British workplaces, discussion paper, Centre for Economic Performance, LSE, London

Jones, I S (1986) Apprentice training costs in British manufacturing establishments: some new evidence, *British Journal of Industrial Relations*, **24** (3), pp 333–62

Lee, D (1982) Beyond deskilling: skill, craft and class, in *The Degradation of Work?*, ed S Wood, Hutchinson, London

Lemaire, S (1993) Regards sur l'apprentissage, *Education et Formation*, **34**, pp 3–10

McKinlay, A (1985) The 1937 apprentices' strike: challenge from an 'unexpected quarter', *Scottish Labour History Society Journal*, **20**, pp 14–32

Marsden, D W and Ryan, P (1991) Initial training, labour market structure and public policy: intermediate skills in British and German industry, in *International Comparisons of Vocational Education and Training for Intermediate Skills*, ed P Ryan, Falmer Press, London

Marsh, A (1965) *Industrial Relations in Engineering*, Pergamon, Oxford

Ministry of Labour (1927) *Report of an Enquiry into Apprenticeship and Training in 1925–26, Volume 6*, HMSO, London

More, C (1980) *Skill and the English Working Class, 1870–1914*, Croom Helm, Beckenham

Rainbird, H (1990) *Training Matters*, Blackwell, Oxford

Ryan, P (1987) Trade unionism and the pay of young workers, in *From School to Unemployment? The labour market for young people*, ed P Junankar, Macmillan, Basingstoke

Ryan, P (1991) How much do employers spend on training? An evaluation of the 'Training in Britain' estimates, *Human Resource Management Journal*, **1** (4), pp 55–76

Ryan, P (1993) Pay structures, collective bargaining and apprenticeship training in post-war British and German metalworking industry, paper presented to CEPR conference on Human Capital and Post-war European Economic Growth, Dublin, March

Ryan, P (1994) Training quality and trainee exploitation, in *Britain's Training Deficit*, ed R Layard, K Mayhew and G Owen, Avebury Press, Aldershot

Ryan, P (1995) Trade union policies towards the Youth Training Scheme: patterns and causes, *British Journal of Industrial Relations*, **33** (1), pp 1–33

Ryan, P (1998) Is apprenticeship better? A review of the economic evidence, *Journal of Vocational Education and Training*, **50** (2), pp 289–322

Ryan, P (1999) Apprentice strikes in British engineering, 1937–68, working paper, University of Cambridge

Senker, P (1993) *Industrial Training in a Cold Climate*, Gower, Aldershot

Stevens, M (1994) An investment model for the supply of training by employers, *Economic Journal*, **104**, pp 556–71

Webb, S and Webb, B (1920) *Industrial Democracy*, Longman, London

Wigham, E (1973) *The Power to Manage*, Macmillan, Basingstoke

Zeitlin, J (1983) The labour strategies of British engineering employers, 1890–1922, in *Managerial Strategies and Industrial Relations: An historical and comparative study*, ed H F Gospel and C R Littler, Heinemann, Oxford

Zeitlin, J (1989) The internal politics of employer organization: the Engineering Employers' Federation, 1896–1939, in *The Power to Manage? Employers and industrial relations in contemporary historical perspective*, ed S Tolliday and J Zeitlin, Routledge, London

Zeitlin, J (1990) The triumph of adversarial bargaining: industrial relations in British engineering, 1880–1939, *Politics and Society*, **18** (3), pp 405–26

Zeitlin, J (1994) Reforming skills in British engineering, 1900–40: a contingent failure, paper presented to Colloquium on Skills and Training, Centre for History and Economics, King's College, Cambridge

Part 2
Theoretical Approaches
to Apprenticeship

4

Nietzsche, Marx and Mastery: The Learning unto Death

Glenn Rikowski

Mastery – One has attained to mastery when one neither goes wrong nor hesitates in the performance.

(Friedrich Nietzsche, 1982: 212)

Introduction

The concept of 'apprenticeship' requires analysis in terms of its end state: mastery. Apprenticeship viewed as a 'new learning paradigm' demands that the concept of the fully developed apprentice – one who has become a 'master' – be clarified. The apprentice-master couplet is not of the polar variety, as in the examples given by Hamlyn (1971: 16–19), such as knowledge-belief and thick-thin. Polar concepts can only be understood relative to each other (ibid). They suggest a continuum, where one implies the existence of the other, in the way that 'hot' implies 'cold'.

This is not the case with apprenticeship-master. Here the *temporal* break – where the apprentice at a certain point *becomes* a master – occasions an ontological break: apprentices 'come out of their time' and become different persons. As Parkin (1978) noted, apprentices learn the process of 'self-generating skill', which involves learning how to undertake continuous learning. The master, by contrast, is (ontologically) a continuous learner where the problems to be solved are generated by engagement with the trade through the application of skill and knowledge with an underlying confidence and attitude (summarized as 'craft pride') towards production and the product. The apprentice *learns* how to become a master. Hence, there is a need to understand mastery as the terminal point of apprenticeship.

Three types of mastery are articulated in relation to three forms of apprenticeship: classical apprenticeship, modern apprenticeship and post-modern apprenticeship. These forms of apprenticeship are depicted as 'real-ideal types' which are not drawn in an abstract, de-historicized way – as a process of 'pure' conceptual analysis – but are grounded within a basic historical account of the development of British apprenticeship from World War I. This historical analysis is not provided here, but can be found in an earlier, and much longer version of this chapter (Rikowski, 1998). Secondly, the whole analysis is driven by perspectives on mastery drawn from Nietzsche and Postone's (1996) rendering of Marx's concept of capital. This analysis, allied to the historical outline in Rikowski (1998), illustrates what is at stake in the new (post) Modern Apprenticeships that have been introduced in Britain in the last few years. (Post) Modern Apprenticeships are based on perennial apprenticeship; there is no terminal point to apprenticeship. Hence, *mastery is never attained*. There is a 'master', but its name is 'capital'. In (post) modernized apprenticeships, apprentices learn unto death in reaction to the 'needs' of a blind, globalizing and dominating social force which is 'without an ego' (Postone, 1996) and whose drives are *infinite:* capital. We learn for, with and through capital in (post) modernized apprenticeship.

The following section starts to build up the main argument by introducing Nietzsche's perspectives on mastery. These perspectives are then utilized as one of the means for appraisal and understanding of developments within British apprenticeship.

Nietzsche and the horizon of the master

Nietzsche's writings contain many perspectives on mastery. In his contrasts between 'slave' and 'master' morality in *Beyond Good and Evil* (1990/1886, section 260) Nietzsche is concerned with a broad analysis of these concepts which function as standards for ascertaining the value of individuals. The task is to show how this project has relevance for a narrower conception of mastery set around craft performance. Nietzsche addresses this utilitarian – and more conventional – sense of the notion of mastery in *The Gay Science* (1974/1882). For Nietzsche, these two perspectives are both inferior to a third perspective on mastery. This third view is mastery as continuous self-overcoming. Through the work of Richardson (1996) and Scott Johnston (1998), and through Nietzsche himself, a typology of mastery, utilizing the three perspectives, is sketched out. It is used to inform later discussion.

A useful starting point is Nietzsche's views on 'normal health' and the horizon of the master as prefix to what he says about 'craft' and the craftsman. Richardson (1996: 129–30) provides a sketch of this first, 'lower' order of mastery. In this conception, the horizon of the master has clear boundaries (of location, practice or social affiliation) which configure his life. These boundaries function to reproduce him as a definable member of a group within which he was born and/or socialized. This 'group holds...

mastery because its energies are committed to a simple and well-organized system of practices' (Richardson, 1996: 129). The group helps to organize the drives of individual members and creates members in its image. Thus: 'each master is raised to be a simple and stable structure of drives himself, also willing growth in an activity with which he identifies – his role' (ibid).

The horizon of the master is set by role, status and identification with practice. Nietzsche held that such an horizon functioned as a boundary within which individuals could flourish and grow in terms of their designated activity. Mastery is nurtured within a closed social sphere through apprenticeship. When it is attained there is minimal scope for re-definition of practice by individual masters. This is because the master aims to 'conserve' a particular practice and way of life. Indeed, reverence for practices built up over many generations is basic to this form of mastery.

Although Richardson (1996) sketches out this type of mastery in relation to politics, he is at pains to stress that it has more general application within Nietzsche's work. This can be seen when we turn to what Nietzsche has to say on mastery in its craft form. In *The Gay Science,* Nietzsche (1974/1882, section 366: 322–23) explores the relationship between mastery and craftsmanship. He notes that 'every craft makes crooked' (ibid). Using 'craft' in a broad sense to mean specialization in employment, Nietzsche argues that:

> Every craft, even if it should have a golden floor, has a leaden ceiling over it that presses and presses down upon the soul until that becomes queer and crooked. Nothing can be done about that. Let nobody suppose that one could possibly avoid such crippling by some artifice of education. On this earth one pays dearly for every kind of *mastery*... For having a speciality one pays by being a victim of this speciality.

> (1974/1882: 322–23)

This perspective on mastery is castigated by Nietzsche for stunting the life force of individuals, for not engendering an expansive creativity and for restricting individual growth and development. For these ends, argues Nietzsche, individuals need to smash through narrow horizons set by occupation, trade or tradition in search of the 'great health'. They need to overcome themselves and increase their capacity for self-development. In effect, they need to become masters of a very different kind. The case of the craftsman illustrates the poverty, life-denying nature and baseness of the 'normal' type of mastery.

Nietzsche expends considerable energy, spread throughout his works, on exploring the conditions necessary for the rise of a master type who breaks the bonds of society. He examines history (especially ancient Greece), individuals (such as Goethe and Napoleon) and contemporary societies and culture in an attempt to gain insight into the becoming, the formation of such masters. At the heart of this form of mastery is self-mastery, but self-mastery which is self-regarding and not subsumed under a conserving imperative which seeks to eternalize a particular social group, practice or way of life. Nietzsche acknowledges that education or training could be one of the forces making for self-overcoming, yet education and training are 'firmly rooted in the social and cultural' and: 'To self-overcome requires the very overcoming of education, as far as education is itself a product and a minion of the dominant society and culture' (Scott Johnston, 1998: 73).

This expanded form of mastery has no horizon, no boundaries – unto death. It is a process and trajectory. Nietzsche acknowledged that it involved playing a 'dangerous game' as it entailed continual dissolution, re-definition and recomposition of self. It also involved a 'war against society', including education, as the self-overcoming individual 'has the locus of existence entrenched firmly within' (Scott Johnston, 1998: 78). Thus, Nietzsche's injunction (in *Ecce Homo*, 1979/1888) to 'become what one is' involves placing a 'will to create and live within one's own truths' as the centre of one's life-activity and process (Scott Johnston, 1998: 78). In turn, this involves a form of mastery with a 'new system of valuation provided by and for this individual [which] takes its point of reference from the individual, and not the outward society, church, state, nation, or culture' (ibid). Hence: 'Static being gives way to a dynamic becoming. Every moment of every day of every year is spent in self-overcoming' (ibid).

It is a lifelong vocation. The parallel with lifelong learning is startling, and we return to this in due course.

Three models of apprenticeship

Drawing upon Parkin (1978), Richards (1988) and the historical analysis given in a much longer version of this chapter (Rikowski, 1998) it is possible to distil the notions of classical and modern apprenticeships, and to bring out basic contrasts. Classical and modern forms of apprenticeship can be characterized as follows.

(Old) classical apprenticeships:

- time-serving;
- training by 'sitting by Nellie' (observation of the master) and learning by doing (participation in production);
- evening classes (not compulsory);
- emphasis on indentures – document signed by parents, apprentices and employers – which laid out rights and duties of the three parties;
- methods of entry through trade unions or informal links (sons of employees);
- specialized training in a single trade;
- inculcation of 'craft pride' and 'craft mysteries'.

(New) Modern Apprenticeships:

- training to standards of craftsmanship (through module system);
- supervised off-the-job training;
- compulsory day release for college study;
- contract of employment;
- emphasis on attainment of formal qualifications (eg, City & Guilds);
- 'scientific' entry: tests, structured interviews, application forms and stipulated qualifications;
- flexibility: trade specialism, but some training in other trades;
- results-oriented and importance of quality.

The features outlined above do not describe the actual state within the apprenticeship system for all instances between two points in time. They can be most usefully viewed as 'real-ideal types' – as they are based on historical analysis in Rikowski (1998) and not de-historicized concepts – which illustrate the development of apprenticeships over the 1920–1980 period (ibid).

It was generally acknowledged by most authors who made interventions in the apprenticeship debate during 1920–80 that the shift from (old) classical to (new) Modern Apprenticeships started in the 1930s. Butler (1933) was the first to use the term 'new apprenticeship'. The shift to (new) Modern Apprenticeships was uneven. In some large 'enlightened' firms the change had taken place before World War II. The 1964 Industrial Training Act was designed to speed up the shift.

The third type of apprenticeship is based on what has been known as Modern Apprenticeship, but which seems more like a (post) Modern Apprenticeship which can be described as follows:

(Post) Modern Apprenticeships:

- training to standards of NVQ level 3;
- contract of employment;
- 'scientific' entry: structured interviews, application forms, etc;
- flexibility 1 – expanded form (eg, mixing GNVQ with NVQ, customizing NVQs for firms immediate or medium-term needs);
- flexibility 2 – increasing importance of core, key or transferable skills for: internal flexibility in-company; transferability within and between companies and industrial sectors; for retraining (in case of unemployment); and for progression (including higher education entry);
- set within a lifelong learning context and trajectory (as in Berkeley, 1994).

For (post) Modern Apprenticeships, it is the last three factors that are particularly important. This becomes clear in the following discussion.

First, there is a certain continuity between the three forms of apprenticeship. They are all about self-generating skill, apprenticeship as 'learning how to learn' and the application of lessons learnt in production. Fuller (1996) shows how this applies specifically to (post) Modern Apprenticeships.

Secondly, although they all have the drive towards 'self-generating skill' in common, the first two types are separated from (post) Modern Apprenticeships in one key respect. They both assume that a point is reached when apprentices attain the ability for self-development in relation to trades. For (post) Modern Apprenticeships, the model suggests that learners are always going to be subject to the vagaries of rapid technological and labour market changes. Capacity for self-generating skill will be continually tested and developed to meet new labour process and labour market challenges. This relates to a third point about horizons.

In classical apprenticeship, the *modus operandi* for apprentices is to 'learn how to learn' within a single trade. This is self-generating skill within a narrow horizon, and because of its narrowness Marx viewed classical apprenticeship as 'craft idiocy' (1977/1867). In Modern Apprenticeship, the horizon is extended, for flexibility, to two or three trades, but is still within a principal form of self-generating skill as practice. It is in (post) Modern Apprenticeships that the horizon changes dramatically – to the infinite. The horizon is always just distant. It shifts with rapid technological change, globalizing labour and commodity markets and the always present possibility (as impending necessity) for labour power transferability, extension, progression or transformation. The horizon of the (post) modern apprentice dissolves into infinity; there are no defined boundaries, no absolute limits to the possible demands of capital as exerted through the world-and-beyond market. This implies both lifelong learning and *lifelong apprenticeship*. 'All that is solid melts into air' (Marx and Engels, 1973/1848: 83) and the form of self-generating skill as current practice is always provisional. As we shall see, this view has significant consequences for mastery.

A final observation is that there appears to be a retrospective evolutionary, or at least developmental, force at work in the movement between the three forms of apprenticeship. Apprenticeship, as represented in the shift between the three modes, seems to become increasingly subjugated to a deepening of the capital relation. The historical account offered in Rikowski (1998) illustrated this. Classical apprenticeships gave way to modern ones as relative surplus value production, through the mechanization of production, increasingly dominated the process of value creation. This was a long drawn-out process, hastened by the Industrial Training Act 1964. But Modern Apprenticeship was deemed to be insufficient as an adequate form of apprenticeship for globalizing capital, by leading employers and by the Tory Government. (Post) Modern Apprenticeships signify a world dominated by capital in a deeper sense: they herald an opening up of skilled labour power more fully to the colonization of capital within personhood. With this, we now turn to explore mastery.

Nietzsche, lifelong learning and the end of mastery

It is now possible to appraise the three forms of apprenticeship sketched out previously by returning to a consideration of mastery through Nietzsche. For Nietzsche, the first two types of apprenticeship – classical and (new) modern – would have had a special significance. They were basically preparation for a narrow 'trade mastery'. As I argued in an earlier paper (Rikowski, 1997), Nietzsche was concerned with the 'breeding' and maintenance of a cultural elite, while allotting the masses or 'herd', with their 'slave morality', a life of disciplined toil as an element of the material foundation upon which the elite could thrive and develop as self-overcoming 'artist-warriors'. Thus, although Nietzsche would have viewed the first two types of apprenticeship as preparation for forms of mastery which were pathetic, stunted deformations of character, he would nevertheless have recognized their utility. The moral outlooks involved in the forms of mastery arising from the first two types of apprenticeship, with their conservatism and loyalty to trade practices, are based essentially on the 'morality of utility' (Nietzsche, 1990/1886: 1997). Nietzsche had contempt for this form of mastery precisely because it was bounded and relatively fixed within a narrow sphere of activity. The individuals are 'self-developers' and 'overcomers' within a very limited horizon. They are enmeshed in a form of mastery not worth having, but which, through the productive activity they engender, can provide a foundation for culturally richer and more vibrant individuals who become masters in a fuller sense.

What is clear about the forms of mastery arising from the first two types of apprenticeship is that they are attainable. Masters are socially recognized as such when they 'come out of their time'. The temporal break is established. This is not the case with (post) Modern Apprenticeships.

For (post) Modern Apprenticeships, the formal end of the apprenticeship does not signify mastery for a number of reasons. First, mastery is not built into the process, but flexibility and adaptability are the prime movers. Secondly, and following upon this, it is assumed that the trained skilled worker will skip around the labour market and between labour processes with a lightness of touch and the capacity to learn in a range of situations. Hence the stress on core or key skills, progression and lifelong learning. Mastery, however, is denied. Despite the fact that all three forms of apprenticeship incorporate self-generating skill and the associated knack of 'learning how to learn', within (post) Modern Apprenticeships there is no end point to *learning* how to do this. (Post) Modern Apprenticeships incorporate lifelong learning but lifelong learning is incompatible with mastery. These points require development.

(Post) Modern Apprenticeship necessarily incorporates lifelong learning: it is an aspect of the post-modernization of apprenticeship. It establishes learning above the status attached to specific occupations, and sets in motion the ceaseless learning process unto death. Furthermore, in contemporary Britain all education and training policy is bathed in the drive to establish a lifelong learning culture, as the recent Green Paper testifies (DfEE, 1998). Thirdly, leading companies, such as Rover Group (see Berkeley, 1994), specifically place (post) Modern Apprenticeships within a lifelong learning context and trajectory. Now, mastery implies control over learning, including the decision not to learn further if accumulated learning allows completion of goals as decided by the learner. With mastery, the emphasis is on the practical application of 'lessons learnt' to goals designated by the master. This may involve ceasing to learn new material in order to complete tasks within limited time frames or, in relation to some lessons already learnt; to 'forget what is known' (Nietzsche, 1982/1881) in order to act habitually as master of a creative process. Both processes may result in the denial of lifelong learning. Furthermore, lifelong learning appears as a post-modern form of 'learning for its own sake'. This passes the drive to the process rather than to the learner and makes a mockery of control, destiny, desire – and mastery. The outcome of all this is that (post) Modern Apprenticeship, incorporated within lifelong learning, implies lifelong apprenticeship. It therefore precludes mastery.

For Nietzsche, (post) Modern Apprenticeship must be preferable to the two previous types as it configures a richer, fuller type of individual, even though such individuals fall short of the 'great health' and the drive to mature mastery. Charitably, one could argue that (post) Modern Apprenticeships are more likely to open up the individual to a fuller form of life and provide a firmer basis for any real self-overcoming. However, the movement towards (post) Modern Apprenticeship also represents a deepening of the capital relation; (post) Modern Apprenticeships are particularly concerned with responding to various demands of capital (as is education and training generally as purposed in recent government policy statements and official reports) (Ainley, 1999). Thus, a Nietzschean perspective on (post) Modern Apprenticeships points to the hopelessness of this form of apprenticeship for self-overcoming. Self-overcoming Nietzschean-style involves struggling against educational institutions and base utility, and entails the denial of lifelong learning as the process of lifelong certification and the end of mature mastery. Even apprentice trainers are simple lifelong learners.

(Post) Modern Apprenticeship is an aspect of lifelong learning. But as lifelong learners within capitalism we only become lifelong apprentices. (Post) Modern Apprenticeship is hence a springboard to lifelong apprenticeship and a denial of mastery. This does not mean there is no master within (post) Modern Apprenticeship, but to divine who or what exercises mastery we have to turn from Nietzsche to that other great materialist philosopher of the 19th century: Karl Marx.

Marx: capital as master of the soul

In the *Grundrisse* (1973/1858) Marx's descriptions of the 'universal individual' sometimes sounds eerily like the more eulogistic and fanatical characterizations of the 'lifelong learner' and lifelong learning in contemporary education policy statements and reports. The worker as 'universal individual' has the ability to undertake a wide range of work and has 'general industriousness' (Marx, 1973/1858: 325). To this extent these individuals constitute a 'new species' (ibid). Marx emphasizes that universal individuals are both the outcome of capitalist development and point towards a different, multi-faceted form of transhuman development through the struggle for communism. Capitalism, argues Marx, provides the substratum for the development of the new species. This is based on the fact that, objectively, capitalists (as personifications of capital) require a flexible and adaptable workforce able to quickly take up a wide range of employments as and when required in response to changing labour process and product demands. The drive to create universal individuals – or lifelong learners – is an inherent and infinite drive (as are all of capital's drives), though bounded by the material manifestations of other drives (counteracting, sometimes contradictory) flowing from capital, and by the shifting (relative) barriers of time and space.

Universal individuals from the 'standpoint of capital' represent a form of 'universal prostitution', as their powers are utilized by capital for its reproduction and expansion. Lifelong learners are experiments in the realization of universal individuals. Post-modern apprentices herald their possibility. Insofar as lifelong learners as post-modern apprentices have real existence then they simultaneously point towards a deepening of the capitalization of humanity which entails a progressive transhumanization (the 'human' as a form of capital – human capital), and towards a future human sociality which actively dissolves capital. This is because, for Marx, universal individuals can only develop to a point limited by the social relations flowing from the domination of capital (1973/1858: 241–42). The further development of these individuals rests upon the systematic suspension of barriers integral to capital, leading to the dissolution of capital and abolition of its rule over the lives of individuals. Within the rule of capital, both lifelong learners and post-modern apprentices (two aspects of the same form of personhood) are harbingers of the death of the capitalization of humanity and of the humanization of capital. They point towards transhuman life forms – 'new species' (Marx) – which are at first *horrific* as humans capitalized and capital humanized, and second *liberatory* as new transhuman life forms unburdened by the demon force of capital and open to extended possibilities for collective, democratic and self-generated forms of transhumanity.

As capitalized transhuman life forms we are dominated by capital. Capital is the master of altered (trans-) human souls. This has been the case for some time – certainly throughout the 20th century. Lifelong learning and (post) Modern Apprenticeship are both signs and forces of a deepening of this process. They are signs of deep, and deepening, possession. Classical and modern apprenticeships are indicators of less developed forms of transhuman capitalization, which is why representatives of capital came to loathe them as limited models of capitalized transhuman existence.

The problem with this is that it is difficult to explain how humans evolve as altered forms of humanity – become transhuman life-forms – through the development of capital. The evolution of apprenticeship: classical–modern–post-modern: mirrors this process but does not explain it. So, how does capital *become* human and humans *become* forms of capital? How does capital *become* master of the transhuman soul?

Only a brief outline can be given here. First, it is necessary to view capital as totality, as a globalizing and beyond-global force. There is no human 'beyond', and capital is a blind dominating extra-human force, without ego (Postone, 1996). Secondly, although capital is an extra-human, alien force it is created by humanity – by the expenditure of human labour power as real abstraction. The real abstraction (abstract labour) arises from the fact that capital appears first in the form of value, its value-form as surplus-value (Marx, 1977/1867; Neary, 1999) materialized as socially average labour power producing an excess of value over-and-above that represented by wages. Thirdly (and Marx makes light of this) in the actual labour process, which is also a valorization process, humans develop their abilities as forms of labour power. They develop their personhoods as they create an alien force – capital – which then comes to dominate them (Marx, 1992/1844; Postone, 1996). In labouring within the capitalist labour process, labourers' subsume their wills under capital (frustrating immediate desire and life-activity). They produce the elementary forms of capital as value-to-surplus-value incorporated within the commodity-form of capital. In the process, they develop their 'selves' in, through and in the form of capital (Marx, 1973/1857: 90).

There is also a process of the social production of labour power (schooling, training, workplace and work-based learning) which is premised on the production of future capitalized souls in labour process space. The social production of labour power in capitalism projects humans as capitalized entities. It incorporates the drive to produce 'work-ready', 'employable' beings as capital-creating life-forms at minimum cost. We then sell our labour-power as a force to be capitalized within the labour process.

We consume capital in its commodity form (food, housing, household goods and the other paraphernalia of contemporary existence). We flow through capitalized transport. We are dependent on the state-form of capital (in innumerable ways). Our quality of life is dependent on capital in its money-form (market dependency). In all these ways, and in all these forms, we become and are capital. However, because even capitalized life-forms have consciousness, the domination of capital within personhood and within transhuman collectivities is always in question. We have the capacity to find the weaknesses in the master within our souls and the known capitalized transhuman universe.

Conclusion

What this analysis shows is that Nietzsche's third form of mastery is impossible. There is no 'outside', no hiding place for self-overcoming beyond capital. Mastery cannot be established outside capital. Capital engenders destruction from within by transhuman capitalized life-forms as universalizing individuals – expansive lifelong learners. As a consequence, we require a politics, new forms of collective action, effective subversion and a new conception of class struggle. Capital and class struggle are not just 'out there', but are contradictory forces within personhood as labour power. Labour power, that 'abominable commodity', reflects the reduction of personhood to a form of capital. However, it is also the foundation of capital – and hence capitalism. Although capital has a tendency to reduce persons to labour power, labour power, as an aspect of personhood, is under the sway of individual and collective acts of willing and desire. Capital has this big weakness, and it is our big hope.

References

Ainley, P (1999) *Learning Policy: Towards the certified society*, Macmillan, Basingstoke

Berkeley, J (1994) *Developing the Next Generation for Work: A 'Modern Apprenticeship' case study*, Education & Careers, Rover Group Limited, London

Butler, R (1933) Training for industry: the New Apprenticeship, *Industrial Welfare and Personnel Management*, **XV** (176), pp xiv–xvi

Department for Education and Employment (1998) *The Learning Age: A renaissance for a new Britain* (Cmnd. 3798), The Stationery Office, London

Fuller, A (1996) Modern Apprenticeships, process and learning: some emerging issues, *Journal of Vocational Education and Training*, **48** (3), pp 229–48

Hamlyn, D (1971) *The Theory of Knowledge*, Macmillan, Basingstoke

Marx, K (1973) [1857] *General Introduction (to the Grundrisse)*, tr M Nicolaus, Penguin Books, Harmondsworth

Marx, K (1973) [1858] *Grundrisse: Foundations of the critique of political economy* (rough draft), tr M Nicolaus, Penguin Books, Harmondsworth

Marx, K (1977) [1867] *Capital: A critique of political economy – Volume One*, Lawrence and Wishart, London

Marx, K (1992) [1844] Excerpts from James Mill's 'Elements of Political Economy', in *Karl Marx: Early writings*, Penguin Classics, Harmondsworth

Marx, K and Engels, F (1973) [1848] *Manifesto of the Communist Party*, Pelican Books, London

Neary, M (1999) Youth, training and a theory of human resistance, forthcoming in

Post-modern Excess in Educational Theory: Education and the politics of human resistance, ed M Cole, D Hill and G Rikowski, The Tufnell Press, London

Nietzsche, F (1974) [1882] *The Gay Science*, tr W Kaufmann, Random House, New York

Nietzsche, F (1979) [1888] *Ecce Homo: How one becomes what one is*, tr R Hollingdale, Penguin Classics, Harmondsworth

Nietzsche, F (1982) [1881] *Daybreak: Thoughts on the prejudices of morality*, tr R Hollingdale, Cambridge University Press, Cambridge

Nietzsche, F (1990) [1886] *Beyond Good and Evil: Prelude to a philosophy of the future*, tr R Hollingdale, Penguin Classics, Harmondsworth

Parkin, N (1978) Apprenticeships: outmoded or undervalued?, *Personnel Management*, **10** (5), pp 22–25 and 41

Postone, M (1996) *Time, Labour and Social Domination: A reinterpretation of Marx's critical theory*, Cambridge University Press, Cambridge

Richards, G (1988) A study of the recruitment of engineering apprentices in Coventry, unpublished PhD thesis, University of Warwick, Department of Sociology, Coventry

Richardson, J (1996) *Nietzsche's System*, Oxford University Press, Oxford

Rikowski, G (1997) Nietzsche's school? The roots of educational post-modernism, paper presented to the Education Research Seminar, 'A Marxist Critique of Post-modernism in Education', Inter-Area Group, School of Education, University of Brighton, 19 November

Rikowski, G (1998) Three types of apprenticeship, three forms of mastery: Nietzsche, Marx, history and capital, University of Birmingham, School of Education Research Papers

Scott Johnston (1998) Nietzsche as educator: a re-examination, *Educational Theory*, **48** (1), pp 67–83

5

The Nomad's Apprentice: Different Kinds of 'Apprenticeship' among Kyrgyz Nomads in Central Asia

Stephanie Bunn

Theory

The classic approach to learning in psychology and the social sciences takes knowledge, whether social, skill-based or intellectual, to be a discrete body of information which the learner can absorb or digest and then later retrieve and apply. Rather like learning a language from a 'Teach-yourself-how-to' book, where in front of you, as given, is the grammar and vocabulary and you hope that by studying hard and learning all the rules you will eventually be able to speak. If only it were that easy! Most learning, of course, happens in the way that most humans learn their first language – on the job – in the process of living life itself. As an apprenticeship in living.

Apprenticeship as a metaphor for understanding learning, and learning as it takes place in apprentice-type situations have particular significance for anthropology. Recent thinkers on the subject – Esther Goody, Michael Coy, Jean Lave, Gisli Palsson and others – all emphasize the context-based, processual nature of learning. Their work is important because it takes a new look at what was an outmoded subject – apprenticeship – bringing our attention to the importance of practical, skill-based learning. Through this reconsideration of learning through practice, many new insights have been shed onto the nature of learning itself. This is true for both pedagogical learning and the 'learning' of culture.

Jean Lave in particular stands out for challenging the long-held assumption that learning, and culture, is simply a transfer of knowledge, usually between one head and another. She emphasizes how schools as teaching institutions have channelled the way we understand learning, often causing us to assume that learning is best if done by individuals away from 'real life' (not on the job), in a 'neutral' situation (like a school), so that the more generalized, abstract, condensed knowledge we are taught there can be applied to many different situations.

In contrast, she looks to learning through apprenticeship as a way of learning through practice – 'situated learning' as she and Wenger call it (Lave and Wenger, 1991). Apprentices learn from masters, people who know how to do the job well themselves. They learn through physically engaging, integrating skill and knowledge, in a way that reminds us, as Sigaut says, that skill can never be condensed and written down in a book (1993). It is almost impossible to learn a skill, riding a bike for example, by following instructions in a book. This processual, practical and physical way of learning involves the apprentice in a variety of working relationships – 'a community of practice' – and 'concerns the whole person in the world' (Lave and Wenger, 1991: 49–50). Instead of the passive reception of information of a pre-given, fixed curriculum which, Lave suggests, is how teaching is practised, apprenticeship shows how learning is achieved by 'scaffolding' or, to use a different phrase, following Vygotsky's conception of the 'zone of proximal development' (1978), Lave and Wenger use the term 'legitimate peripheral participation'. This is where novice apprentices begin to learn at the edge of the work, as their mentor, or master, structures or scaffolds simple activities for them to do which slowly enable them to learn, and then discriminates and structures more complex skills at levels they can manage until, through time and experience, they are ultimately drawn right into the centre of action as they become fully skilled workers themselves.

Palsson, writing of apprenticeship among Icelandic fishermen, develops Lave's ideas further. He too challenges the notion of learning as 'the transmission of a culture, mental code or script that exists prior to and independent of human activities' (1994: 903). He emphasizes how mind and body are not separate in skilful practice, referring to this kind of knowledge as intuitive (1994: 907). The great skill of an experienced, well trained Icelandic fishing skipper enables him to act as if his technology, and his surroundings, were an extension of his person (1994: 910). The attentive, intuitive ability that comes from this level of skill enabling a skipper to 'think like a fish' and find a fishing ground by 'some kind of whisper' is described as 'the state of "fishing mood"' – an understanding that is impossible to explain or verbalize. This kind of 'state', which develops out of skilled action, can only begin to be understood as one moves away from the cognitive approach to learning. I will return to similar understanding when I discuss the Kyrgyz hunting with eagles.

The great interest aroused by the work of Lave, Wenger, Goody and others has led to a movement in anthropology where much research into learning inevitably uses the apprentice model. This has had some great benefits, as with the work of Palsson, but it also has limitations.

Practice

This chapter will examine the relationship between learning in the family and learning through apprenticeship among Central Asian nomads, particularly the Kyrgyz, among whom I have done field research for over five years. Kyrgyzstan is a small, independent republic in the CIS, south of Kazakhstan and west of China. It is crossed by the Tien Shan mountain range from east to west and over 85 per cent of the land is above 1,500 metres. The Kyrgyz are, or were, nomadic pastoralists, keeping sheep, horses, cows and, formerly, Bactrian camels and yaks. Like most other Central Asian nomads, they traditionally lived all year round in yurts (Kyrgyz: *boz uy* – felt tents), travelling with their animals from winter to summer pastures. Their domestic activities and craft traditions were determined largely by the central role that animal husbandry played in their way of life. Their domestic skills centred mainly around herding animals and processing animal products such as milk, meat, skin and wool.

While the nomadic lifestyle remained almost unaltered for possibly more than 2,000 years, everything began to change after the Russian revolution and Stalin's collectivization programme of the 1930s. At this time most people were sedentarized (sometimes forcibly) and moved into collective farms based in villages in the valleys. Today, the shepherds and their families live in tents only during the summer months when they move the flocks up into the high mountain summer pastures – the *jailoo'oo*.

Despite this, many traditional domestic activities are still carried out, including textile craft work and tent-frame making. While most families worked for the collective farms, much of this work still involved shepherding, and traditional ways of working and living were most appropriate to the land and climate and were still much in evidence at independence in 1991. Ironically, the new freedom of capitalism and the influx of the global market economy through privatization and development may soon do more damage to traditional skills than 70 years of communism.

There is traditionally very little specialization of work among Central Asian nomads. Most shepherd families need to be widely skilled and adaptable to be fit and contributing members of the pastoralist community. Men need to be able to ride, to know everything about herding animals, especially sheep, including understanding the weather, the seasons, the pastures, animals' health, breeding times, when to move flocks and so on. A shepherd could scan the landscape and tell you about all its occupants, even at a far distance; could kill a sheep and precisely cut it up into an age-old prescribed system of parts; could tell by the movement of wild animals and the stars exactly when to move pasture, and so on.

Women traditionally need to be able to have children and look after them, cook and process all food stuffs – there are 20 to 30 different milk products alone – and make all clothes and tent furnishings. As Kyrgyz lifestyle has changed, women's role and work has often remained more intact than their men's, probably because whatever extra work women take on, they still retain their domestic identity. Men, on the other hand, have suffered strong dislocations of identity when no longer working in the mountains as shepherds. A Kyrgyz man, I was told many times, wants to be in the mountains, with his animals and horses, with one or two wives and many children.

Traditional understanding has been added to by Soviet 'scientific' and medical knowledge, which has sometimes been beneficial, as in terms of animal medicine or milk treatment, but sometimes damaging. For example, the push for twin lambs has resulted in over-grazing of pastures, and the increased use of motor vehicles, along with discouragement of use of the yak and camel, has led to erosion of mountains by wheel tracks. One of the key successes always hailed as being introduced by the Soviet Union is education and literacy. Luria, Vygotsky's 'apprentice', based much of his research on the benefits in thinking said to arise from the widespread literacy programme of the USSR in Central Asia. Before the Soviet Union, the Kyrgyz were largely an oral culture (Luria, 1976).

Kyrgyz children begin to learn adult skills and roles almost as soon as they can walk, through watching, imitating, playing and participating. There is no separation of children from adult life as in Western Europe or America. Children are allowed to be around adults when they work, stay up late and take part as soon as they are able. Children accompany parents on horseback almost from the moment they are born. Two-year-olds run around galloping as if riding a horse. They will sit on the *sarai* fence and watch horses being lassoed and trained. Four-year-olds may try to milk calves while their older brothers and sisters milk its mother for real. They watch their fathers kill and cut up a sheep and help clean it, chase sheep into the fold, go with their brothers on hunting trips. Until the age of 5 or 6, children are quite free and are indulged in many ways, allowed to do much of what they want – especially the boys. They often go to stay with their grandparents in the countryside or mountains.

After 5 or 6, they are ready to live in the community, making the step into adult society and, traditionally, begin to help their mothers, if a girl, or fathers, if a boy, although sex roles are not absolute. Seven is the age at which they now begin to attend school. By 16 years, they are considered to be adult – a boy can cut a sheep, hunt, get married. The traditional way of 'educating' children is still taken very seriously in many areas. It is important to understand that whereas in Russian (the Kyrgyz second language) there are two possible words for 'education': *obrazovaniya,* which means education, and *vospitaniya,* which means upbringing, in Kyrgyz, the education of a child can only be translated by one word – *tarbiya* – which very definitely means only upbringing, or preparation for life. In traditional Kyrgyz nomadic societies, there were no special educational institutions, only the family and the community. There are very definite beliefs about how you should bring up children into adulthood, including the moral and ethical climate in which they should be brought up. Such behaviour is particularly represented and illustrated by the actions of old people – by grandparents and aged, respected relatives. The older generation think you should not show your bad side to young children, or shout at them.

Mahabba, with whom I spent some time, once said to me that her father-in-law, Alpymysh, told her off if she shouted at or hit her children. Instead, if he wanted one of his grandchildren to behave, he would sometimes pretend to be angry, holding a short monologue, speaking to himself and throwing his hat on the ground. All the children behaved well in front of him. At special celebratory meals, *besh barmak,* where a sheep is killed and guests are invited, adults take great care about how they talk in front of children, because it will influence them. The conversation will be about how to be a good Kyrgyz person, proverbs and stories about wisdom and good behaviour are told. A young son who brings the water for washing hands at the beginning and end of the meal will be given *bata beroo'oo,* a blessing, special advice for his life, by each guest in turn. Children of guests, especially the very young, may come in and sit, and are often invited by an aged matriarch to come and sit with them at the *tor,* the place of honour, where they are lovingly covered in smacking kisses and fed choice pieces of meat, while witnessing the conversation which goes on.

It is a feature of Kyrgyz 'education' not to give people advice directly, but to say it 'to the walls', then people will be more likely to hear. There is a proverb that reflects this:

> *Keregem saga aytam, kelinim sen uk,*
> *Oo'oglum saga aytam, oo'olum sen uk.*
> I say to you – if I speak to my *kerege* (yurt wall), my *kelin* (daughter-in-law) will listen to me,
> I say to you, if I speak to the *u'uk* (yurt roof poles), my son will listen to me.

Most moral and ethical advice is conveyed in this way, as if speaking to a third person, or through stories and moral tales.

As it is in philosophy, so it is in learning other skills – and it is usual not to force children to learn a skill, but to let them wish to do it of their own accord. The intention is that the child will see and express a wish to learn. Then they can be taught. Of course, like all philosophies of life this is not always adhered to, but it is aspired to.

Traditionally, older people had responsibility for transmission of religious and genealogical knowledge to the new generation. Children may go when very young to stay with their grandparents until they are 5 years old or so. Thereafter they will still visit them often, in the summer months if their grandparents work in the summer pastures, or in the villages if their parents live in the high mountains, and the children need to go to school in the winter. Children, accordingly, have very great affection for their grandparents. Many Kyrgyz words reflect this role of older people in the education of young people. Teenagers may call their parents *baike,* older brother, or *eje,* older sister, for example, and their grandparents 'mother' and 'father'. In this way the child becomes apprentice to the adult.

Goody (1989), writing of the development of apprenticeship in Africa, suggests this practice of sending children to live with relatives represents an intermediate stage in the development of apprenticeship and of domestic skill teaching within the family, which occurs as a result of greater specialization in the domestic economy. I do not think this is the case among Kyrgyz nomads. In the first place, it reflects the special role grandparents have in the upbringing of the younger generation. Secondly, as outlined above, traditional Kyrgyz pastoralism does not involve great economic specialization. Most people need to be widely skilled and adaptable. Nomadic pastoralism in Central Asia has always been a part of a wider economy which depends on a relationship with settled oasis societies. Within this context, raw materials such as horses and furs were traded and it was the settled societies which provided specialist goods in exchange. Most Kyrgyz specialists, and there are a variety of specialist roles, relate less to the economy and are more a part of reciprocal family relationships and involve special cultural skills which are admired and given status, not money.

Specialists

Specialists include the blacksmith, the yurt master (nomadic felt tent-maker), the shaman (though such an occupation does not really exist now), the epic poem singer (*manaschi*) and sometimes the animal trainer (a horse trainer, or a hunter with eagles). To learn to become one of these one has to stand out from an early age, and usually one has to undertake some kind of apprenticeship, most commonly from childhood. Some epic poem singers will only take one apprentice in a lifetime. A blacksmith may take two or three at once. This is said to reflect the different nature of the skills involved. The Kyrgyz word for apprentice is *oku'uchu* – a word that means learner or student. It is possible to be known as an *usta,* a master, simply because you are good at crafts that do not involve apprenticeship. This is especially the case in 'women's crafts'. A great felt-maker, or an embroiderer will be known as such, for example. But to become one does not involve any concrete training, and is simply a part of the domestic life that a girl grows into if she has the talent and the inclination. To become especially skilled in almost any area of Kyrgyz life, one has to have 'birth talent' – the skill is seen to be in one's blood. Alpymysh, for example, was a hunter. 'Anyone can be a shepherd', he said. 'To be a hunter is very hard. One in a hundred people will be a hunter'. If he did not hunt, he would become ill.

Illustrations

Yurt master

Sapar is a yurt master living in Red Flag Village, which recently reverted to its former name, White Poplar (Holy Poplar). He was the youngest son of Toktosun Ismailov, a great yurt master, and made his first yurt (*boz uy*) from start to finish at 16. Then he left this work and went to Balykchi to teach there in the driving school. In accordance with the traditional role of the youngest son, five years ago he moved home to live with and look after his parents. This was the point at which he decided to make his living from being a yurt master. (Making yurts is a part of the economy – they are bought and sold. In the present economic climate in Kyrgyzstan, very fragile since independence and mass privatization, having this trade has saved Sapar from the poverty that many of his neighbours are facing).

White Poplar was like a school for yurt masters. Sapar's father has taught at least 12 men to make *boz uys*. He himself had learned from Begmat, an old man who had given him the specially formed rod which acted as a form for the curve of the trellis pole. To become a yurt master, you simply have to want to learn. Sapar's relative, his 'second brother' was, at the time I was there, learning from him. He could already bend the wood into shape using the vice and thread up the trellis frame. To learn how to make a *boz uy,* you must work with the master for a year. You need to learn how to care for the trees the wood comes from, how to cut wood, how to bend and form it, how to make the *tunduk* (roofring) and so on. All this, I was told, you can learn in one month, the time it takes to make one *boz uy*. But you must do it for a year. At the end of the year, Sapar will say to his relative, 'Go away', and give him some equipment, and say 'Go to your house and do it'.

Now Sapar's son Erydan is watching his father, wanting to learn. Sapar didn't say, 'You must be a this, or a that'. He worked and looked for a reaction. If he thinks his child is interested, he helps his son to learn. All the time Erydan is behind his father, watching how to do it. The fathers do, and the sons sit behind them, and they begin to do. At 14 years old, Erydan began to help yurt making; but even at 2 or 4 he had begun to watch. First of all, he began to make the *kyk,* the fermenting sheep's dung for bending the wood. Gulbar said of her husband, 'Sapar doesn't teach his sons. He waits till they have an interest. But both sons are interested. When he is away, they begin to do the work. Sapar at first doesn't say anything. When they begin to work, then he says how to do it. Perhaps he understands when they can or can't do it'. In the present uncertain economic climate, Sapar's family is one of the few in the village that is not terribly poor. People from all over the country, and beyond, go to him for *boz uys*.

The hunter

Alpymysh is a shepherd and a hunter. Now his sons do the shepherding, and he concentrates on hunting, which he finds altogether more personally satisfying (see above). He traps marmots, has hunted snow leopards and sometimes hunted with eagles, the most prestigious form of hunting. Eagles have to be captured as young birds and specially trained. Then they are used for hunting foxes or wolves. To learn to train an eagle, one first has to learn under an eagle hunter. When he was 15, Alpymysh watched an old hunter in his village, and learned from him. The hunter taught him and gave him an eagle for himself. But his mother made him give it back, saying he was too young. One has to be ready to hunt. Alpymysh could have been a yurt master. From 13–14 he watched a yurt master and subsequently built his own *boz uy*. But he wanted to be a shepherd and a hunter.

Since then, Alpymysh has trained other eagles, breaking his teeth and scarring himself climbing rock faces and crags in the mountains in order to find young eagles to train. When I first visited Alpymysh in the summer pastures, he was training a young eagle. To train an eagle, one has to understand the mind of the animal. 'It understands everything I say', he said, and then spent the next half hour in a dark shed talking to it. To train an eagle, one has to know everything about it – its diet, the condition of its feathers, when it will be ready to hunt and when it needs to rest. One eagle Alpymysh had trained came back to visit the place it had worked with him every year for ten years after he released it. In this situation, I wonder, who is the master and who is the apprentice? This special relationship reflects the unique relationship nomadic people have with animals, and their notion of control, will and work. Kyrgyz people often talk about the importance of nature, mountains and balance and in the mountains do not put themselves outside nature or see themselves as separate. They are not controlling it. And so it is in their understanding of learning both for children and for special animals. These are not relationships of control as we understand them. Yet there is a loss of control, when the learner comes forward to learn from the skilled person. And this forms the beginning of the learning relationship – for the eagle and the child – and the man.

The shyrdak master

Textile work, such as making felt carpets and embroidery, is women's work. The quality and variety of textiles made by Kyrgyz women for use and decoration of tent interiors is awe-inspiring. Any article for use in the tent, from pot holders to bed covers to felt carpets, is traditionally made with comparable effort and skill. Some of the most impressive Kyrgyz textiles, and where their craft work is sometimes hailed as 'high art', are the special felt wedding carpets known as *shyrdak*. These are made by a woman, or her daughter, for the daughter's wedding. A great *shyrdak*-maker rightly qualifies for the name *usta* or master. And yet there is no apprenticeship to be a felt *usta*.

One has to have a birth talent and simply grows in to becoming one, as with all other Kyrgyz domestic activities, through working, copying and helping one's mother. In truth, all Kyrgyz women could traditionally do most of the tasks required – hand-spinning, dyeing, quilting, felt-making. But what singles out an *usta* is her ability to draw the uniquely balanced and intricate patterns, by eye, with no stencil, and cut them out by hand. Most women will be able to sew together *shyrdak,* but an *usta* is required to cut out the pattern. Some women are famous all over Kyrgyzstan. Yet they do not have apprentices as such, though other women will come and watch and help. The Soviets awarded such women with medals, and gave them titles and certificates. They were encouraged to make work to sell to the Artists' Union and to Intourist shops and *beriozkas*; but this did not improve the quality of their work.

It is an interesting facet of this and many of the Kyrgyz crafts that they are not traditionally made for sale, but only for gifts. In *shyrdak,* the work is self-motivated and made with hopes and wishes for the future marriage in mind. If one is not working for money, but to make a piece of work for one's self or as a gift, one's attitude of mind can be quite different, and that feeling, sewn into the work, will make a difference. To sell a *shyrdak* is still, in many areas, considered shameful. Ironically, it is one area where development workers are putting in foreign money to set up small workshops – with limited success. The work is mass-produced, and women are being diverted from works of great skill to making small tourist artefacts which are quite trivial in comparison.

This is a significant point for much Kyrgyz apprenticeship. Skill is not always so directly connected with economic activities. Many essential features of nomadic high culture were not connected with trade. The motivation for making such work and for becoming skilful is uncomplicated by profit motives. This shows an important dimension to being skilful and to apprenticeship that is often overlooked – the love of being skilful and of making – the love of the job and the desire to give. This tends to get sidelined in the work of Lave and others, who focus on economic and political considerations.

The manaschi

All the practices and beliefs of how to grow up and become a good Kyrgyz adult are embodied in the still-living Kyrgyz oral epic, *Manas*. This is an oral poem of over half a million lines which has been ongoing and evolving for at least 1,000 years, and is still being sung today. This poem centres around the Kyrgyz hero, Manas, who led the Kyrgyz from the Altai mountains to the Tien Shan (where they still live) 1,000 years ago. It contains many elements of Kyrgyz history, from their migration, to different battles and wars, through to all the upheavals of the Russian conquest and the formation of the Soviet Union. It was banned by the communists before World War II but survived and still exists. Kyrgyz politicians, academics and writers alike allude to *Manas* when talking of the new future of Kyrgyzstan, as a model for the future nation, and all refer to its wealth of knowledge. For a people who have not recorded their history or laws in writing, *Manas* is 'the main spiritual treasure, where everything that the people had gained was stored up' (Masayev, 1994: 91). And so say many other thinkers and writers.

Within the poem are many details of how to live and be Kyrgyz; from how to find your way by the stars, to how to bring up children, to how to play *ordo,* the adult game of knucklebones which embodies key ideas about strategy. One could say it embodies the Kyrgyz world view, their history and beliefs about how to live. And yet the poem or song itself is not didactic – not a set of rules or instructions, or a teaching mechanism – it is an ongoing, changing story, sung for the joy of being Kyrgyz and a part of the context rather than a description of it.

Manas is sung by special epic poem singers known as *manaschi*. It is a mixture of memorized episodes which are improvised around a theme. *Manaschi* are said to have special skills: a heightened memory, a special emotion. As for an apprentice, a *manaschi* may choose only one person from the many different communities of a tribe. If people see a special quality in a child, an expressive gift, artistic ability, a special memory, a love of singing *Manas,* they may try to send him to a *manaschi*. Thus, in the Kyrgyz community, some people look at the child and try to define him – his future, and so on. A grandparent may do this when they name a child. A *manaschi* will look for a child with these qualities. Not every child can sing *Manas*.

Traditionally, the *manaschi* moved from community to community, singing *Manas* there, staying for one or two months, being looked after by the community. If he had an apprentice, he would take the child/apprentice with him to his performances and on his travels. Most *manaschis* claim that Manas and his 40 *choros* (warriors) came to them in a dream and chose them to sing *Manas*. Often, they say that when they woke up they knew the whole of *Manas*. But I've seen young children of 3 or 4 singing *Manas* with their mothers, who teach them long sections by heart. And in order to learn, young children become pupils to *manaschis* and hear and learn the skill and secrets of the singing. They learn small epic poems and tales with simple poetic forms, progressing step by step. There are special rituals for preparation of a singer – a great *manaschi* will find a child and afterwards give him special gifts, even keeping back a part of the tea that he drinks, and giving it to the child, saying something like 'My quality I transfer to you!', 'My quality is in you now'. There are other rituals, special tests, sayings, tales and games when the singer chooses his pupil. As an apprentice, the child will learn ways of performing, separate lines and verses by heart, different episodes and so on. As he progresses, he learns some well-known episodes by heart, and performs them. From this stage, he progresses to creating his own improvised versions and then knowing all the events in the epic from start to finish, at which point he will become a master. The difference between these masters, *chinigi manaschi* (literally, true *manaschi*) and *chong manaschi* or great *manaschi,* is simply the quality and inspiration of performance.

In terms of learning and culture, epic poems such as *Manas* are unique, since they both embody the wisdom and learning of the Kyrgyz and at the same time teach it. An apprentice *manaschi,* at the same time as he learns how to sing *Manas* and all that it implies, is also learning its content. And as he learns and sings it, he reinforces the content of the poem to the children, younger and older than himself.

Conclusion

The Kyrgyz word for apprentice is *oku'uchu* which means learner, but a master may also call an apprentice 'my son'. Herein lies the key to the traditional Kyrgyz approach to learning and apprenticeship. In many ways, Lave and Wenger's concept of a 'community of practice' is most apt here, and yet also most visibly flawed. Kyrgyz learning does take place in the community, but this community might as well be called the home or the family as the workplace.

It is difficult to draw the boundary between the child and the apprentice, or between upbringing and teaching. The relationship of father to son, mother to daughter and master to apprentice is very similar, especially in a society where relations between grandfather, father and older brother begin to blur. The *manaschi* is like a father or a grandfather to his apprentice. A *shyrdak* 'master' becomes so simply by growing into womanhood. The only 'rule' seems to be that women are rarely apprentices.

The importance of the concept of 'birth talent' is also overlooked. If we accept the diminishment of the role of master that Lave suggests goes alongside 'community of practice', then the model does not allow for societies where masters are considered to be unique and irreplaceable, and destined to be so from birth.

It is also very useful to look at the nature of learning when the economic imperative is not foremost, to see what other factors play a part. Developing a skill by choice, or developing a 'birth talent', are important features of learning – as is to make for the enjoyment of it, for one's family, or for a gift. These factors can influence how a skill is developed and the quality of the work. One flaw in Lave's argument is that her framework does not allow for the student who studies maths for the love of it (as opposed to doing it to meet a need for calculations in shopping/dieting) or the place of creativity and intuition in learning.

In Kyrgyzstan, these factors are important and an integral part of why one becomes a 'specialist'. Through considering them also we should be able to develop our understanding of the nature of learning and apprenticeship further, which could lead us on to ask deeper questions about the relationship between learning and the environment, intuition and skill, learning and invention and so on.

References

Goody, E N (1989) Learning, apprenticeship and the division of labour, in *Apprenticeship: From theory to method and back again*, ed M W Coy, SUNY Press, New York

Lave, J and Wenger, E (1991) *Situated Learning: Legitimate peripheral participation*, Cambridge University Press, Cambridge

Luria, A R (1976) *Cognitive Development*, Harvard University Press, Cambridge, MA

Masayev, S (1994) *The Epos 'Manas'*, Sham Press, Bishkek

Palsson, G (1994) Enskilment at sea, *Man (N.S.)*, **29**, pp 901–27

Sigaut, F (1993) Learning, teaching and apprenticeship, *New Literary History*, **24**, pp 105–14

Vygotsky, L S (1978) *Mind in Society*, Harvard University Press, Cambridge, MA

6

Conversation and Instruction within Apprenticeship: Affordances for Learning

Michael A Forrester

Introduction

Presupposed in the idea of apprenticeship rest the concepts of instruction and learning. Despite being the focus of psychological and educational enquiry for the last 100 years, the study of learning processes remains fraught with difficulty. Progress and advancement on the issue often remain focused on very restricted contexts, eg, in designing artefacts to aid instruction (Chee, 1995), or in restricting the idea of apprenticeship to cognition and thinking (Collins and Michalski, 1989; Pontecorvo and Girardet, 1993). As others have noted, one constraint on developing conceptually rich theories of learning is the emphasis on abstraction – the focus on the ability to abstract to a novel situation following experience on a selected number of examples (Laurillard, 1993).

One can argue that the most interesting thing about 'learning in general' is that there is no such thing – at best one can only claim that people display a disposition for the possibility of learning, as to learn about something always takes place in a particular context. However, it may be helpful to distinguish two approaches to investigating learning within psychology: either a focus on performance learning or consideration of the experience of learning. Displaying that you have learned something always rests upon specific criteria for what it might mean to demonstrate the said learning, ie, perform what has been learned in context. In contrast the experience of learning is an ongoing dynamic event noticeable by the learner (eg, learning by mistake, recognizing that something is not quite correct and so on). We appear to work with at least two rather odd assumptions about learning: one that adults and children simply accumulate 'learning' – it just happens if you spend enough time in an educational context, another that learning can take place and not be noticed. The former assumption certainly underscores the tradition of the apprenticeship while the latter seems a very unlikely idea, given that whatever else learning might be, it is noticeable.

What is missing is a theoretical understanding of the predispositions and perceived possibilities within learning contexts, a way of directly addressing and examining how participants themselves engage in the learning process. My suggestion is that conversation and dialogic contexts are the primary mechanisms which enhance or even produce learning. Conversation also happens to be the central site for investigating the learning process. The aim here is to consider the nature of learning in conversational contexts, bringing together ethnomethodologically informed conversation analysis (Sacks, 1992) and the affordance metaphor from perceptual psychology (Gibson, 1979). Arguably, by looking in detail at certain conversations where 'learning moments' occur we can better understand the conversational practices which facilitate or constrain participants' learning. Minimally, the analysis below focuses on instances where participants in a learning situation comment 'Ahh' or 'Aa-ha – I see' during talk involving explanations and accounts. Such expressions are generally warranted as demonstrating that somebody is learning or understanding something.

The emergence of discourse analysis within social psychology has engendered a growing interest in the study of talk within and beyond institutional contexts. Interestingly, while discourse analysts note the influence ethnomethodology has had on this work, there is a less than wholehearted commitment to conversational analysis's form of empirical scepticism. Maintaining an ethnomethodological focus, the object of enquiry for conversation analysis should be 'the set of techniques that the members of a society themselves utilize to interpret and act within their own social world'. In other words, there has to be clear evidence in participants' own talk that they themselves orient to whatever representations, categories, models or metaphors become the basis for analysis. And part and parcel of the formulating criteria for participant-based analysis is attention to the sequential nature of talk-as-social-action, particularly the principle of accountability. All behaviour concerned with communication will be accountable and will follow appropriate conventions for politeness, signalling participation, monitoring of actions and so on.

Certainly studying the process of learning, focusing on participant oriented criteria for what constitutes noticing something, displaying recognition of relevant information, producing a justifiable account of ongoing learning, and other such associated social practices for enhancing learning in context may offer a unique way into understanding the 'zone of proximal development'. Within developmental and educational psychology Vygotsky's ideas now have considerable prominence. Essentially, Vygotsky's theoretical framework emphasized the grounding of thinking and learning in practical activity, his claim being that the very mechanisms underlying higher mental functioning derive from internalization of social relationships. Learning takes place in the zone of proximal development, defined as the distance between a learner's existing level of knowledge as determined by their attempts to solve a problem independently, and the level of potential development as determined through problem solving under adult assistance/guidance, or in collaboration with more experienced peers. It is this idea which underlies subsequent research, focusing on the strategies shown by a more competent dyad member and how these are eventually taken over by a less competent participant in order to regulate and monitor his or her own behaviour.

However, despite a growing literature on the outcomes from learning in the zone of proximal development, we remain largely ignorant of the dynamic process implicit within 'interactional zones'. What is often glossed over is the fact that participation in conversation is always dynamic – ongoing immediate action, each move or act pre-figured in the immediate context of its local history. With this in mind one can consider re-formulating the study of conversational participation in light of Gibson's (1979) concept of affordance.

As is well known in psychology, in contrast to the then dominant information processing approach, Gibson (1979) formulated a radically innovative theory of perception and action. Arguing for an 'ecological perspective' where organism and environment are always and already 'coupled' together, Gibson claimed that perception and action shouldn't be understood as somehow impoverished. Rather, one 'resonates' with the environment and the environment 'affords' (provides for, occasions) actions and events making possible this (and not that) perception of the world. An important point about the notion of affordances is that they make possible, or have the potential for, some sets of actions and not others. Furthermore, this detection and production of affordance structures is an immediate (non-cognitive) phenomenon inherently part and parcel of the ongoing dynamics of events and actions. We could benefit from considering participants' orientations to the production and recognition of structural patterns in talk as social affordances: immediately recognizable projections, predictions and perceived consequences of making this (and not that) utterance at any given time. Considering conversation as a dynamic context for events and actions, we might benefit from re-conceptualizing affordances as social constructs: patterns of action, behaviour and sequence which have directly recognizable consequences and implications.

Social affordances and conversation

We can start with the suggestion that the predominant orientation of sensory-cognitive processes leads to our engaging in constructivist conversational processes which build upon our skills or predispositions to detect and extract relative invariance and change (detecting affordances). In conversations, and in our ongoing constructions of them, we make available and use patterns and structures of talk so as to signal, identify and emphasize particular aspects which should be picked up, ignored, made recognizable or whatever. The very construction of a conversation is presupposed upon the realizability or not of specific social affordances. For example, in a learning conversation participants' conceptions of the ongoing 'conversation as coherent unit with the potential for learning' will be an intersubjective accomplishment (Vygotsky, 1979). Depending on our expectations and ongoing interest during the conversation (particularly as listener, but also as critical self-monitor when speaking) we may ask ourselves, 'Is this a point worth developing? Why have we taken this turn now? This is clearly irrelevant, we must get back to the topic', and so on. Criteria for this kind of ongoing decision making will depend upon the history of the interaction between participants, relative status, success in similar discussions previously or whatever.

Most importantly however, the immediately drawn inferences realizable by participants will rest upon the dynamics of the talk itself – the social affordances made available or suppressed. There is a significant sense in which participants themselves produce opportunities for learning during conversation. For participants, at some level potentially beneficial elements of conversations have to be recognized 'directly' during the ongoing interaction – akin to Gibson's (1979) affordance metaphor. We simply 'know' that if we talk with some people we are very likely to learn something (and not with others).

It is important to emphasize that the way the concept of affordance is being employed here is in a socio-cultural sense. When we engage in conversation with someone, the *way* we speak and listen, *when* precisely we speak and listen, whether we use certain kinds of intonational emphasis, the sensitivity we display to structural entities in the talk (eg, adjacency pairs, preference organization and so on), together interpenetrates and co-produces the social affordances realizable as dynamic conversational constraints and possibilities. We have been encultured into our everyday understandings and social practices in part through the processes and procedures involved in recognizing and displaying social affordances.

Structuration and conversational affordances

In one sense the idea of conversational structure as possessing 'affordance-like' qualities is part and parcel of the endemic structuration of social life. We can consider particular elements in conversation to envisage how structuration occurs. In Schegloff and Sacks' (1973) study of closing sections in talk they pose the problem of how it is that two people manage to succeed at closing a conversation, that is given the observation that the continuation of speaking turns could go on indefinitely (without a precise mechanism for solving the closing problem). Given it is the production of recognizable 'affordance structures' in conversations which is our interest, the participants must somehow organize their co-convergence at a point in the conversation where one speaker's turn completion will not occasion another speaker's talk, and will at the same time not be heard as the other's silence. What is needed are techniques or methods for providing ways to introduce previously unmentioned mentionables (such as 'Oh, by the way, one of the reasons why I came by to see you today was…') which makes recognizable the structural properties of a closing section, itself then permitting appropriate 'terminal exchange' adjacency pair inclusion (eg, 'OK?', 'OK, bye…, bye'). The specific way in which adjacency pair sequences are employed as social affordance structures requires that the first utterance of such a pair is recognized as having a particular 'first pair part' status. So if a participant wished to methodically provide for 'closing section implicativeness', that is indicate quite clearly that she is concerned to move towards providing the opportunities for initiating those distinct patterns identifiable as closing sections of conversation, then there are highly conventional and immediately recognizable procedures for doing this. Schegloff and Sacks (1973) point out that because of the organization of turn-taking, 'unless close ordering is attempted there can be no methodic assurance that a more or less eventually aimed-for successive utterance or utterance type will be produced'. It is in this sense that we can consider the relationship between the recognition of 'structural affordances' in talk and procedures and processes produced by participants in order that they can accomplish both the talk itself and whatever communicative aims it fulfils. The idea of structuration helps focus on the dynamic online nature of such processes: participants are oriented towards the accomplishment of talk and themselves provide and produce 'structuration' strategies.

Thus, in the example referred to above, the reason why two utterances are needed is that a current speaker can display that she understood what a prior first pair part was aimed at, and subsequently whether she is willing to go along with it. In addition, whoever used the first pair part can see whether what she intended is understood and has been (or will not be) accepted for its 'closing section' implicativeness. Recognition and display of conversational patterns can not only be considered for their 'structural regularities' but as dynamic potential 'online' affordances oriented to by participants.

Participation in conversation and the recognition of learning

It is worth reiterating the dynamic nature of conversational contexts, particularly when we consider learning processes. And learning is always demonstrable. You cannot claim to have learnt something unless you can display and communicate what has been learnt. Furthermore, while there are undoubtedly many well-learned skills which take on the appearance of being 'unconscious', we need to keep in mind that at some time in the past their earliest accomplishment was defined by those around us, through the medium of conversation, as the first instances of learning (to walk, to ride a bike and so on). Also, the goals of learning (in the dynamic ongoing process of participation as learner) are altered by the process of trying to achieve them. The learning process is intrinsically interwoven with communication and, arguably, is always public, that is demonstrable (at the very least to oneself).

As mechanisms for learning, conversations always remain pre-dispositional and potentiating. One cannot always be assured that those aspects you, as participant, are constructing for noticeability, will in fact be noticed and taken up. Further, it is simply not always realizable to subscribe to strict criteria of goal accomplishment: there is always the potential that the dynamics of the conversational context will create possibilities for the structuration of learning not envisaged before, or at the start of, the interaction. Conversations, by the very nature of their openness and flexibility, always contain the potential for unrealized affordances for learning. This helps us understand why it often seems that on the one hand learning 'just happens', yet on the other, very specific procedures, techniques and strategies are employed by those committed to enhancing the learning of another.

Studying learning in conversation: an example from an educational context

In order to provide a flavour of how conversational analysis and a social affordance metaphor of learning processes can be usefully combined, consider an interaction between an adult researcher and a 9-year-old child where the latter is learning how to estimate. Within mathematics education, learning to estimate and approximate have become topics of considerable interest since the introduction of calculators into the classroom. As part of a series of studies into how children learn estimating skills, an in-depth analysis of the process of acquiring one particular estimation task (estimating as part of proportional reasoning) was carried out at the University of Kent (reported in Forrester and Shire, 1994; see also Forrester and Pike, 1998). The extract examined here focuses solely on an instance where the child displays a specific orientation to learning something in context – in particular by saying 'a-ha' in the sense of 'I see what you mean'. In other words, the use of this expression as an indication that suddenly, where before you did not quite understand something, you now see what it means, or you recognize the significance of whatever it is. It can be argued that the act of producing this expression in the way described is warrantably understood by others, that you are learning something.

Background to the interaction

The background to the immediate context discussed below is one common to a great deal of research conducted in educational institutions. A researcher (in this case a researcher who had spent a number of years teaching mathematics at primary school level) was conducting a series of studies within the everyday context of the school programme. As part of one study, he asked a child (selected randomly by a class teacher) if she would be happy to learn a particular kind of mathematics task using a computer (in a quiet corner of a large classroom). The adult and child had not met before, but both participants in the teaching session were well versed in the conventions and procedures for behaving appropriately in the school classroom.

The context of the interaction was one where the adult was instructing the child how to understand a proportional reasoning task which involved estimating how much distance there should be between a series of numbers presented on a computer screen. The child's task was to re-arrange the balloon-numbers (the numbers were presented on balloons attached to strings and arranged on a line) so that the amount between each number was represented approximately by their positioning on the screen. Keeping in mind the significance of the immediate sequential history of an ongoing conversation, in the extract below we can consider structural and social affordance aspects of the talk leading up to and surrounding the child displaying a specific instance of learning in her use of 'a-ha'. This occurs at line 23 (towards the end of the extract) and follows immediately on from an extended stretch of speech from the researcher Chris.

Conversation analysis conventions (after Psathas, 1995)

Code	*Transcription conventions employed:*
↑ or (↓)	Marked rise (or fall) in intonation
Underlining	Used for emphasis (parts of the utterance that are stressed)
Upper-case letters	Indicate increased volume (note this can be combined with underlining where appropriate)
:::	Sounds that are stretched or drawn out (number of :: provides a measure of the length of stretching)
([ ])	Overlaps, cases of simultaneous speech or interruptions. Where appropriate, the spacing and placing of the overlap markers indicate the point at which simultaneous speech occurred
(.)	Small pauses
(1.4)	Silences with the time given in seconds
°	Shown when a passage of talk is noticeably quieter than the surrounding talk
=	When there is nearly no gap at all between one utterance and another

1: Lorna: [now i'll do:: h (1.0) these two again because (1.0)
if:::::these are a different numb::er (.)   then i might need
these spaced out a little bit more (5.0) and i moved this a
little way (2.5) so i could space them all (.) [on there

2: Chris: [well how
much did you say there was between seventy two an- ..
ninety five [you] worked that out just now didn't you

3: Lorna: [.h] = u:m::::: i think it wa::s (2.0) i'll do it again (2.0)

4: Chris: well it was twenty three (1.0) thats what you [said before

5: Lorna: [twenty
three::

6: Chris: okay .. [so there was-

7: Lorna: [twenty] three::=

8: Chris: =twenty three there (2.5) how much was there ↑there
(1.0) between fifty and sixty ↑seven (2.0)

9: Lorna: five

10: Chris: no (.) between <u>fifty</u> and sixty seven =

11: Lorna: = oh ! fifty one fifty (.)seventeen

12: Chris: seventeen so there was seventeen there and twenty three
↓there (3.5) an::d also (.) we said tha::t seventy two (.)
was just <u>under</u> (.) halfway between fifty and a hundred

13: Lorna: ↑i need to move <u>this</u> one (.) a littl- a little bit closer (.)
because (.) seventee:n (.) is less (1.0) than twenty three
[and that::s a smaller gap]

14: Chris: [a:::h i see (.) no:w by <u>this</u> one you mean the fifty] don't
you (2.).hh but wha- what do we know about where we
put the fifty right at the beginning (6.0)

15: Lorna: cos i'm going to (.) make out wh' that is and then move
(.) .h ↑if its the same i'm going to move it a little bit
closer [anyway

16: Chris: [but if (.) but if you move that a little bit cl<u>oser</u>
(1.0) that won't be halfway betwee:n nought and a
hundred anymore (7.0)

17: Lorna: but i::m (.) doing it (.) in be<u>tween</u> ↓now (4.0)

18: Chris: how do you me::an = ((spoken in a flat tone of voice))

19: Lorna: = bigger and smaller (1.0) like (1.0) you (.) said (1.0)
we're doing ..

20: Chris: yeah (.) °okay° (.) well you're doing very well ((spoken
quickly as reassurance)) (3.0) .hhh .. i was just thinking
(1.0) that if- if you were to move <u>THAT</u> one (2.0)
instead of <u>that</u> one (1.0) then you could keep that
halfway (1.0) and you could (.) you could (.) get over
your problem (.) about (.) seventeen (.) being smaller
than (.) twenty three (.) ↑see what i mean (2.0)

21: Lorna: i could move those two [over there↓

22: Chris: [exa::ctly you just move those
across a little [bit

23: Lorna: [a::[:h !

24: Chris: a:::h ! you got it ! .. that's r[ight !

25: Lorna: = [i see what you do

26: Chris: okay =

The talk leading up to the moment the child exhibits this understanding of
the nature of the talk possesses distinct structural features. Consider first
the long pauses before lines 14 and 17 (six and seven seconds respectively).
Pauses of this length are particularly noteworthy for participants, often indicating specific difficulties with the 'doing' of the talk. In both cases, these
pauses lead immediately to attempts by Lorna (the child) to give a realizable
account of what she is doing, accounts which Chris orients to as unaccept-
able, as evidenced in his response. For the first, in line 16, Chris's utterance
overlaps her account and begins without any affiliative orientation to what
she is saying. In fact, the slight pausing and repeat of 'but if' emphasizes his
following assertion that her solution is not really appropriate at all.

The nature of Lorna's tentative reply (after a noteworthy seven-second
pause) exhibits signs of her increasing uncertainty, the stretching on 'i::m';
the staccato pauses and the lowering of pitch and emphasis on 'between'.
Significantly, after a marked and noticeable four-second pause by Chris, he
then asks what she means, speaking with a noteworthy lack of intonation
contour and sound stretch on the word 'mean'. Here, not only is there no
affiliation but also little attempt to provide a framing for facilitating the
child's answer. In everyday conversation people often employ a monatomic
flat tone or pitch change in speech, as a 'to-be-noticed' feature (often
emphasizing 'matter-of-factness') indicating a lack of empathy or affiliation.
This interpretation is borne out by Lorna's immediate response (note the
latching between lines 18 and 19). Again she has staccato-like pauses (now
longer) and she can only reply that as far as she understood she was simply
doing what she was instructed to do.

We then move immediately to the extended utterance that leads to the child finally understanding the nature of the task. Line 20 begins with a specific orientation to the interactional trouble being displayed by the child – replying affirmatively, saying 'OK' quietly and then commenting on how well the child is doing at the task. After a three-second gap Chris, speaking slowly, begins by simply talking about how he sees the task and then, with frequent and careful pausing, spells out in some detail how Lorna could get over her problem. His talk is very measured, deliberate and relates specifically to the pragmatics of what is currently on the screen and potential solutions to the problem.

Importantly, when Lorna then indicates her understanding (by actively doing it onscreen and talking about the move she is making – line 21), Chris is quick to overlap/interrupt with a particularly noteworthy emphasis on 'exactly' and an indication of how easy the task now is, given her suggestion, leading to her distinct 'a::ah' in lines 23/25. It is important to note that Lorna's interruption at the end of line 22 is followed quickly by Chris repeating her 'a-ah' and finally her interruption and assertion that she now sees what is to be done. There is a mutually displayed orientation to what it is to understand the problem as well as displaying that understanding intersubjectively, ie, shared meaning. Intersubjectivity becomes a mutually shared accomplishment, worked up in a process where participants display a sensitivity to the social affordances of talk (eg, their orientation to what was presupposed by Chris's use of a very flat intonational contour).

Concluding comments

In the extract considered above, the structuration of a learning moment is mutually co-constructed with respect to the social affordances displayed and recognized during the ongoing talk. During interaction there is a continued and constant orientation to the immediately recognizable warrants presupposed by participants' actions and responses. We are both compelled to display orientations to these structures, yet at the same time seek to make manifest, through skilful employment of structural phenomena, as yet unrealized movements in the conversation, topic introductions, shifts, re-introductions and so on. By examining in micro-detail the structural organization of talk as it leads up to the such instances of learning it is possible to highlight those presuppositions which underpin the process of intersubjectivity – as a mutually worked-up orientation to activity by both participants.

Socio-cultural perspectives on learning emphasize participation in structured and supported problem-solving contexts, where the greatest benefits are from interactions where participation itself changes understanding (Pontecorvo and Girardet, 1993; Roth and Bowen, 1995). Certainly, learning as the transformation of social relations into internalized cognitions encompasses numerous contexts; conversational, non-verbal, participation in practical action and so on. But learning with and from another person demands and compels the display of appropriate behaviour as performance. As yet, we know rather little about the micro-details of dynamic processes of the zone of proximal development within which learning through participation is realized. Hopefully, using conversation analysis as methodology and bringing to bear the metaphor of the affordance we may be in a better position to understand the learning that occurs through the medium of conversation. Learning first to recognize, display and orient to, and then produce conversational structures is interdependent with understanding the social affordances presupposed in their deployment. In a study of the early emergence of conversational skills, Wooton (1997) makes the point that acquiring the ability to project conversational structure is interdependent with displaying an orientation to moral accountability. Rudolph (1994) reminds us that the very construction of an apprenticeship rests upon the mutual construction of discourse strategies. Employing conversation analysis may provide a methodology for understanding how the detection of learning affordances in talk underscores the transformation of apprentice into expert.

References

Chee, Y S (1995) Cognitive apprenticeship and its application to the teaching of small talk in a multimedia interactive learning environment, *Instructional Science*, **23**, pp 133–61

Collins, A and Michalski, R (1989) The logic of plausible reasoning: a core theory, *Cognitive Science*, **13**, pp 1–49

Forrester, M A and Pike, C (1998) Investigating estimation in the mathematics classroom: a conversation analytic approach, *Journal for Research in Mathematics Education*, **29**, pp 334–56

Forrester, M and Shire, B (1994) The influence of object size, dimension and prior context on children's estimation abilities, *Educational Psychology*, **14**, pp 451–65

Gibson, J J (1979) *The Ecological Approach to Visual Perception*, MIT Press, Harvard, MA

Laurillard, D (1993) *Rethinking University Teaching: A framework for the effective use of educational technology*, Routledge, London

Pontecorvo, C and Girardet, H (1993) Arguing and reasoning in understanding historical topics, *Cognition and Instruction*, **11**, pp 365–95

Psathas, G (1995) *Conversational Analysis*, Sage, London

Roth, W M and Bowen, G M (1995) Knowing and instructing: a study of culture, practice and resources in grade 8 open-inquiry science classroom guided by a cognitive apprenticeship metaphor, *Cognition and Instruction*, **13**, pp 73–128

Rudolph, D E (1994) Constructing an apprenticeship with discourse strategies: professor-graduate student interactions, *Language in Society*, **23**, pp 199–230

Sacks, H (1992) *Lectures on Conversation Analysis*, Blackwell, Oxford

Schegloff, E A and Sacks, H (1973) Opening up closing, *Semiotica*, **8**, pp 289–327

Vygotsky, L S (1979) *Mind in Society*, Harvard University Press, Cambridge, MA

Wooton, T (1997) *Interaction and the Development of Mind*, Cambridge University Press, Cambridge

Part 3
Apprenticeship as a
Model of Learning

7

Making Meaning: Language for Learning

Edwin Webb

Addressing the mysteries of learning, whether knowledge or skills, might be said to be the 'business' of education and training. Such learning, to an overwhelming degree, demands and operates through linguistic intelligence. It is the prime means by which we acquire and demonstrate understanding, conceptualize categories of reality and make sense of the world of experience. And within whatever other instructional methods are employed in education and training, language will feature as a fundamental means by which learning is communicated, implemented and assessed.

Language, of course, is not the only means by which we process experience and convert it to working sense. We derive information through all of our sense modes, and not all of that information needs to be embodied in language in order that we can 'make sense' of it and act upon it. We have available to us a range of representational possibilities. Bruner (1967), for example, established a three-fold classification for our systems of representation: *enactive, iconic* and *symbolic*. By all of these means we engage with experience and variously process information. Within the symbolic, however, language both preponderates, overwhelmingly, and has its own unique functioning.

Consider, for example, the following commonplace statement: 'One picture is worth a thousand words'. Whether or not one would regard this as true, in the case of any given picture, the *thought* that 'one picture is worth a thousand words' is one that can be constructed *only in language itself*. From the established thought, of course, it may well be possible to devise a pictorial representation of that conception as an alternative mode of expression. But the conception itself is a linguistic conception. A similar example is provided by various images on my new computer screen – an example which, in my case, insists upon itself and to which I shall return later. Those screen images represent (re-present) in an abbreviated and alternative form their functions. I can 'think' with these graphic images once those functions are understood; and that will be an understanding which *in the first place* is established verbally. Representation without understanding remains meaningless.

Such an acknowledgement compels us to look at language within *any* context of learning. The context of apprentice-learning involves its own language operations of training and the development of knowledge and skills. It subsumes also, however, the trainee's previous experience of language and the grounding of that experience within compulsory-age schooling – a process of education which, while serving its own intrinsic aims, should contain within it an essential preparation for further learning. That preparation will be general, not specifically vocational, but it will be based on prior experiences of learning and on established perceptions and understandings. At the point of entry to apprentice-training that general disposition towards learning will be both called upon and tested out.

What is in question here is the nature of that preparatory language experience which the learner will bring to apprentice-training and, within a wider context, to the challenges and opportunities of a projected learning society committed to lifelong learning. What, specifically, may be challenged is the kind of preparation that certain aspects of the statutory National Curriculum impose upon pupils and their relationship to the 'business' of learning.

Apprentice-learning

The traditional history of 'apprenticeship' is in its root meaning of the Latin *apprehendere* – to seize, or lay hold of – by which the novice was bound to a master for a fixed term of instruction in order to learn a craft or trade. The same root, however, provides us with two of the essential verbs of learning itself: to *apprehend* and to *apprise*. To apprehend ('seize' with the mind) is to understand, to perceive or construct meaning. To apprise is to inform ('give form to'; that is, 'to shape').

Within the etymology of 'apprenticeship' there is, therefore, a complex of interactive processes which supplies a suggestive model for learning itself. In apprehending something, properly, we learn not only to do something (as we might through instruction, mimed copying, repetition, practice), but we learn also to understand the principles of operation together with that shaped knowledge which informs what we are doing. Without these essential understandings we would be unable to vary the activity. Thus at the heart of learning there is meaning – a making sense of what we are learning to do. In learning to do something we show, or fail to show (to another or even to ourselves) the extent of that understanding.

Let me illustrate some of these processes of learning with a personal and, for some time yet probably, a pressing example, one which I introduced earlier. I sit now at a newly delivered and installed computer. I do what I can do with it, which is to create this 'folder' of words (which until a few days ago, for me, was a 'file' of words) using a system whose operation I understand to the extent that I can do what you (in a reprinted form) are now looking at. There are many other things, however, which this computer is capable of doing, as well as different, quicker ways of doing things – if only I understood what my advanced technicist colleagues clearly do understand. The monitor screen of this 'new' machine displays buttons, icons and other visuals which do not feature on my 'old' machine. Some of them do not 'mean' anything to me. Until I can establish such meanings I will not understand how to use the resources they contain. Lacking direct instruction, were I simply to 'have a go' with them, freely experimenting to see what happens when I employ each device, the perception and comprehension of my learning would still entail operations of verbal thought, however reduced. They would be of the order: 'I see, if I click on this image, then this happens....' Even though many of these visuals are displayed as icons – and have been designed, therefore, to represent immediately and visually what they 'do' – until they are made meaningful to me (shaped to and via a language I understand) they will remain to me a mystery.

'Mystery' invokes, in turn, many related aspects of the history of medieval craft and trade guilds, which I will not pursue. I will remark only that the end as well as the beginning of some learning, for some learners, can remain steeped in, if not completely composed of, such mystery – which is incomprehension. It is no wonder that we draw from *apprehendere* also our notion of a different experience of apprehension: that sense of gloomy foreboding and impending failure. The process of learning, if we are to succeed in the endeavour to help learners develop a 'preparedness to learn' is thus, precisely, a movement from apprehension to apprehension – from unease to perception and understanding.

These fundamental aspects of learning which I have sketched, educed from meanings implicit to 'apprenticeship' (not the history of its actual practice) have both a general application and a particular focus. For learning to proceed effectively, the learner must be able to recognize meaning in what is learned. Such recognition is more than a simple identifying of what one has seen or heard: it is re-cognition, a thinking-through (again) in order to arrive at comprehension and the application of that understanding. Where this does not happen, though facts and information can still be acquired (I *know* – that is, can state – many things I do not understand) that knowledge will be inert. Learning, then, in the sense in which I am identifying it, is not a matter of reception, but of reflexion – that activity of consciousness which works over selections of its content and composes meaning. And critical to the establishment of meaning will be language.

Language for meaning

There is a question I have posed, over the years, to many groups of pre-service and in-service teachers, within both the secondary and further education sectors, as well as to groups of people from industry and commerce. That question is: 'What do we use language for?' Without exception the first response received is always 'to communicate'. Subsequent responses go on to specify particulars within this function of language: to convey information, to ask questions, to describe something, to explain, and so on. Other responses take us into the interpersonal: to present an impression of oneself, to belittle, to challenge authority, and many more. Occasionally other perceptions are forthcoming, such as a recognition that language can be used to confuse someone, or to conceal something. All of these responses are true – but partial, and they remain so even when I prompt the groups to think about the *prime* function of language. And that, to put it at its simplest and most profound, is: *to make meaning*.

Without the making of meaning there is little or nothing to communicate in language. In face-to-face communication, of course, there are many other factors at work in addition to the strictly linguistic. The tone, pace and other paralinguistic features of voice will contribute to the auditor's shaping of an impression of the speaker; as gestures and movements will contribute to a 'reading' of the individual – leading to judgements, among other possibilities, as to that person's trustworthiness; the seriousness of what is said; an impressionistic evaluation of the person. In face-to-face communication one can amend or withdraw what one has said; discussion can qualify meanings and negotiate understandings in fluent and immediate interaction – or can halt at cross-purposes and ill-temper if things go wrong. The processes of discussion, none the less, are those of the exchange, negotiation and resolution of meaning. Talk is constructed out of the immediacy of these shared possibilities.

Writing, however, is a composition of meaning in which one's thinking (and therefore one's responsibility) is most exposed. The negotiation of meaning is, first, with oneself, an activity sometimes referred to as 'intrapersonal communication'. Intrapersonal communication is *thinking*. At the risk of then complexifying this simple formulation, I shall add that such an operation is actually reflexive; it involves *thinking about thinking*. I must think about the thoughts I have. It is not enough just to 'have' them. I must test them out, ask questions of them, try to shape and refine them, give them expressible form – all in the endeavour to compose my thinking and arrive at a linguistic formulation that represents those thoughts as closely as possible. The form of the language thus composed is the thought. To change the language is, however marginally, to change the thought. I think *in* language about meanings which I have thought, and am thinking, *in* language. If I fail to make meaning, I fail to make sense.

Language expressed, given voice or put into writing/print, is utterance; that is, an 'outering'. Until given in these forms we can conceive of linguistic thinking, following Vygotsky (1986),[1] as 'inner speech', an internalization of language continuing to operate as the genesis of thought. There may be, as Vygotsky also conjectured, a further stage of thinking in which 'post-language symbols' replace 'inner speech'. These represent thought-units, derived from language but freed now from the conventions and constraints of word-meaning and rule-governed grammar. We might perhaps experience something approaching this recognition on those occasions when we know we have something to say, some incipient, pre-conscious thought or idea, but cannot yet 'say what it is'. Only through a concentration of and upon language can the thought be bodied-forth at all: 'I talk so as to find out what I think. Don't you? Some things one can't judge of 'til one hears them spoken.' Cited by the Danish philologist, Otto Jesperson (1922: 252) from Housman's novel *John of Jingalo* (1912), this young girl's remark captures perfectly the nature of that interpenetration of language, thought and meaning which I have elaborated elsewhere (Webb, 1992). To make utterance, in speech or writing, is to endow thinking with form, so that it is communicable, enabling us to apprise ourselves and others of that thought.

English in the National Curriculum

Because we have separate words for language, thought and meaning, it is easy to conceive of them as different in nature, different 'things' as it were, established through that process known to sociologists as 'reification'. Yet linguistic thinking cannot operate these reified units of analysis as independencies, nor is linguistic thinking possible in the absence of any one of these coordinates. It is important to re-establish the essential interconnectedness of language, thought and meaning for three reasons at least. The first is that the re-conception of learning, personal and vocational, within a culture of life-learning and lifelong learning, will be dependent upon developing and extending capacities for linguistic thinking. Second, because their separation leads to conceptions of practice, for teaching and training, which lead to a failure to integrate the learning itself. Third, because learning, to be evident at all, must be communicable. And even though some learning can be demonstrated by direct practice, in what the learner can do, any explanation of that practice, together with thinking-through to possibilities of changing that practice, will entail language-operations as well as the functional doing.

Yet precisely this separation of language from its coordinates of thought and meaning now characterizes a good deal of the prospectus for education and training. Since the inception of a National Curriculum for compulsory education (through the Education Reform Act of 1988), the major part of the public debate on English within the curriculum has centred upon the matter of standard English. The General Requirements of the revised Orders (HMSO, 1995: 2) currently in place assert that: 'In order to participate confidently in public, cultural and working life, pupils need to be able to speak, write and read standard English fluently and accurately.' No argument is advanced in support of this assertion.[2] It is intended to be taken as axiomatic and self-evidently true. The insistent stress upon the formalities of learning and producing standard English dominates and controls the entire movement of the English Orders.

In relation to our thinking however – that reflexive process that includes thinking about our thoughts – there are two qualifying observations that need to be made. To think *in* a standard form of English, as I have expressed it elsewhere (Webb, 1995: 206–07), 'is to think those thoughts only of which the prescribed form is capable'; and 'to be committed, or condemned, to write and speak in one way only is actually to be sentenced to a singular mode of thinking, of reflection, of sharing and exchanging'. To think *in* standard English is to conceive thought within the semantics of the form. There is a corollary truth too: it is quite possible to write perfectly correct standard English which is in fact meaningless. George Orwell, in several of his essays (and most notably in his 1946 essay, *Politics and the English Language,* 1968: 56–70), drew sharp attention to this observation and the practices which should alert us to such emptiness. Disciplines within the domain of academic writings yield their own examples, as I once had the temerity to illustrate (Webb, 1980).

The imperative that pupils should learn to speak and write standard English 'accurately' within the present English curriculum, translates into a concentration upon the singular *form* of this version of language. That in turn has emphasized the direct teaching of grammar and the development of the learner's explicit 'knowledge about language'. Yet the director of the Language in the National Curriculum Project, set up to train teachers in the teaching of 'knowledge about language', admitted that there is no convincing evidence of the kind required that such knowledge does, or will, in fact enhance language competence (Carter, 1991: 16).

However great its dominance as the written mode of public language, the dominating drive of the English Orders to establish, or impose, a given form of language from the beginning of compulsory education onwards actually disestablishes the essential interrelationship between language and thinking. Thinking should *evolve* into that form of language which most accurately presents itself, rather than be cast from the beginning into a prescribed form that will predetermine essential characteristics of the thought itself. The insistence upon, or imposition of, standard English now starts at the very beginning of primary education, and its pre-eminence is successively and ever more weightily reinforced throughout later stages of formal education. Yet standard English is not essential to thinking to oneself, nor is it necessarily required for the purposes of 'informal situations' of talk (HMSO, 1995: 18). Informal communication, whether in speech or writing, can go on effectively in language forms other than that of fully expressed standard English requirements.[3] What is not given anywhere within *English in the National Curriculum* is any kind of rationale for standard English itself.

There is one. It attaches itself most powerfully to contexts of writing, rather than speech, and validates standard English as a *meaning*-form instead of a *feature*-form of language. In trying to make meaning as explicit *as possible* in writing, to an unfamiliar audience especially, the writing will successively approach and assume the conventions of standard English in order to make the thinking communicable to others. This is a matter not simply of eradicating ambiguity or slackness of expression, but of testing the taken-for-granted, so that one cannot excuse oneself by 'saying', as it were, 'You know what I mean.' Writing can supply a context for thinking itself. Vygotsky, again, provides invaluable insights, which James Britton (1987: 23) usefully summarized as follows:

> Vygotsky believed that mastery of the written language – learning to read-and-write – had a profound effect upon the achievement of abstract thinking. The *constancy* of the written language, grafted, so to speak, upon the *immediacy* of the spoken language, enables a speaker to *reflect* upon meanings and by doing so acquire a new level of control, a critical awareness of his/her own thought processes.

The development of writing within *English in the National Curriculum,* however, reduces to the Key Skills of planning, drafting, revising, proof-reading and presenting of the final text (HMSO, 1995: 15, 23). Whether or not these are actual skills, or whether they are just programmatic stages of writing (which one *might* follow sequentially), they are presented as 'operations' rather than as opportunities for engaging reflexively with one's thinking. In practice, in school and college, writing comes down to a matter of presentational form – the 'final polished work' which will be 'neat and legible' (ibid: 23).

The mechanization of language

It is commonplace to talk and write of language 'skills', as in the National Curriculum example of Key Skills cited above. Skills of various orders and types are firmly embedded in many formal programmes and syllabuses of education, just as we have seen the proliferation of many other so-called 'skills': social and life skills, coping skills, communication skills, core skills, and so on. The impetus in all these cases, including that of language, for the re-casting of complex operations of human consciousness and action, aims at a mechanization both of what is to be learnt and the manner of its teaching and learning. It reduces and simplifies at the risk of distorting and falsely representing.

Skills are not detachable in this way. Nor are they impersonal. They need to be re-contextualized within a culture of learning that will break down the divide between personal learning and vocational learning. Professor Bob Fryer's report (from the National Advisory Group for Continuing Education and Lifelong Learning) represents one recent attempt to describe learning in ways that foster and sustain personal identity. The inclusiveness of its description might provide useful hints for a re-tuning of vocational learning. *Learning for the 21st Century* (1997) borrows from the Royal Society of Arts' Campaign for Learning the following definition of learning:

> Learning is a process of active engagement with experience. It is what people do when they want to make sense of the world. It may involve an increase in skills, knowledge and understanding, values and the capacity to reflect. Effective learning leads to change, development and the desire to learn more.

The danger of the *reductio* by which the interpenetration and essential connectedness of language, thought and meaning are recast as sets of separable skills is that it systematizes through procedures rather than through a reflexive thinking-through, an active working-over of experience. It is, at best, second-hand learning. For the skills model of learning applied to language suggests not only that the identified skill is directly teachable, but that (in the mercantile language of much educational metaphor today) it can be 'delivered' through instructional modes. Yet more than 70 years ago, A N Whitehead (in *The Aims of Education,* 1932) pointed to the falseness of separating skills from that act that subsumes them. Fifty years later, taking his cue from Whitehead, Holt (1977: 18) expressed the matter more combatively:

> The baby does not learn to speak by learning the skills of speech and then using them to speak with, or to walk by learning the skills of walking and then using them to walk with. He learns to speak by speaking, to walk by walking.... Talking is not a skill, or a collection of skills, but an act, a doing. Behind the act there is purpose... we talk because we have something we want to say, and someone we want to say it to, and because we think or hope our words will make a difference.

What applies here to talking, in the context of language skills, can be extended also to those multifarious acts we call reading and writing. They are all to do with the making of meaning (in speech and writing) and the 'reading-into-meaning' of others' speech and writing. And all of these processes of establishing meaning are interactional in nature. Such acts are not skills: they are 'a process of active engagement with experience' by which people 'make sense of the world'.

The nomination of language-competencies as skills does not make convincing sense; their definitives are, in fact, reifications which have been separated out from more inclusive acts and activities. It would be better to think more holistically here, perhaps along the lines of Howard Gardner's 'linguistic intelligence'. Of the different modes of intelligence which Gardner (1984) identifies and elaborates, the 'linguistic' could then be seen, at least, as inextricably bound up in the realization of the individual's fuller development, rather than be seen as impersonal skills which one learns to perform. For 'linguistic intelligence' does not operate alone. In Gardner's own terminology, the linguistic is a powerful shaper and mediator of the 'interpersonal' and 'intrapersonal' intelligences which he identifies, and may be a contributor certainly to the development of 'logical intelligence' – and it is possible that language contributes elements towards the development of others of these multiple intelligences too.

Towards a reintegration

Training for employment, including apprentice-training, which concentrates exclusively upon the acquisition of discrete skills may well contain the seeds of its own obsolescence. The model of apprentice-learning, whether vocationally directed or embedded within lifelong learning, must involve more than the acquisition of knowledge and the operation of skills. It must promote the individual's capacity to *think* through 'active engagement with experience'. The development of language and thinking must operate interactionally; enforcing correctness of expression upon unreflexive thought that has not yet established itself will not work. Developing that reflexivity of thinking must be the prime concentration of vocational training as well as formal education. The literacy of learning requires an active promotion of the inseparables of language, thought and meaning.

The new learning age will demand such reflexivity of its participants. Traditional writing demands what Vygotsky (1986: 181) called 'a double abstraction' – abstraction from 'oral speech' and abstraction 'from the interlocutor'. Writing, in this tradition, is a solitary occupation, and it is the exclusive experience of writing which composes formal education. It requires great discipline and extensive experience of language to produce writing which, in making meaning *explicit,* promotes and develops reflexively our capacity to think – in the absence of the challenges of an interlocutor. For this promotion we need to devise and introduce, I suggest, new forms of 'interactional writing'. There are possibilities. Contemporary technologies of writing, for example, can make the 'interlocutor' virtually present; and it may be that we shall learn from these still-emerging technologies of communication and learning (e-mail, computer-mediated communication (CMC) conferencing) new ways of generating methods for interactional writing. At the least, we are beginning to recognize, perhaps, that such communications as these actually put an even greater stress upon capacities for writing of a changed order – one in which meaning is not only 'made' and 'sent', but can be composed and negotiated interactionally with others. Further, one may presume that the immediate future of lifelong learning, as well as vocational training, will incorporate increasingly such technological possibilities for education and training. Reconstructing writing as an interactional mode of communication, to develop language and thinking reflexively and concurrently, is a necessary supplement to the traditional model of writing as a solitary activity composed of skills to be learnt, rehearsed and then deployed. There are opportunities here for real engagement and interaction – and challenges to the constitution of traditional classroom practices (see, for example, Tweddle *et al,* 1997).

As in the case of writing, so will the notion generally of learning founded upon language-interaction need to be developed, at all stages of education and training, so that the making of meaning for the individual becomes the central preoccupation of the undertaking. Without this concentration, especially in the realm of linguistic thinking, the apprentice-learner will fail to make sense of the world of personal experience – and will fail to make sense of the world of work.

Notes

1. In a note to this revised edition of Vygotsky's *Thought and Language,* the translator, while retaining the title of the first English version (1962), comments that *'Myshlenie i rech* should be rendered in English as Thought and Speech'. In a recent discussion with Russian academic colleagues at St Petersburg, they offered the view that 'Thinking and Speaking' would provide an even more precise representation.
2. The National Curriculum Orders nowhere define standard English, offering only brief pointers as to what 'distinguishes' it 'from other forms of English'. There remains the argument, advanced for example by Milroy and Milroy (1985), that standard English is in fact 'defined' by sets of attitudes and ideological practices, including intolerance of variation, rather than as a discrete, describable variety of English.
3. John Mullan (*The Guardian,* 7 September 1998: 4), for example, has commented on the 'informality' of many e-mails received, comparing them with 'the terrors of letter-writing'. A singular feature (and possible advantage?) of e-mails which he notes is: 'They do not require elaborate composition but encourage what the novelist Samuel Richardson called 'writing to the moment' – a kind of instantaneousness that catches the present-tense thoughts, and changes of mind, of the writer.'

References

Britton, J (1987) Vygotsky's contribution to pedagogical theory, *English in Education,* **21** (3), pp 22–26

Bruner, J (1967) *Towards a Theory of Instruction*, Belknap Press, Harvard, MA

Carter, R (1991) *Knowledge about Language and the Curriculum: The LINC Reader*, Hodder and Stoughton, London

Fryer, R (1997) *Learning for the 21st Century: First report of the National Advisory Group for Continuing Education and Lifelong Learning*, NAGCELL, London

Gardner, H (1984) *Frames of Mind: The theory of multiple intelligences*, Heinemann, Oxford

HMSO (1995) *English in the National Curriculum*, HMSO, London

Holt, J (1977) *Instead of Education*, Penguin, Harmondsworth

Housman, L (1912) *John of Jingalo*, Chapman & Hall, London

Jesperson, O (1922) *Language: Its nature, development and origin*, Allen and Unwin, London

Milroy, J and Milroy, L (1985) *Authority in Language*, Routledge and Kegan Paul, London

Orwell, G (1968) *The Collected Essays, Journalism and Letters*, IV, Penguin, Harmondsworth

Tweddle, S, Adams, A, Clarke, S, Scrimshaw, P and Walton, S (1997) *English for Tomorrow*, Open University Press, Buckingham

Vygotsky, L (1986) *Thought and Language*, tr Alex Kozulin, MIT Press, Cambridge, MA

Webb, E (1980) The snaffle and the bit: language and education, *New Universities Quarterly*, **34** (3), pp 342–57

Webb, E (1992) *Literature in Education: Encounter and experience*, Falmer Press, London

Webb, E (1995) Poetry, experience, tradition, *The Use of English*, **46** (3), pp 205–17

Whitehead, A N (1933) *'The Aims of Education' and Other Essays*, Williams and Northgate, London

8

Beyond the Institution of Apprenticeship: Towards a Social Theory of Learning as the Production of Knowledge

David Guile and Michael Young

Introduction

Traditionally, the idea of apprenticeship has been associated with the process of skill formation within craft and industrial production and, to a lesser extent, within certain professions. Apprenticeship in these different contexts has usually been characterized by a constellation of both legal and contractual rules and relations governing the status of employment, associated workplace entitlements and a combination of formal and informal educational processes which help to socialize workers into specific workplace and occupational cultures. We have defined these arrangements in a recent article as the 'institution of apprenticeship' (Guile and Young, 1998a). Apprenticeship as an institution, irrespective of its workplace context, is also an educational process and like formal education has been assumed to rest on a transmission model of learning. However, unlike formal education, the institution of apprenticeship is also assumed to be underpinned by the dual assumptions of *learning by doing* and a *master as the role model,* rather than any model of curriculum or formal instruction. Furthermore, it is also assumed that as a model of work-based learning, apprenticeship will produce different outcomes of learning compared with programmes based in schools and colleges.

There is gradually emerging, however, a body of literature that has suggested that the concept of apprenticeship does not have to be restricted to the range of occupations and contexts with which it has traditionally been associated (Brown *et al,* 1989; Guile and Young, 1998a; Lave and Wenger, 1991; Teles, 1993). Once a 'situative' perspective on learning is adopted (Greeno, 1997), the idea of apprenticeship can be used to conceptualize both the process of learning and the practices, tools and resources that support learning. As we shall suggest in this chapter, apprenticeship offers a way of conceptualizing learning that does not separate it from the production of knowledge or tie it to particular contexts. It can therefore be the basis of a more general theory of learning that might link learning at work and learning in classrooms, rather than see them only as distinct contexts with distinct outcomes.

Following the recent work of cultural anthropologists such as Jean Lave, we are interested in the potential of apprenticeship for conceptualizing learning as a social process. Our particular interest is in exploring how far this reconceptualization can lead to the development of new pedagogic criteria for what we have referred to elsewhere as 'reflexive learning' (Guile and Young, 1998a). The concern of this chapter, therefore, is in the main conceptual rather than substantive. Building initially upon recent developments within socio-cultural activity theory (Vygotsky, 1978), we introduce the concept of the 'zone of proximal development' to argue that despite its traditional association with work-based learning, the concept of apprenticeship can also shed light on pedagogic processes of classrooms. Such an analysis, therefore, offers three possibilities which we can only begin to point to in this chapter. First, it forms the basis of a critique of 'transmission models'; second, it can indicate similarities and differences between work-based and classroom-based learning; third, it can suggest the basis of new types of relationships between the two. We begin, however, by using Vygotsky's concept of the zone of proximal development to analyse the model of learning traditionally associated with the 'institution' of apprenticeship, before proceeding to examine two alternative conceptions of the zone of proximal development – what we will refer to as the 'societal' and the 'transformatory'. We argue that these conceptions offer a new perspective on the process of learning that relates to emerging features of learning in an era of 'reflexive modernization' (Beck et al, 1994).

Existing approaches to learning have tended to rely on behaviourist and individualist assumptions and be dependent on transmission pedagogues. They also tend to treat the concept of knowledge transfer as a decontextualized process, or associated with cognitive science accounts of learning as the stable individual mastery of well-defined tasks. However, new models of learning are emerging within social psychology (Greeno, 1997), the philosophy of education (Prawat, 1993) and sociolinguistics (Gee, 1992) which emphasize its 'situative' or social character. They focus upon the context of learning and the importance of ideas as a resource for learning, and they argue that all learners require opportunities to transform social practice and develop new ideas. Neither should be the privilege of an elite; they should be possibilities for all learners. Drawing, in particular, upon recent work in the philosophy of education, we introduce the notion of 'ideas-based constructivism' to illustrate how this shift towards a social theory of learning can be the basis for seeing knowledge production as integral to the process of learning. In addition, we draw upon ideas derived from socio-cultural psychology to highlight two aspects of the potential of information and communication technology (ICT): first, if the potential for learning of ICT is to be realized, it has to be on the basis of a social theory of learning; second, ICT offers promising new ways of integrating learning with the production of knowledge and hence of overcoming the barriers between school and work-based learning. Finally, we outline the criteria that might inform such a social theory of learning and production of knowledge and offer some brief considerations about the implications of our ideas for learning in schools and colleges and the new relationships between school and college-based learning and learning in workplaces.

Apprenticeship, learning and the zone of proximal development

The concept of the zone of proximal development is central to Vygotsky's theory. He defined it as:

> the distance between the actual development level as determined by independent problem solving and the level of potential development as determined through problem solving under adult guidance or in collaboration with more able peers.

(1978: 85)

Vygotsky was concerned with the progress that students make with their studies as they relate their 'everyday' concepts – the understanding that emerges spontaneously from interaction with other people and in different situations – to the 'scientific' concepts that they experience through textbooks and the formal curriculum. Vygotsky saw scientific concepts as those ideas whose analytic purchase had been deepened over a long period of time. As Kozulin (1990) has argued, the concept of the zone of proximal development was an integral part of Vygotsky's programme to account for the complex interaction between scientific concepts and everyday concepts and hence the development of intellectual and practical expertise. He also saw it as a framework to identify the pedagogic structure(s) needed to assist learners to move beyond the stage of mastery that they were capable of on their own.

Over the years the concept has been modified, developed and given a broader interpretation within socio-cultural activity theory both in the United States (Brown *et al,* 1989; Griffen and Cole, 1985; Lave and Wenger, 1991; Rogoff, 1990; Schribner and Cole, 1971; Wertsch, 1981) and in the Soviet Union (Davydov and Radzikouskii, 1985; Leontiev, 1978). Following the tradition of Vygotsky's own empirical research, most writers have restricted the use of the concept to understanding child development. It has, however, been applied in two quite different ways within contemporary curriculum theory. One interpretation has favoured a 'practical problem-solving' approach to teaching and learning, while the other has focused upon the important role of ideas within teaching and learning (Prawat, 1993).

It is our contention, however, that there are common processes that underlie learning in all contexts and for all ages and that Vygotsky's concept of the zone of proximal development is a useful way of highlighting similarities as well as differences between learning in formal and informal contexts. Moreover, we believe that more recent interpretations of this concept help to throw light on the complex relationship between the role of ideas, practical problem solving and the production of new knowledge that could be the basis for reconceptualizing an approach to learning in vocational education (Engestrom, 1996b; Lave and Wenger, 1991). We also feel that the concept, in particular, provides a useful way of taking further some of our ideas about linking school and work-based learning (Guile and Young, 1998a). From our point of view, the appeal of Vygotsky's approach lies in the emphasis it places on the idea of mind *in* society, its associated focus on cognitive development in specific contexts and the pedagogic practices that underpin such development.

Learning and the institution of apprenticeship

As we stated earlier, apprenticeship has traditionally rested upon a transmission model of learning which was supposed to develop work-related knowledge and skill. We begin, therefore, by exploring the ideas about learning implicit in the institution of apprenticeship. It is our intention to question the traditional assumptions of apprenticeship as an institutional approach to learning that is radically different from learning in formal education. One helpful way of approaching this issue, we believe, is to distinguish between the process, the types and the outcomes of learning and the arrangements for learning.

Most studies in cognitive psychology, cultural anthropology and anthropology of education portray apprenticeship as lacking an explicit theory of instruction and not dependent upon any formal teaching (Coy, 1989; Schribner and Cole, 1971). Learning is seen as a natural process which happens over time and occurs via observation, assimilation and emulation and without any substantial intervention from more experienced others (Raizen, 1991). However, two slightly different emphases emerge within this literature. For some commentators, learning appears as a result of direct interaction between apprentices and their environment. This interaction can take the form of observation, trial and error, conditioning and so on. A different interpretation emerges from those studies which originate from socio-cultural activity theory. They are more inclined to stress the idea of mediation as an integral aspect of the learning process (Schribner and Cole, 1971) and accord more importance to the interaction between experienced adults and apprentices as a process that facilitates practical participation in, and eventual understanding or mastery of, different activities.

None the less, despite the existence of these slightly different interpretations of the process of learning within apprenticeship, both groups have assumed that formal and informal contexts involve different types of learning and result in different outcomes of learning. Resnick has argued that there are three broad characteristics of mental activity outside formal education which stand in contrast to learning typical of formal education. These, she suggests, are that 1) learning in formal educational contexts is an individual process; 2) it involves a purely mental activity based on the manipulation of symbols; and 3) it results in the production of generalized concepts. Learning in *informal* contexts, in contrast, is a collaborative process; it usually involves the manipulation of tools (machinery, computers, etc) and it leads to highly context-specific forms of reasoning and skills (Resnick, 1987).

These distinctions about the different process of learning and the forms and outcomes of learning in formal and informal contexts help to sustain the overriding and widely held belief that expertise in apprenticeship is developed through the gradual accumulation of experience under the guidance of an established master within an unspecified 'zone of proximal development'. Consequently, it tends to be assumed that the concept of knowledge developed within apprenticeship is restricted to a combination of trade or craft knowledge handed down by the master and the implicit knowledge ('action oriented skills' – Zuboff, 1988) that is part of all practical activity.

Research from other branches of social science, eg, post-compulsory education and training and management science, however, has adopted a different perspective on the processes of work-based learning and the skill development that take place within the institution of apprenticeship. By focusing on the arrangements for apprenticeship, it has identified models of apprenticeship that embrace formal and informal learning within structured on- and off-the-job training provided by employers (Brown *et al*, 1994; Fuller, 1996; Gherardi *et al*, 1988). It has also highlighted that in practice, work contexts vary widely in the learning processes and forms of learning that they make available. Some workplaces are relatively routine and require little explicit knowledge, whereas others are highly knowledge-intensive. Also, work contexts vary according to whether the explicit knowledge involved is of a 'traditional' craft type or more associated with a developing body of 'theory' (Gott, 1995). As a consequence, a general theory of learning not only needs to take account of differences in the degree of expertise needed within specific occupations, but also in differences in the content and quality of such expertise. Moreover, the nature of workplace practices and the demands they make on apprentice learners are likely to be quite different when different forms of knowledge or work are involved.

In an attempt to address the need for a more systematic relationship between formal and informal learning and for analysing the instructional basis of apprenticeship learning, Gherardi *et al* (1998) have employed the concept of the 'situated curriculum'. Fuller (1996) has also tried to identify the conditions that may support a more effective relationship between formal and informal learning. Such arrangements have become necessary because the evolution from pre- to post-industrial societies has generated new demands upon the institution of apprenticeship. In addition to the acquisition of craft-based skill through workplace learning, employers have increasingly required apprentices to acquire more formal types of knowledge to help them cope with industrial change and the demands of knowledge-intensive work. Consequently, there has been a slow realization that the emergence of new contexts for, and new demands upon, apprenticeship and the need to enhance workplace learning with more formal types of learning calls for a reassessment of the traditional assumptions about both types of learning and their relationship to apprenticeship. Among other matters, it has become apparent that the transmission model of learning traditionally associated with apprenticeship, ie, involving learning by doing and the master as a role model, always implicitly involved a zone of proximal development, albeit an informal zone, since apprentices were being moved beyond the stage of 'mastery' they were capable of on their own (Guile and Young, 1998a). This implies greater similarity between the process of learning which occurs within apprenticeship and formal learning than had previously been accepted to be the case. Furthermore, given that far more attention has been devoted to identifying how workplaces can serve as 'environments for learning', there has been greater interest in the value of contemporary learning theory as a theoretical resource for analysing learning in formal and informal contexts.

Reconceptualizing the zone of proximal development

Over the last decade researchers from many fields within social and psychological science have begun to adopt new perspectives on the process of learning. One of the main reasons for this interest has been the way in which the zone of proximal development has been reconceptualized in neo-Vygotskian theory. Cole (1985) for instance has suggested that culture and cognition create each other within the zone via a dynamic interrelationship between people and social worlds as expressed through language, art and understanding.

Accordingly, Cole laid the foundations for extending the application of the concept to human development in general, rather than restricting its use to analyses of child development. Cole's interpretation of the zone of proximal development has offered contemporary researchers a way of examining the processes through which cognition is developed among individuals and groups in different types of formal and informal context (Engestrom, 1996b; Lave, 1996; Rogoff and Wertsch, 1984). In addition it provided a new perspective on the process of learning. Instead of focusing upon the content of formal or informal learning, it encouraged researchers to investigate how learning may occur through common processes in different contexts.

As we have recently pointed out (Guile and Young, 1998a), Cole's original argument that culture and cognition create each other within the zone of proximal development has been expanded by both Lave and Engestrom. Instead of focusing upon apprenticeship purely as an 'institution', Lave, working in collaboration with Wenger, has developed it to emphasize the dynamic interrelationship between social, cultural, technological and linguistic practices. This breakthrough was made possible because Lave and Wenger extended the zone of proximal development to highlight the social and cultural basis of learning (Lave, 1996; Lave and Wenger, 1991). This approach enabled them to highlight how, over a period of time, social, cultural, technological and linguistic practices afford individuals and groups opportunities to learn. Although Engestrom's work has not been directly concerned with apprenticeship, he shares with Lave an interest in overcoming the limitations of much of contemporary learning theory (Engestrom, 1987, 1995; Engestrom *et al,* 1995; Lave, 1993; Lave and Wenger, 1991). Engestrom also took the zone of proximal development as his starting point; however, he was interested in how people developed the capability to do something they had not previously accomplished. This led him to adopt what Lave and Wenger (1991) have described as a transformatory perspective on the zone of proximal development. His studies on the social transformation of the organization of work begin to identify how individuals and groups, through critically interrogating their work contexts, collectively produced new understandings and hence new knowledge (Cole and Engestrom, 1994; Engestrom, 1993, 1996b). It is our contention that taken together the contributions of Lave and Engestrom and recent work in the philosophy of education provide the basis of a more comprehensive social theory of learning.

A societal perspective on the zone of proximal development

As we have argued elsewhere, and in contrast to the more normative interpretations of the zone of proximal development referred to earlier, Lave and Wenger developed their 'societal' perspective on the zone of proximal development, by highlighting the historical and social dimensions of learning, and 'connecting issues of socio-cultural transformation with the changing relations between newcomers and old-timers in the context of a changing shared practice' (1991: 49). This emphasis on a historical and social perspective is important in reconceptualizing learning, especially in a period of continued social change. First, it directs attention to the distance (and potentially, the links) between the everyday activities of individuals and the historically new forms of social practice that need to be collectively generated as solutions to everyday problems. Second, it identifies learning as a social process, and by broadening the concept of 'social' beyond immediate contexts of interaction, it acknowledges the contribution that technological and other external 'resources' can make in support of such learning processes, as well as how learning is shaped by wider social forces and can shape them. This reconceptualization of the process of learning led Lave and Wenger to identify how social structures and social relationships influence the process of learning over time; the importance of relationships between one context of learning (or 'community of practice', to use their term) and another; and the opportunities available for learning within such communities, and the human and technological resources needed to support them. They come to conceive of learning in terms of 'participation [since it] focuses attention on ways in which it is an evolving, continuously renewed set of relations' (1991: 51). Furthermore they argue that participation:

> can be neither fully internalized as knowledge structures [within individual minds] nor fully externalized as instrumental artefacts or overarching activity structures. Participation is always based on situated negotiation and re-negotiation of meanings in the world. This implies that understanding and experience are in constant interaction – indeed, are mutually constitutive.
>
> (1991)

Viewing the relationship between learning, activity and socio-cultural contexts as a mutually constitutive process within 'communities of practice' leads Lave and Wenger to challenge the idea that expertise in a given field is invariant and consists of mastery of discrete tasks and skills. This leads them to reconceptualize intelligence as a distributed process as well as an attribute of individuals. Their argument suggests that zones of proximal development are constituted by such resources as physical and cultural tools, as well as other people, and that these resources are used, or brought together to be used, to shape and direct human activity. It follows that, from their perspective, intelligence and expertise are acquired through a process of accomplishment, rather than being a matter of self-possession. As Lave observes, when people undertake activity 'they are skilful at, and are more often than not engaged in, helping each other to participate in changing ways in a changing world' (Lave, 1993).

This is not to deny that individuals develop particular forms of 'knowledgeability' (ie, forms of knowledge and skill). However, Lave and Wenger (1991) emphasize the collective basis through which individuals develop a social identity, learn new forms of social practice and become 'knowledgeable'. By 'knowledgeability' they mean the combination of knowledge and skill required to successfully operate within a 'community of practice'.

Lave and Wenger argue that learning is not a distinct mental process. It is better understood as a relational process which is generated socially as well as historically in social formations where participants engage with each other as a condition and precondition for their existence (Lave and Wenger, 1991). Thus learning becomes a matter of emerging identities developing within different 'communities of practice'. Such a perspective adds another dimension to reformulating existing ideas about skill transfer. Conventional approaches usually assume contexts are invariant. They also rely upon a narrow transmission model of teaching and play down the importance of the meaning given to skills and knowledge by learners. The assumption of such approaches is that the message to be transferred is always unproblematic and clearly understood; it follows that there is a need to address how new knowledge might be produced within the contexts between which the knowledge or skill is to be transferred. On the other hand, as recent research has shown, accomplishing the transfer of learning and crossing organizational boundaries is a complex and challenging process (Engestrom and Middleton, 1996). It involves people developing the capacity to think beyond the immediate situation they find themselves in and understanding why it might be both possible and necessary to generate new knowledge.

A transformatory perspective on the zone of proximal development

As we have noted earlier, in order to address how people learn to do things that they have not previously accomplished and, in the process, generate new understandings and new knowledge, Engestrom elaborated further the idea of the zone of proximal development being collective and the basis for learners to transform the situation they find themselves in (Guile and Young, 1998a). Engestrom concentrates upon identifying how collaborative activity is needed to reconfigure workplace activity and the knowledge that employees have (Cole and Engestrom, 1993; Engestrom, 1996b). He recognizes that many existing approaches to learning assume that it involves the circulation of existing knowledge rather than the production of 'knowledgeability' and also argues that considerable variation exists in the fundamental imprint of the different groups with their different goals and circumstances, on what it might mean 'to know' on a particular occasion, in a particular context, or within the culture of a particular organization. Consequentially, he broadens his framework of analysis from a sole focus upon 'expert' definitions of what is to be learned and how it is to be learned.

He emphasizes the importance of encouraging learners to identify contradictions or puzzles within their existing knowledge or workplace practices as a way of developing new knowledge. It is these 'problems' which

Engestrom sees as legitimate starting points for exploring and designing solutions and therefore as a basis for new learning (Cole and Engestrom, 1993).

Engestrom's studies of the transformation of health centres in Finland (Engestrom, 1993) and learning in work teams (Engestrom, 1996a) highlight the relationship between different modes of learning, the types of outcome arising from each mode and the influence of context and conditions upon each mode of learning (Guile and Young, 1998b). Although he accepts Lave and Wenger's premise that learning is a social and reflexive process that leads 'communities' to change their identities over time, he implies that learning within 'communities of practice' is likely to be a slow continuous evolution of practice rather than transformative. Nevertheless, as the health centre and work team studies demonstrate, crisis points often occur because the 'communities of practice' end up confronting conflicts or problems that are not immediately resolvable (Cole and Engestrom, 1993).

Engestrom's research indicates that two conditions need to be met if people are to expand their understanding and transform existing 'communities of practice'. They are, first, the context of learning must be expandable to include the existing organization, its purposes and 'tools' of work, as well as its location in the wider community. This avoids limiting the focus of learning to 'here-and-now' problems and relatively 'quick fixes'. It also enables new possibilities for the organization of work to be extensively debated and their likely implications for other related activities to be considered prior to any process of change (Engestrom, 1996b). Second, if the context of practice is to be taken into account, it is vital that participants feel they are able to question, criticize or reject some aspects of accepted practice and existing wisdom.

One common thread runs through both Lave and Wenger's and Engestrom's argument about the process of learning. Both view learning as a mediated activity which will benefit from access to linguistic, technological and social resources that are not necessarily part of the context of learning itself. In contrast to Lave and Wenger who endorse the appropriation and exploitation of those resources which are already available within existing 'communities of practice', Engestrom retains an explicit role for concepts and learning technologies (ICTs) that may be located externally to an organization's existing culture and environment. He recognizes the value of concepts and ideas which may be external to a community but be the basis of frameworks for reconceptualizing the felt dilemmas and contradictions within the community of practice. As Engestrom's field studies indicate, unless these conditions prevail, it will not be possible for participants to construct a vision of the past and the future of their specific activity systems, nor will they be able to produce new knowledge (Engestrom *et al*, 1996).

The idea of reflexive learning

There are several conclusions that follow from our preceding argument. First, if participation in communities of practice is a critical aspect of developing 'knowledgeability' or working out the meaning of an idea in the context of its use, it raises questions about how communities of practice are established and sustained. Second, the idea that concepts and access to learning technologies (ICTs) are important in workplace learning stands in stark contrast to the traditional assumption that apprenticeship only involves a process of learning by doing with a master as the main role model. Clearly there are certain workplace situations where this model may still apply (Lave and Wenger, 1991); however, increasingly in modern workplaces, in which continuous change is the norm, this idea is less and less tenable (Hirschorn, 1986; Shaikin, 1996; Zuboff, 1988). Third, if concepts are important to the process and outcomes of learning, it suggests that the traditional emphasis in apprenticeships on developing 'tacit knowledge' and 'action-orientated' skills will be inadequate, on its own, to enable apprentices or for that matter other employees to operate effectively in future in workplaces (Gott, 1995; Zuboff, 1988). Fourth, if the first two observations are taken together, they imply that learning by doing may well be an inadequate model for describing work-based learning or apprenticeship.

Learning by doing or problem solving has been emphasized as a foundation of both apprenticeship and school-based vocational education. Moreover, as Prawat (1993) has argued, the educational benefits of extending 'learning by doing' are widely accepted in learning research. Writers from such diverse fields of study as cognitive and constructivist psychology (Brown *et al,* 1989; Steffe, 1990), as well as philosophy and psychology of education (Floden *et al,* 1987: 465–506) have all developed different rationales for focusing upon practical problem solving as the paradigmatic context for promoting higher order thinking in classrooms. This has led, Prawat suggests, to an emphasis upon the assimilation of knowledge through the use of existing schemata to interpret problematic situations and by a reliance on available routines. In essence, he argues, this implies an *informative,* rather than a *transformative* relationship with the world (Prawat, 1993).

The critical question from our point of view is how powerful learning experiences will lead individuals and groups to develop a more *transformative* relationship with the world that is based around collaborative activities which can be provided in formal and informal contexts. At the heart of this question is the relationship between what Vygotsky distinguished as 'scientific' concepts, ie, those which emerge from collaborative activity between apprentices/students and more experienced adults and are immersed in disciplinary or multidisciplinary fields, and the 'everyday or spontaneous' concepts, ie, those concepts which emerge from reflection on such everyday experiences as play, work, interpersonal interaction and so on. As different generations of socio-cultural theorists have made clear, this distinction between 'scientific' and 'everyday' concepts is consistent pedagogically with both 'societal' and 'transformatory' notions of the zone of proximal development (Engestrom, 1991; Wertsch, 1985). Learning becomes a process of mediating in new contexts, ideas or concepts which have been meticulously worked up and debated over a period of time in other social contexts in relation to other practical problems.

Certainly, both concepts refer to learning processes. However, as Kozulin and Presseisen (1995) have recently made clear, while the learning in a generic sense can emerge from any of the latter processes, 'learning activity', ie, grasping the meaning of scientific concepts and using them to transform understanding and social practice, does not occur spontaneously. Consequently, from our point of view, the challenge is to redefine the relationship between theory or scientific concepts and practice or everyday concepts. Yet, as writers from such diverse fields as cognitive psychology and sociolinguistics have begun to argue over the last decade or so, not only do ideas, or 'scientific concepts', play a crucial role in directing attention to important aspects of the environment that otherwise would go unnoticed (Neisser, 1976), their transformational potential only occurs when they are discussed and applied in a social context (Gee, 1992).

The US philosopher of education Prawat introduces the concept 'ideas-based constructivism' to encapsulate this process. It is his contention that all forms of learning are enhanced when ideas or concepts that emerged from other contexts can be drawn upon to clarify thinking, knowing and, ultimately, help to transform social practice. Prawat's ideas fit in well with our distinction between the 'societal' and 'transformatory' perspectives on the zone of proximal development and the value of the concept of 'legitimate peripheral participation'. In Lave and Wenger's work, meaning is developed through immersion into and exploration of different forms of social practice and this may lead to a fuller and richer understanding of the 'ideas' which lie behind specific social practices. In the case of Engestrom, 'communities of practice' should be encouraged to use ideas to transform situations by enabling participants to question, criticize or reject some aspects of accepted practice and existing wisdom.

Such a development is only likely if ideas or concepts external to a situation can be called upon to clarify thought and understanding of purposes. This raises two key questions. First, how do 'communities of practice' use ideas to serve such purposes? Second, given the rapid emergence of ICT as a resource for learning and hence access to new ideas, how do 'communities of practice' use ICT to transform thinking and practice?

Certain clues as to the answer to the first question have been provided by Engestrom. He has argued very persuasively that connecting ideas to practice involves using a learning cycle that explicitly incorporates context, cognition and contradiction (Engestrom, 1995). The learning cycle Engestrom proposes is based upon his concept of 'expansive learning' (Engestrom, 1987) and enables individuals and groups to connect the current level of their understanding about practice to emerging ideas as to how to transform practice and hence to generate new knowledge about practice. Within his learning cycle, ideas represent what Neisser (1976) has referred to as 'anticipatory phases of activity'. In other words, they direct attention to aspects of the cyclic process of questioning, modelling, revising practice, etc and in the process become part of the cycle and help to determine how further information and/or responses, etc are accepted and used. Unlike Kolb's (1984) much better-known 'learning cycle', which emphasizes learning either as a process of natural reflection or formalized procedures and specifically directs participants to rely on 'everyday concepts', Engestrom's 'learning cycle' adopts a transformatory perspective. This encourages 'communities of practice' to find ways of connecting 'scientific' and 'everyday' concepts to achieve changes in understanding and social practice.

A partial answer is provided to our second question about the use of ICT as a resource for learning by the work of the Helsinki Centre for Activity Theory (Engestrom *et al*, 1995, 1996). They indicate an awareness that new conceptual and technological resources must be used sensitively within 'communities of practice' if they are to complement the forms of learning already being engaged in within communities; however, they do not specifically address the use of ICT as a resource for learning and the production of new knowledge. In fact, this dual role of ICT is rarely addressed in the social and psychological sciences. One of the most imaginative contributions to our understanding of the role of ICT as a resource for learning comes from the work of Pea (Pea, 1993; Pea and Gomez, 1992). His work makes it clear that although ICTs can be used to enhance individual learning within given parameters, they can also be used to create the possibility of 'communities of practice' being extended to become *distributed communities of learning*.

These insights about the potential use of ICT need to be set in the context of our earlier discussion about reconceptualizing apprenticeship as the basis of a social theory of learning. Contrary to the assumption of traditional approaches to apprenticeship, namely that learning is implicit and informal and pedagogy is irrelevant, we have argued that it is possible to identify how pedagogic structures are embedded within workplace activity. Lave and Wenger (1991) stress the idea of situated learning which sensitizes us both to the negotiated character of learning as a social practice and to how opportunities to participate within workplace cultures influence whether and how we learn. Hence, their emphasis upon the social character of the zone of proximal development. Engestrom, however, goes one stage further with his idea of 'transformative' learning which, rather than only focusing upon the transmission of existing knowledge, acknowledges the importance of new knowledge being produced within workplace communities as part of the process of learning. The critical issue for Engestrom is that although transformative learning has to be designed, design focuses on more than formal teaching and has to take into account the context as a whole. He retains a role for a theory of instruction as well as a focus on the social processes, relationships and resources that are needed to support learning. Instruction in this sense involves ensuring that the goals of learning are clear and people are encouraged to think beyond the immediate circumstances. This ensures that the zone of proximal development is collectively organized to facilitate the transformation of context, cognition and practice. Nonetheless, unless *communities* enable their members to extend the sources of information to which they have access and expand their socio-cultural basis, they will not develop new forms of 'knowledgeability' nor will they begin to use ICT to produce new knowledge (Guile and Young, 1998b). As we have argued elsewhere, such activity can be described as a process of 'reflexive learning' (Guile and Young, 1998a) and is the 'micro' expression of the 'macro' process of 'reflexive modernization' (Beck *et al*, 1994).

Conclusion

This chapter was stimulated by two issues, one theoretical and one practical. Theoretically, it arose via recent developments in socio-cultural activity theory, from the possibility of using apprenticeship as a conceptual model for a social theory linking learning and production of knowledge. Practically, it is an attempt to respond to the recent policy interest in apprenticeship and the possibilities it may provide for overcoming the separation of formal and informal learning and of educational institutions and workplaces. Thus, it has tried to provide a more unified perspective on the different types of learning traditionally associated with these different contexts.

The chapter has examined some of the assumptions underlying the institution of apprenticeship and the possibilities it might offer when freed from its historic legacies, for overcoming barriers to learning opportunities in post-compulsory education and training and constituting part of a strategy for the UK becoming a learning economy.

If young people are to develop the new kinds of skills and knowledge that are emerging as essential to a learning society, they will need to be able to use ICT as a resource both to access information as well as to collaborate with others within distributed communities of practice to produce new knowledge (Lundvall, 1996). We have argued that exploiting the learning potential of ICT will involve radical changes to how we organize education and training. More fundamentally, it will involve exploring the implications of recognizing learning as a *social* process. This chapter, therefore, argues that critical to any such changes is that policy-makers, users and education and training providers rethink their ideas about learning and pedagogy as well as developing a more critical approach to the potential of online learning. To this end, the chapter draws upon the twin notions of 'community of practice' and 'ideas-based constructivism' and suggests a transformative approach to Vygotsky's idea of the zone of proximal development as the basis for a social theory of learning. Such a theory, it argues, could provide a way of linking work-based and school- and college-based learning together as changes in work and society become *the ideas* for reflecting on changes in pedagogic practice, and the disciplines of subject-based knowledge become the *criteria* for interrogating changes in work and society.

We are not the first to suggest that the concept of apprenticeship might serve as the basis of an alternative learning paradigm for formal education and training (Brown *et al,* 1989), or online learning (Teles, 1993). We draw on Prawat's distinction between 'problem-based' and 'ideas-based' approaches to learning to differentiate between our and earlier approaches. The former refer to those attempts to introduce a practical approach to problem solving as the paradigmatic context for promoting higher order thinking in classrooms and elsewhere. This, we argued, leads to an *informative* relationship with the world, since 'communities of practice' are encouraged to accept a problem as it is posed to them, by a teacher or other adult, and to use existing conventions, beliefs and practices to explain how to address them. The latter refers to our argument that learning should either encourage 'communities of practice' to identify problems which need to be solved, or where problems have been identified for them to solve, they should think about their relation to the problem and pose alternatives to it. Such an approach, we have suggested, implies a much more *transformative* relationship with the world. This transformative approach, we contend, can only occur when the learning process explicitly involves the use of both 'scientific' and 'everyday' concepts. Although the former may direct attention to aspects of a problem that may otherwise go unnoticed, they are ultimately only valuable when they can be used to help transform everyday problems.

Furthermore, we argued that the educative purposes of ICT have to be rethought in relation to both the changes occurring in work as a result of the introduction of ICT, and in relation to the new potential for learning ICT generates. The recognition that both 'ideas' and ICT are equally important resources for 'communities of practice' led us to argue that such 'communities' must have a stake in the development of new practices if they are to establish their own future identities, develop their capacity for lifelong learning and the production of new knowledge and hence contribute to the creation of a learning society. Accordingly, we suggested that our concept of *reflexive learning* encapsulated the process whereby 'communities of practice' can connect ideas to practice. We suggested this might happen in two ways. First, through the use of a 'learning cycle' that specifically incorporated context, cognition and context; second, by using ICT to create the possibility of a 'community of practice' being extended to become a *distributed learning community.*

References

Beck, U, Giddens, A and Lash, S (1994) *Reflexive Modernization*, Polity Press, Cambridge

Brown, A, Evans, K, Blackman, S and Germon, S (1994) *Key Workers: Technical training and mastery in the workplace*, Hyde, Bournemouth

Brown, J, Collins, S and Duguid, P (1989) Situated cognition and culture of learning, *Educational Researcher*, **18** (1), pp 32–42

Cole, M (1985) The zone of proximal development: where culture and cognition create each other, in *Culture Communication and Cognition: Vygotskian perspectives*, ed J Wertsch, Cambridge University Press, New York

Cole, M and Engestrom, Y (1993) A socio-historical approach to distributed cognition, in *Distributed Cognition*, ed G Saloman, Cambridge University Press, Cambridge

Coy, M (1989) *Anthropological Perspectives on Apprenticeship*, SUNY Press, New York

Davydov, V V and Radzikouskii, L A (1985) Vygotsky's theory and the activity orientated approach in psychology, in *Culture Communication and Cognition: Vygotskian perspectives*, ed J Wertsch, Cambridge University Press, New York

Engestrom, Y (1987) *Learning by Expanding*, Orieta-Konsulti, Helsinki

Engestrom, Y (1991) Towards overcoming the encapsulation of school learning, *Learning and Instruction*, **1** (1), pp 243–61

Engestrom, Y (1993) Developmental studies on work as a testbench of activity theory, in *Understanding Practice*, ed S Chaicklin and J Lave, Cambridge University Press, Cambridge

Engestrom, Y (1995) *Training for Change*, International Labour Office, London

Engestrom, Y (1996a) *Innovative Learning in Work Teams: Selected papers on expansive learning*, Centre for Activity Theory and Developmental Work Research, Helsinki

Engestrom, Y (1996b) Developmental work research as educational research: Looking ten years back and into the zone of proximal development, *Nordisk Pedagogik: Journal of Nordic Educational Research*, **16**, 131–43

Engestrom, Y, Engestrom, R and Karkkainen, M (1995) Polycontextuality and boundary crossing, *Expert Cognition Learning and Instruction*, **5**, pp 319–37

Engestrom, Y and Middleton, D (eds) (1996) *Cognition and Culture at Work*, Cambridge University Press, Cambridge

Engestrom, Y, Viorkkunen, J, Helle, M, Pihlaja, J and Poiketa, R (1996) The change laboratory as a tool for transforming work, *Lifelong Learning in Europe*, **2**, 10–17

Floden, R E, Buchmann, M and Schwille, J R (1987) Breaking with everyday experience, *Teachers College Record*, **88**, pp 465–506

Fuller, A (1996) Modern Apprenticeships: process and learning. Some emerging issues, *Journal of Vocational Education and Training*, **48** (3), pp 229–49

Gee, P (1992) *The Social Mind: Language, ideology and social practice*, Bergin and Garvey, New York

Gherardi, S, Nicolini, D and Odella, F (1998) Towards a social understanding of how people learn in organizations: the notion of a situated curriculum, *Management Learning*, **29** (3), pp 273–97

Gott, S (1995) Rediscovering learning: acquiring expertise in real-world problem solving tasks, *Australian and New Zealand Journal of Vocational Education Research*, **3** (1), pp 6–20

Greeno, J G (1997) On claims that answer the wrong question, *Educational Researcher*, **26** (1), pp 5–17

Griffen, P and Cole, M (1985) Current activity for the future, in *Children's Learning in the Zone of Proximal Development*, ed B Rogoff and J Wertsch, Jossey Bass, San Francisco, CA

Guile, D and Young, M (1998a) Apprenticeship as the social basis of learning, *Journal of Vocational Education*, **50** (2), pp 173–92

Guile, D and Young, M (1998b) The concept of learning and learning organizations (unpublished)

Hirschorn, L (1986) *Beyond Mechanization*, MIT Press, Harvard, MA

Kolb, D (1984) *Experiential Learning: Experience as the source of learning and development*, Prentice Hall, Englewood Cliffs, NJ

Kozulin, A (1990) *Vygotsky's Psychology: A biography of ideas*, Harvard University Press, Cambridge, MA

Kozulin, A and Presseisen, B Z (1995) Mediated learning experiences and psychological tools: Vygotsky's and Feurestain's perspective in a study of student learning, *Educational Psychologist*, **30** (2), pp 65–75

Lave, J (1993) The practice of learning, in *Understanding Practice*, ed S Chaiklen and J Lave, Cambridge University Press, Cambridge

Lave, J (1996) Teaching as learning, in practice, *Mind Culture and Society*, **3** (3), 9–27

Lave, J and Wenger, E (1991) *Situated Learning*, Cambridge University Press, Cambridge

Leontiev, A N (1978) *Activity, Consciousness and Personality*, Prentice Hall, Englewood Cliff, NJ

Lundvall, B A (1996) *The Social Dimension of the Learning Economy*, DRUID Working Paper No 96.1, Aalborg University, Denmark

Neisser, U (1976) *Cognition and Reality*, Freeman, San Francisco, CA

Pea, R D (1993) Distributed intelligence, in *Distributed Cognition*, ed G Saloman, Cambridge University Press, Cambridge

Pea, R D and Gomez, L (1992) Distributed multimedia learning environments, *Interactive Learning Environments*, **2** (2), pp 73–109

Prawat, R (1993) The value of ideas, *Educational Researcher*, **31** (7), pp 5–16

Raizen, S (1991) Learning and work: the research base, paper presented at the United States Department for Education and The Overseas Education Centre for Development Conference, Phoenix, Arizona: Linkages in Vocational Technical Education and Training, April

Resnick, L (1987) Learning in and out of school, *Education Researcher*, **16** (9), pp 13–20

Rogoff, B (1990) *Apprenticeship in Thinking: Cognitive development in social contexts*, Oxford University Press, New York, pp 3–25

Schribner, S and Cole, M (1971) Cognitive consequences of formal and informal learning, *Science*, **82** (1), pp 553–59

Shaikin, H (1996) Experience of the collective nature of skill, in *Cognition and Culture at Work*, ed Y Engestrom and D Middleton, Cambridge University Press, Cambridge

Steffe, L P (1990) Mathematics curriculum design: a constructivist's perspective, in *Transforming Children's Mathematics Education: International perspectives*, ed L P Steffe and T Wood, Erlbaum, Hillsdale, NJ, pp 389–98

Teles, L (1993) Cognitive apprenticeship in global networks, in *Global Networks*, ed L Harrison, MIT Press, Cambridge, MA

Vygotsky, L S (1978) *Mind in Society*, Cambridge University Press, Cambridge

Wertsch, J (1984) Children's learning in the zone of proximal development, in *New Directions for Child Development*, ed B Rogoff and J Wertsch, Jossey Bass, San Francisco, CA

Wertsch, J V (1981) *The Concept of Activity in Soviet Psychology*, M E Sharp, Armonk, NY

Wertsch, J V (ed) (1985) *Culture Communication and Cognition: Vygotskian perspectives*, Cambridge University Press, Cambridge

Zuboff, S (1988) *In the Age of the Smart Machine*, Heinemann, Oxford

9

Apprenticeship *à la mode*? Some Reflections on Learning as Cultural Labour

Phil Cohen

Starting points

It is an encouraging sign of the times that many of the questions raised by what used to be called 'the new vocationalism', and which were sidelined at the time it was introduced, are today finding their way back onto the agenda of academic, if not yet political, debate. During the 1980s when Thatcherism was in full flood, a surprising number of erstwhile radical educationalists were being carried along in the first flush of enthusiasm for the enterprise culture and the promise of what it could do for those who had been failed by an educational system still permeated by anti-industrial values. There was, it seemed, little room for a wider-angled view of what was at stake. In this brave new world, apprenticeship was just another dirty word to put alongside trade unionism, socialism and Marxism, part of the accumulated ideological baggage which was supposedly holding back the innate spirit of free enterprise of the British people, and therefore fully deserving to be junked.

Today, under the sign of 'modernity', apprenticeship is making a comeback bid, as a name for what might constitute a more viable and open-ended form of learning to labour under post-industrial capitalism – an antidote to what has so far been on offer under the rubric of the new vocationalism. *En route* Modern Apprenticeship has been approximated to the middle-class paradigm of career. The 'modern apprentices' are dressed up in business suits, and cheerfully consign their overalls (and the blue-collar culture of manual labourism) to the dustbins of history.

At first sight it is difficult to tell whether this piece of re-description is simply another exercise in political impression management – on a par with calling polytechnics universities as if this somehow disguised the fact that we have a two-tier structure of higher education – or whether it does in fact correspond to a substantial change in the form and content of training. Is the re-valorization of the term a rather cunning way to deploy a sentimental image of artisan culture to disguise the pervasive deskilling and loss of control over the overall labour process that has resulted from the introduction of new informatics and corporate management strategies? Or are we dealing with a rather disingenuous nominalism, an exercise in wishful thinking – if only we change the name then the reality it denotes will change too? Or does 'apprenticeship *à la mode*' represent a genuine piece of social engineering, indicating the best possible future for a new generation of young workers? How, in any of these cases, are we to disentangle the mythography of apprenticeship from what is practised in its name?

I do not think the question is resolvable by interviewing trainees or by observing what goes on in the schemes to which this term is once more being attached. Valuable and indeed indispensable as do-it-yourself ethnographies of learning are (Heath, 1983), the answer will ultimately depend on what is meant by 'apprenticeship' in the first place. The term has been subject to a great deal of conceptual inflation and is surrounded by an aura of imagery which cannot fail to arouse the most diverse expectations. That is why a good place to start the enquiry is to ask just what apprenticeship has meant historically and what it has come to represent today. What kind of story, about work, gender, identity, learning, growing up, the nature of mind and body, does apprenticeship tell?

A short history of apprenticeship: from mimesis to masquerade

In the account I am going to give, apprenticeship is considered not just in its narrow legal/contractual or institutionalized form, but in its wider sense, as what Foucault (1988) has called a 'technology of self', or what Bourdieu (1977), more mindful of its social dimensions, has called a 'habitus'. Each general form of labour and learning has its own special kind of social routine organizing certain, largely unconscious, frames of mind and body into specific dispositions of skill and competence, which in turn are associated with particular kinds of identity work. Although this process is most visible in customary rules and rituals of initiation into workplace cultures, or in the knowledge/power structures of schooling and training, it is no less present in the contexts of family and community life, where sexual and generational divisions of labour are reproduced – and sometimes challenged. Even where they are not locally dominant, the social relations of apprenticeship have often furnished a referential model for these other, more informal kinds of learning activity; as a cognitive frame or code, apprenticeship becomes embedded in the making and telling of life stories within communities of practice centred around hobbies, sport and all manner of physical and social recreation (Bertaux and Thompson, 1993; Rogoff 1990).

Yet we cannot understand the vicissitudes of apprenticeship in this wider sense outside its changing articulation to other equally deep-rooted codes, in particular those of inheritance, vocation and career. Each of these codes constitutes a distinctive culture of informal learning, relaying a particular set of relations between cultural capital and cultural labour; each code also has its own autobiographical register, throwing a diachronic grid over the key experiences of identity formation as well as synchronically regulating access to subject positions *vis-à-vis* knowledge and power (Cohen, 1997).

For example, the apprenticeship code unfolds life as a step-by-step struggle for mastery over a given body of knowledge or skill. The inheritance code forges a set of quasi-congenital links between origins and destiny, making each child a chip off the parental block – you have your mother's hands, your father's sense of humour. Vocation privileges the life journey as an endless quest for the discovery or fulfilment of an authentic inner self; career sets the infant's feet competitively upon the first rungs of a symbolic ladder of incremental achievement even before it has learnt to walk.

In understanding how these codes operate singly or in combination, it is important to make a distinction between two orders of representation within and across which their paradigms operate: mimesis and masquerade. Although in the so-called post-modern turn they are often fused or confused, it is important to distinguish them in principle, because they hold very different implications for how we understand the learning processes entailed (Bakhtin, 1994; Lotman, 1990).

Mimesis is a practice of simulation and/or emulation which claims to master or comprehend external reality through a model or instrument which reproduces its essential features in a scaled-down, and hence manipulable version. Children's toys, automata, puppets, maps, diagrams, scale drawings, role models, realist art and literature and natural scientific explanations all function in this mode. Fitness is here a matter of likeness, a sense of appropriate correspondence or analogy between map and territory, labour and product, or more generally between what is fashioned and the material from and about which the process of production draws its meaning. Mimesis for most of its history has been an art of direct mirror control exercised over bodies, techniques, environments and materials, and a very masculine art it has been at that.

Masquerade in contrast is a practice of dissemblance or dissimulation, which aims to overcome a perceived lack or absence in the real (eg, the separation of the worker from the means of labour) through a model of indirect mastery inscribed in the process of representation itself. Here the traditionally 'feminine' arts of disguise and impression management hold sway and fitness is a matter of liking (not likeness), a sense of what might be pleasurably related to what, within the chosen symbolic frame. Masquerade enables people to play with difference, to adopt the role of the other, in order to stage-manage their identity in ways which reduce anxiety of influence, and maintain positions of symbolic control in situations where in real economic and political terms they are powerless. The model that figures in masquerade fashions nothing but the desires which it clothes with its own rhetorical devices.

As Benjamin points out (1989), children's play is dominated by the mimetic faculty, but its realm is in no way limited by what one person can imitate in another. The child plays at being not only a shopkeeper or a nurse, but also a windmill, a train or a space capsule. The mimetic faculty, he insists, has a history – one that is bound up with the history of social production, and leads ultimately to its supersession by masquerade.

It is certainly the case that until the advent of industrial capitalism, the vast majority of people in Western societies learnt to labour through mimetic forms of apprenticeship. In the phase of manufacture, or small workshop production, the implements of labour were often thought of as a kind of prosthetic extension of bodily skill, moulded by the customary usages of handicraft (Jennings, 1985). Co-ordinated actions of hand, ear and eye were initially privileged over other parts or techniques of the body as the medium of apprenticeship; for the early labour aristocracy, skill was a function of this specialized dexterity, embodied in a form of cultural capital transmitted from generation to generation – a patrimony of skill that was in your blood and bones. Growing up to be skilled always entailed an apprenticeship to this kind of inheritance (Bisseret, 1981; More, 1980).

Those who laboured primarily with their shoulders, backs, thighs, genitals or feet were, in contrast, treated as an inferior, 'species-specific' type of unskilled worker, almost a 'race apart'. This distinction, which took on moral as well as economic overtones in the Victorian period, was found in many trades and industries. There is the contrast between stevedores and dockers, actresses and prostitutes, the hewers and lumpers of coal. Within the 'race apart', the musculatures of labour were largely trans-valued through their masculinization; only as a vehicle for the assertion of virile forms of strength and endurance (ie, 'hardness') could these otherwise abject forms of labour be invested with a sense of pride in physical prowess (Rule, 1980). In both skilled and unskilled forms, learning to labour thus involved apprenticeship to an inheritance governed by strictly patriarchal rules. The apprenticeships that existed within women's trades tended to be attenuated versions of the masculine forms. As for the 'domestic' apprenticeships served by budding housewives and mothers, here the sexual division of labour assumed its most 'naturalized' and emotionally loaded form (Pollert, 1981; Scott and Tilly, 1978).

As long as rhythms of labour were tightly calibrated to cycles of seasonal production, the functions of nature and the immediate body were bound mimetically to the second nature of the social order and its feudal/patriarchal body politic. Only through masquerade, associated with practices of youth misrule and riotous apprenticeship, was it possible to temporarily suspend or up-end these fixed social hierarchies (Mitterauer, 1992). Many of the early forms of resistance to capitalist work discipline drew upon and extended these practices. In fact, with the advent of machinofacture, learning to labour continued to be an apprenticeship to an inheritance, but the terms and functions of that articulation changed. At first, the new technologies of mass production were regarded as simply bigger and better hand tools. Mechanized functions were 'naturalized' and compared to those of the body, especially in its sexual or reproductive capacities. It is no coincidence that factory workers were called 'hands', but already here the relation is less one of 'natural symbolism' than a calculated metonymy, which will quickly enough become transformed into metaphor (Rabinbach, 1990).

With the advent of fully-fledged Fordism and the accelerated trade cycle, the customary rhythms of employment in the manual trades became increasingly at odds with the tempo of mass production. Handicraft processes were marginalized and increasingly replaced by semi-skilled repetitive work. As this occurred, artisan techniques become increasingly aestheticized and/or feminized, and given a new lease of life under the sign of vocation. Morris, Ruskin and the arts and crafts movement attempt to create a vision of socialism around a return to this idealized pre-industrial body of manual labour, now reconfigured as a mimetic medium of creative self-expression (Joyce, 1991).

Meanwhile in the real world of mass production and consumption, once the commodity becomes 'second nature', mimesis becomes a direct instrument of self-alienation. As living labour becomes increasingly disembodied or, as Marx put it, dominated by dead labour, so the structures of imitation/ emulation which governed the apprenticeships of the 'old' labouring body become both a site for the hyper-exploitation of youth labour, and a brake on the introduction of fully rationalized regimes of social production (Sohn-Rethel, 1978). Patriarchal closures around an imagined community of labour power intensify in popular cultures of resistance to dilution and deskilling; but they also trigger new reactive forms of youth misrule and masquerade which subvert the attempts of 'civilizing missionaries' to conform working-class life and labour to the moral economy of industrial work discipline.

It is no coincidence in fact that historically non-indentured boy labour has been concentrated not in manufacturing but in the distribution and servicing trades. If they have been confined to the lowest paid, least skilled positions within these sectors, this has nothing to do with any real qualities or lack of them which young workers may possess. It has everything to do with customary practice in confining lads to the fetching and carrying of goods, the servicing of clients or customers, or lending a helping hand to the adult worker. Sometimes all three menial tasks were combined in the same job, sometimes there was a progression from one to the other, but the essential point is that boy labour was proto-domestic labour: it was modelled on women's work in the home. This was underscored by the social relations of the workplace. The new lad was expected to make the tea, run errands, sweep up and generally serve as a skivvy to the older men, whether he was officially 'mated' to them or not. He was also subjected to a good deal of teasing, often of a sexual kind, designed to show him up as soft or incompetent in various ways. All this was part of the initiation of the 'virgin' worker, something that had to be endured in order to eventually make the grade as a fully-fledged 'workmate'. Normally this would involve the apprentice demonstrating that he was just as 'hard' as the older men were and, by extension, emulating their supposed sexual prowess with women.

Sexual apprenticeships in fact complemented the occupational form. In some trades the sexual initiation of the young worker was undertaken by an older woman at work, egged on by her workmates. Usually the women chosen for this task were unmarried and regarded as especially unattractive; certainly the initiation rites contained a sadistic, castratory element. In the second stage, however, the sexual apprentice gets his own back in exercising his new-found mastery of technique over younger, preferably virgin girls (and/or through rituals that feminize younger weaker boys). Finally, the sexual improver finds a 'steady' and graduates to the phase of courtship, essentially a form of apprenticeship to marriage and the role of the family wage earner. This tripartite system is summarized in Table 9.1.

Table 9.1 Traditional masculine code of apprenticeship: from the youth wage to the family wage

Gender identity narrative	Occupational identity narrative
1. Initiation of virgin boy by older woman	'Feminization' of virgin worker 'mated' to older man
2. Practice of sexual mastery over younger girls	Counter-display of masculine 'hardness' *vis-à-vis* younger lads
3. Going steady – courtship as apprenticeship to marriage	Making the grade as a workmate among the men

The linkage between techniques of masculinity and manual labour was thus forged through a radical disavowal of the despised quasi-feminine status assigned to male youth by the generational division of labour. The mimetic forms of apprenticeship are split: one way they point to an imposed and 're-gressive' identification with women's work (and the world of childhood) and by the other route, they constitute a no less imposed but 'progressive' identification with men's work (and the world of adulthood) entered through an active repudiation of everything associated with the 'proto-domestic'. The mimetic split is resolved through a process of more or less ritualized masquerade: an imaginary sexual division is constructed in order to maintain a real generational one, while displacing the terms of an otherwise all too Oedipal confrontation between the old hands and the noviciates whom they are training to one day replace them. It is through the intervention of this social imagery that the apprentices' position of peripheral participation is legitimated within the real community of practice in the workplace (Lave and Wenger, 1993).

Through the inter-war period these grids of apprenticeship and inheritance largely held, and continued to forge quasi-congenital links between growing up, working and class; this provided stable – and highly unequal – sets of gender, and generational identification; life histories, however personally complicated, could be related through a coherent and readily accessible narrative grammar. The post-war settlement permanently destabilized this culture of manual labourism, with very different consequences for boys and girls. It inaugurated a double-edged programme of modernization; this involved conserving some of the most archaic structures of the nation state, by nationalizing its cultural ideology and giving it a popular/democratic face (Joyce, 1991). At the same time the no less archaic forms of labour's habitus (including male apprenticeship) were to be swept away and replaced by the meritocratic code of career and a new non-possessive form of individualism (Cohen, 1997).

The triumph of the new vocationalism did not however mean that the mimetics of manual labour entirely withered away. Some elements are subsumed as shadowing, or mentoring, under the new training regimes. At the same time the grid of apprenticeship/inheritance takes on a new lease of life outside production as a source of vicarious identification with techniques of mastery over nature and the labour process, in a kind of defiant masquerade that camouflages real absences, losses and lacks. In this way, some of the more hidden injuries of gender and class inflicted by the deskilling/reschooling of labour are neutralized, either by parodying their effect on others, or by projecting an immaculate body image 'hardened' by the rigours of manual labour as a new and entirely narcissistic ego and peer group ideal.

Through this process of re-embodiment, the productive capacities of disciplined labour are symbolically reclaimed, by and for the individual worker, albeit in a displaced form (Hochschild, 1983). In dance, in sport and especially in the more physically punishing kinds of male athleticism, the element of degradation in manual labour is transformed into a perverse principle of self-gratification. Or to put it another way, submission to physical self-discipline becomes the male body's own labour of love. *En route* labour learns to mimic capital in its own onward march of repressive productivity.

The growth of youth unemployment as a structural feature of Western economies throughout the 1980s and 1990s cut off a whole generation from any kind of work apart from what was offered by the hidden economy. The collapse of customary transition routes from school to work accelerated the collapse of the culture of manual labourism; as the codes of apprenticeship and inheritance increasingly pulled apart and become enclosed in their own technologies of self-reference, so the links between growing up, working and class not only weakened, but became permanently displaced into idioms of gender and race that hitherto had been subsumed within them.

Among those who could not gain entry to the new post-Fordist work habitus, certain types of traditional manual work now took on a hyper-inflationary value, not so much because of the skill or wage level entailed, but because they require or permit the public display of masculinities which have otherwise become redundant. Certain types – the building worker, the trucker, the rigger, the cowboy, the steel erector and the miner – are repackaged for homeboy consumption. In Country and Western music, in buddy movies, in soft porn magazines and comics, in corporate advertising, in TV serials, their praises are sung, often with strongly homoerotic overtones. This new ideal body-of-labour has little to do with the realities of the jobs, and you do not have to learn any trade skills to become one. It has everything to do with masculine masquerade and nothing to do with the mimetic apprenticeships of manual labour. These figures are celebrated for being ruggedly individualistic, *and* for restoring a lost sense of physical male fraternity and pride; and not just to the working classes, but to the nation as a whole. They have indeed been invented as the standard-bearers of a new white race, which is in fact only the old lost white race of colonial frontiersmen in a new guise. For those who rejected these 'ideal types' of manual labour as sites of identification because they no longer correspond to any realizable aspiration, there is little but the narcissism of minor difference offered by popular youth cultures to fall back on. When apprenticeship is only to and from itself youth ceases to be merely a transitional stage and becomes a referential model for the whole life story. Body politics and performative dramas around the mastery of 'feminine' techniques of impression management and masquerade (and their masculinist disavowal) now take centre stage, to produce a scenario of discontinuous moments. This new situation could be represented as shown in Table 9.2.

Table 9.2 Contemporary code of apprenticeship

Axis of self-reference	Axis of 'the other'
1. Initiation with peers	Rivalry with peers:respect
2. Labouring masculinity	Belabouring race:territory
3. Softening style	Hardening bodies:attitude

Local situated knowledge

Having briefly outlined a general history of this shift from mimesis to masquerade within the code of apprenticeship, I would now like to consider how this might play out within a local context, in terms of the relation between real and imagined communities of practice in the East End of London.

In a series of case studies in ex-Docklands areas we are currently looking at how the cultures of manual labourism have been internally modified in order to sustain strong, and often strongly racialized, practices of class, gender and ethnic identity. In particular we are looking at how these identities are worked through social networks linked to family, neighbourhood or peer group narratives so that male territorialisms and matrilocalisms continue to 'rule OK' in marking the boundaries of real and imagined communities of labour.

In the course of these studies we have come across a significant difference among those children and young people whose informal learning is still largely confined to codes of apprenticeship and inheritance. There are those, predominantly but not exclusively, from the South Asian community who succeed in coming to grips with 'middle-class' codes of career and vocation in school, putting them to work in constructing themselves performatively as educational success stories, without, for all that, translating these codes into styles of identity work in other areas of their lives. And there are those, mainly but not exclusively, from white or black (African descent) working-class families who seem quite unable to take this step, but rather move in the opposite direction, attempting to translate their informal learning codes into ways of negotiating (and sometimes disrupting) the dominant educational success story authorized by the school.

None of the conventional criteria associated with factors of individual motivation, such as pushy parents, inspired teachers, sibling rivalry, or personal ambition adequately explain these differences. Existing models of sponsored and contest mobility do not seem to quite meet these cases either, since the relation between these patterns of code shift and academic performance, let alone occupational success, is at best tenuous and contingent on a whole range of situational and biographical variables that shape access to local opportunity structures (Bertaux and Thompson, 1993).

One possible factor of explanation emerged indirectly from reading the published autobiographies of East Enders, both immigrants and 'native', belonging to an older generation. Many of these writers had become successful in some sphere of public life despite, rather than because of, their experiences of schooling. In almost every case their accounts pivoted on an unexpected situation or event that temporarily upset the predictable course of their lives. Uprooting from homeland, the death of a parent, wartime evacuation, the closure of the docks, a move to a new area, the loss of a friend, a near-fatal car accident, serious illness, whatever the nature of the jolt, it had opened up access to perspectives and resources of symbolic empowerment that would not otherwise have been within their grasp.

These high-fliers did not simply pick up the pieces and carry on as before; they seized the opportunity to refashion the direction of their lives, and they did this by imagining their futures unfolding within a number of quite distinct frames at once. In one context, such as the acquisition of domestic skills (such as gardening or DIY) or in the sphere of religious observance, they might see themselves as following in familiar footsteps, as so many chips off the old block. Through other cultural pursuits they might embark on a quest for a more vocal and 'authentic' self. In yet other domains, for example sex, sport or dance, progress might be described rather differently as a matter of gaining incremental mastery over a given body of techniques, while in their working lives they set out to climb step-by-step up a ladder of professional knowledge and status, to get to the top.

Elements from all these different life-story plots were woven together in a more or less seamless narrative web. Whatever the pattern – and it varied considerably from one account to the next – these differently coded versions of learning and life story were integrated within an overarching myth of origins and destiny that was both strongly aspirational *and* culturally plausible. In many cases these personal 'onwards and upwards' stories were linked to motifs of struggle based in the labour movement and/or the history of Diasporic communities (Thompson and Samuel, 1993).

In this way themes of individual advancement were subsumed or framed within a wider, more collective sense of progress, and many of the wrinkles in individual lives retrospectively ironed out. At the same time this kind of optimistic 'grand narrative' seemed to make it easier for the authors to shuttle back and forth between different codes and contexts and so gain entry into new and unfamiliar worlds of knowledge and experience with some measure of confidence. In default of this, the outcome might well have been very different; the original disruption could have proved all too traumatic leading to its compulsive repetition accompanied by a sense of identity confusion or chronic grievance, a fruitless search for ideal beginnings or impossibly 'happy endings' (Winnicott, 1990).

Among the present generation of young white East Enders there are still those with 'get up and go' who do just that, following customary self-made routes; and there are some who succeed in making the transition into new opportunity structures by giving up on the old ones based on closed networks of kinship and community. Meanwhile those who continue to apprentice themselves to a customary inheritance of labour power find themselves increasingly cut off from the newer brands of educational and cultural goods produced by and for the global city.

Those who fall back on the hidden economy, or whose lives are vulnerable to potentially traumatic disruption, whether through family breakdown, domestic violence, drug addiction, or depression, find themselves in a new kind of fix. The professional support systems designed to put their lives back together again no longer encode principles of hope that would enable them to develop alternative but still culturally plausible narratives of their own future.

The reason is not to do with more than the triumph of individualism; it bears on the fact that many of the larger success stories to which these young people might have turned for inspiration are today politically discredited and educationally out of bounds. Myths of origin and destiny which feature onward marches of the people, the nation or the class are no longer publicly available as foundations for tales of individual progress against the odds, even if they continue to inform private dreams of rescue or revenge. At the same time discourses of social in/justice historically voiced by progressive community and trade union organizations have increasingly been commandeered by racist rhetorics, where they inform trajectories of white flight and, sometimes, fight.

For their Asian peers it is a very different story. Here the grand narratives still carry a strong moral and instructional value. The growth of ethnic identity politics has articulated diverse pursuits of cultural heritage, professional achievement, vocal selfhood and technical mastery into a single 'onwards and upwards' life story line; this makes it possible for some at least to overcome racial discrimination and turn initial experiences of social dislocation or academic failure into an educational success story. These forms of symbolic empowerment have in turn helped generate new styles of leadership from a generation which is as much at home in the global as in the local city. At the same time, in some of these communities inheritance narratives guarded by elders have become more dominant and all-embracing, setting up major tensions with other learning and life stories and alienating sizeable sections of the youth, while at the same time providing those who continue to be excluded from mainstream opportunity structures with compensatory pathways to self-respect.

Contemporary patterns of educational achievement and disadvantage have thus become both more complex and more unstable. Modernized codes of apprenticeship and career have been fused to promote new paradigms of open competitive virtue but come into increasing conflict with closed and often charismatic codings of inheritance and vocation. The grand narratives of political progress and scientific or religious enlightenment that hitherto made it possible for leading sections of the immigrant and working class communities to travel across different cultures of learning, transforming educational failure into success stories on the way, have either unravelled or work against each other to reinforce divisions and inequalities of every kind.

Learning regeneration – a cultural studies approach

This local case study raises a broader question about the narratives of aspiration that are available for the production or dissemination of knowledge and how they are institutionalized in particular regimes of learning and identity work. I am talking here about the stories we tell ourselves about how our lives should go, stories which are embedded in educational and family discourses and work at a quite deep and often unconscious level in scripting the experiences and outcomes of schooling and further or higher education (Chamberlain and Thompson, 1998).

Over the last decade, ethnographic research in the field of cultural studies has amply demonstrated that the social designations of identity of every kind are becoming much more fluid, fractured and contested. Yet very little of this work has been applied to the task of drawing out what this might imply about how people actually learn, whether it's how to dance or knit, make love, ride bicycles or horses, play football or musical instruments, write graffiti or poetry, tell jokes or tall stories, practice safe sex, use computers, conduct experiments, or learn a foreign language.

These are all meaning-creating activities; they involve particular kinds of investment in personal meanings which in turn shape the sense of self (Salmon, 1998). What is learnt is not just a skill but an identity. If you can't manage the identity work entailed you won't manage to succeed in doing the activity. If you cannot see yourself as a budding chemist or rock musician then you're not going to get your head and your hands round a Bunsen burner or a guitar. But until you do take that first step to join what Jean Lave calls a 'community of practice' (Lave and Wenger, 1993), then you won't be able to concretely envisage what is entailed in assuming that identity.

This would seem to lock the argument into an old fashioned chicken-and-egg story, until we realize that we are *always* dealing with a process of double inscription, of a specific articulation, whose terms may change, between a real *and* an imagined community of practice. That articulation is not something given, it involves a process of *cultural labour* through which the means of self-representation are actively fashioned and transformed. How some people learn to culturally labour more productively than others, why some are more able than others to turn the products of cultural labour into realizable forms of cultural capital, how this relates to factors of class, or race, or gender, is thus at the heart of the process whereby educational distinctions are reproduced in and as social divisions (Bourdieu, 1981).

Today we are living in a world in which this process is dominated by the career code whose hegemony goes virtually unchallenged; careerism not only pervades almost every sphere of public and private life, but subsumes and reworks elements of the other codes *en route*. One of the reasons why there is a such a pervasive sense of personal fragmentation is that elements of the other codes continue to influence particular moments or contexts of self-representation yet have to compete for a hearing within the overall voicing of the life history by a career code that grants them only the most instrumental presence.

One of the problems with much recent pedagogic theorization has been the tendency to privilege one code at the expense of others as a source of 'learning universals' (Chaiklen and Lave, 1993). In recent discussions of vocationalism, for example, apprenticeship has been promoted as a normative definition of the work-based learning cycle; other codes are thereby relegated to the pre-, post- or anti-modern margins. In contrast, the debate over lifelong learning has been between the technocratic advocates of cradle-to-grave careerism and the humanistic champions of creative self-fulfilment via experiential learning – a thinly coded variant of vocation. The fact that inheritance narratives continue to articulate most common-sense versions of the life-course is conveniently ignored in most of these debates.

The multi-code model would suggest that these normative theories of socio-cognitive development beg a whole series of important research questions. Not all learning and life-cycles have the teleological and centripetal 'drive' of apprenticeship or career; some are recursive and centripetal (inheritance), others asymptotic and centrifugal (vocation). There is no *a priori* reason why the latter should be treated as less definitive of 'modernity' than the former. Modernity takes many forms (Appadurai, 1998).

Instead, we need to know why one code rather than another has been institutionalized within a given educational or training sector or setting, why one furnishes the preferred images and idioms of a particular profession, and another the grammars of self-narrative used by certain other occupational groups. It is equally important to know how codes shape informal learning in contexts such as sexuality or leisure and how all this is related to race, gender, generational and class positioning.

Approaches based on a single code are not only theoretically inadequate; in so far as they inform educational policies they have practical consequences, often underwriting new patterns of exclusion, or reproducing old ones. The multi-code model suggests that it is only by encouraging the single-minded but simultaneous pursuit of technique, status, roots and self-expression in a journey *across* codes and contexts that more inclusive modes of educational lift-off are likely to be generated (Ranciere, 1991).

Despite this critique of modernism and the question for normative learning universals, my argument does not belong within the post-modern frame. It emphasizes the importance of providing stable homing devices that enable students to reflexively integrate a variety of identity topics and learning resources within an overarching dialogue between self, group and wider society. This is not a narrative about 'decentred' or disinherited subjects being sent on perpetual quests for sites of liminality where they can creatively transgress existing boundaries of knowledge in pursuit of new careers!

The model does not therefore locate the potential space of innovation, either for producing new knowledge or making fresh starts, in the properties of any one code; nor in their simple 'cross-fertilization' or transcendence. Instead, it would suggest looking more closely at *strategic learning conjunctures* where the process of trans-coding occurs and the rights of passage between learning contexts are negotiated *en route*.

Such conjunctures rarely conform to institutional timetables; they do not necessarily reflect official progression routes; the personal transition tactics they make possible neither follow a straight line nor go in one direction. The learning patterns they generate proceed discontinuously and in a capillary fashion like rhizomes; their educational outcomes require other kinds of measurement and evaluation than those provided by the algorithms which quantify the official success and failure stories. We need to know more about how these conjunctures come about, how new learning and life-cycle paradigms are articulated through them, who takes advantage of these opportunities, and what kinds of possibility emerge within them for which groups.

From an epistemic point of view we are dealing with the creation of transitional objects-to-be-known that exist in the borderlands of meaning between the linguistically familiar and the culturally inarticulate (Lotman, 1990). Such transitional objects are produced though a set of code-specific transformations:

- apprenticeships that proceed by permanently deferring the 'moment' of mastery through continual regeneration of skills and competencies;
- open rather than closed inheritances where transmission no longer depends on claims of inherent entitlement based on cultural insiderhood, but on performative statements of identity;
- vocations in which the quest for a fully articulate self gives way to a more evocative dialogue with the other (other gender, class, ethnicity) as both internal condition and external limit to what can be known;
- careers that pursue more fluid and discontinuous lines of desire than those laid down by the structures that govern the professional rat race.

If these trans-codings do not amount to 'learning universals' then at least they point to a convergent frame of mind characteristic of reflexive or late modernity (Beck *et al*, 1994). We might characterize this as the 'art of negative capability' – the ability to entertain ambiguity, uncertainty, and doubt without reaching for premature closure in the name of fact, correctness, or essentialized identity (Milner, 1987). This refusal to reach foregone conclusions is closely linked to skills of improvization and conjecture; in our view this constitutes an important, though largely ignored, factor in considering the conditions of symbolic empowerment critical for successful learning outcomes (Ginsberg, 1990). It points to a potential space of cultural and cognitive innovation that no educational system or society can afford not to nurture.

Beginners please: towards a theory and practice of 'propaedeutics'

Strategic learning conjunctures are thus marked by a break with customary practice, a departure from old habits, a new chapter in the life story, a fresh learning curve marked by a sense of excitement or discovery. But that does not mean these conjunctures are the prerogative of noviciates. What old hands, of any age, may have learnt, and what they may have the ability to teach by example, is precisely how to begin afresh each time. They know this because they have thoroughly grasped the tricks – or if you like the generative grammars – of their particular trades, disciplines, or fields of knowledge (Bernstein, 1974).

In this view, the elementary structures of a given body of knowledge, whether cooking, physics, music or historiography, are constituted by the underlying grammar which makes it possible to create new dishes, discover new natural laws, write a musical composition or make fresh connections between historical facts.

Generative grammars are at the outset largely unconscious; they constitute the primary process of learning out of which secondary, more conscious elaborations arise in the course of instruction and practice (Bateson, 1978). What attracts people to a particular field or subject is, however, often a sense that they have a 'feel for it' at this deeper level – a feel that is then, if all goes well, progressively transformed into a 'knack' – the capacity to choose the most appropriate device in any given circumstance, for 'hitting the nail on the head'.

The propaedeutics – the elementary structures and underlying rules that constitute a discipline – emerge most clearly when they are broken. The mistakes made by beginners and the deliberate deviations from customary practice made by old hands are both integral to the learning process; but in the first case what is being learnt is the normative limits and conditions which govern the surface structure of a practice – the procedures that make it possible to do (or not do) it at all. In the second what is being explored is the deeper structure of unconscious representation that governs the desire to know and makes authoritative innovation – the production of transitional objects – possible.

In many contexts of learning the two levels are often confused. This is partly because in the process of graduation from initial learning to initialized learning (ie, learning which is owned because it has the authoritative stamp of the learner's own signature upon it) there is an intermediate step or stage in which attempts are often made to simulate or emulate the process of innovation by disrupting surface structures in a purely procedural way.

This confusion of levels can become systemic in the case of mentoring schemes where superficial idiosyncrasies of personal style or approach on the part of the mentor or 'role model' are often seized upon as the focus for 'mimetic' identity work while the real tricks of the trade remain ungrasped.

Peer-group pedagogies suffer from a similar disadvantage in so far as they collapse or conflate different instances of imitation/emulation/innovation into a single all-embracing learning gestalt. Finally, models of lifelong learning premised on the ideal of the 'self-starting, self-motivated, self-disciplined student' tend to run together themes from all four codes into a single learning cycle, without considering the tensions and disjunctures that necessarily arise in the process of moving from one 'plot' or context to the next. As in the autobiographies of autodidacts there is never a moment in which lack of knowledge is allowed to function positively as a support for the desire to know (Ranciere, 1991).

Our model suggests an alternative approach in which the framework of 'learning transference' is not primarily provided by the interpersonal relation between teacher and student, or the peer-group dynamic, important though these are, but by the transitional (or trans-coded) objects which serve as their proxy. These 'object relations' are not reducible to specific topics of instruction or identity work – they emerge out of that special communication between 'knack' and 'feel' that goes with learning the underlying tricks of a trade.

By paying more attention to conflicts of affiliation which may arise in this primary process, we believe it may be possible to pre-empt some of the learning difficulties which predispose students to underachieve or drop out.

A final implication of this model is that it problematizes the patriarchal equation between age, status and experience. It highlights the fact that children may in some contexts be old hands who know better than their elders how to proceed. In other situations elders may be more able than younger people to tolerate the frustrations of beginning afresh.

The markers of im/maturity customarily attached to different kinds of cultural performance are undergoing rapid inter- and intra-generational change. This is an important and largely neglected area of education research (Martin, 1995).

The hidden Curriculum Vitae, or learning's other scenes

Although the concepts we have outlined (transitional object, potential space, negative capability, propaedeutics) have much in common with Vygotsky's 'zone of proximal development', they add a psychodynamic dimension which is missing from contemporary accounts of learning based on his work (Vygotsky, 1978).

Our model emphasizes the importance of structures of feeling and fantasy which, although largely ignored in rationalistic theories of instruction, nevertheless can exert a decisive influence on learning outcomes. These psychic structures are neither divorced from nor reducible to social structures – they are culturally embedded and narrativized as code-specific myths of origin and destiny; as such they provide templates for distinctive trajectories of identity work set in motion by the primary learning process.

This hidden Curriculum Vitae constitutes the 'other scene' of the learning and life-cycle, connecting imagined communities of aspiration and remembrance with real communities of practice. It is the constantly shifting interaction of these two registers of 'community' (rather than the simple one-way transition from the imaginary to the real) that shapes the trajectory of educational biographies (Salmon, 1998).

The focus on libidinal investments (and disinvestments) in learning inevitably highlights issues of sexism and racism. The masculinization of apprenticeship, the racialization of inheritance, the grid of feminization thrown over occupational choices by the vocation code, the way these positions are challenged or reproduced in dominant paradigms of career, all thus become highlighted as topics of research and intervention.

There is a further, class-related, aspect to the 'other scene'. The model I have outlined has arisen out of work with groups of mainly unemployed young people who often deal with their lack of real control over learning, labour and life process by adopting magical positions of omniscience associated either with subcultural styles or the staking of counter-hegemonic claims to superior knowledge. It is clear that such groups find it especially difficult to hold onto the beginner's position because peripheral participation plays back so many experiences of exclusion and marginality suffered in the wider society. It is easier to carry over already learnt strategies of self-defence, to drop out or disrupt the learning process, rather than to accept that symbolic empowerment (and educational progress) comes from letting go these ploys. In a culture and society still so dominated by Eurocentric ideals of the 'mastermind', the temptation to play at rival 'civilization games' is correspondingly intense (Rattansi and Donald, 1991).

To counter these arcs of negative transference we need to develop a policy of educational regeneration that challenges structures of exclusion in a focused but still comprehensive way. We have to develop strategic learning conjunctures that are as mobile and context-sensitive as the process of trans-coding itself. In this chapter I have tried to lay the foundations for some further theoretico-practical research that might usefully be addressed to this issue, for example:

- How do patterns of idealization and foreclosure operate within mimetic forms of instruction associated with the apprenticeship code and how are these patterns masculinized as they are transmuted into idioms of masquerade via particular styles of academic performativity?
- Under what institutional and social conditions does the code of inheritance become racialized or de-racialized, and under what terms does it become re-articulated to other codes?
- How might the profession of envy and rivalry orchestrated through the career code be sublimated into more productive forms of emulation via mentoring and peer-group pedagogies?
- How are anxieties of influence both articulated and disavowed in practices of scientific or aesthetic innovation pursued within the framework of vocation, and how might these endeavours be given a less individualistic focus?

These questions are far from academic. They bear centrally on the reformation of contemporary educational discourse around some more substantial notion of stakeholding, and on the production of democratic subjects (Joyce, 1994). They also highlight what is at stake in their construction of popular masculinities beyond the cultures of manual and mental labourism (Connell, 1995). And they resonate with wider concerns about the state of the nation as we approach a new millennium.

In the series of narrative paintings that Hogarth called 'Marriage à la Mode', he tells the terrible story of how an arranged marriage goes off the rails, as the systematic perversion of shared hopes brings out the worst and most excessive forms of self-destructive individualism. The marriage of convenience between different codes represented by Modern Apprenticeship is unlikely, fortunately, to have such drastic consequences for those who embark on it! Yet it may have just as pernicious an effect on the enhancement of their best hopes unless we pay more attention to the discrepant versions of learning and life story that are in play here rather than supposing that they all somehow knit together into a seamless web of learning progression. In this chapter I have tried to indicate something of the contribution which cultural studies can make to thinking through this problem.

Note

The provenance of this chapter is as follows: the basic ideas were first developed in the mid-1980s when I was briefly Acting Director at the Post-16 Education Centre at the Institute of Education, University of London. They were first published by the Centre in a monograph, *Rethinking the Youth Question* in 1988. This text was then reproduced along with others on related themes in a book of collected essays on education, labour and cultural studies, published under the same title by Macmillan in 1997. The present text revises and develops these ideas further in response to recent work on the theory of cultural practice by Jean Lave (Lave and Wenger, 1993) and others. This 'rethinking' has also evolved in the context of a new action research programme on learning regeneration which I am currently directing at the New Docklands Campus of the University of East London. I am very grateful to Phil Salmon at the Institute of Education and to Pat Ainley for their continuing support of this intellectual project over the years, and to Mike Rustin and Alan O'Shea at the University of East London for providing such a welcoming and supportive environment which enabled the new work to be carried out.

References

Appadurai, A (1998) *Modernities at Large*, Hanuman, Calcutta

Bakhtin, M (1994) *The Bakhtin Reader*, Arnold, London

Bateson, G (1978) *Steps to an Ecology of Mind*, Paladin, London

Beck, U, Giddens, A and Lash, S (1994) *Reflexive Modernization*, Polity Press, Cambridge

Benjamin, W (1989) *One Way Street*, Verso, London

Bernstein, B (1974) *Towards a Theory of Educational Transmissions*, Vol 3, Routledge, London

Bertaux, D and Thompson, P (1993) *Pathways to Social Class*, Clarendon Press, Oxford

Bisseret, N (1981) *Education, Class, Language, Ideology*, Routledge, London

Bourdieu, P (1977) *Reproduction in Education, Society and Culture*, tr R Nice, Sage, London

Bourdieu, P (1981) *Reproduction*, Oxford University Press, Oxford

Chaiklen, S and Lave, J (eds) (1993) *Understanding Practice*, Cambridge University Press, Cambridge

Chamberlain, M and Thompson, P (eds) (1998) *Narrative and Genre*, Routledge, London

Cohen, P (1997) *Rethinking the Youth Question*, Macmillan, Basingstoke

Connell, R W (1995) *Masculinities*, Polity Press, Cambridge

Foucault, M (1988) *Technologies of the Self*, Tavistock, London

Ginsberg, C (1990) *Myths, Emblems, Clues*, Hutchinson, London

Heath, S B (1983) *Ways with Words*, Cambridge University Press, Cambridge

Hochschild, A (1983) *The Managed Heart*, University of California Press, Berkeley, CA

Jennings, H (1985) *Pandemonium*, Andre Deutsch, London

Joyce, P (1991) *Visions of the People*, Cambridge University Press, Cambridge

Joyce, P (1994) *Democratic Subjects*, Cambridge University Press, Cambridge

Lave, J and Wenger, E (1993) *Situated Learning*, Cambridge University Press, Cambridge

Lotman, Y (1990) *Universe of the Mind*, Tauris, London

Martin, L (ed) (1995) *Socio-cultural Psychology*, Cambridge University Press, Cambridge

Milner, M (1987) *Eternity's Sunrise*, Virago, London

Mitterauer, M (1992) *A History of Youth*, Blackwell, Oxford

More, C (1980) *Skill and the Working Class*, Croom Helm, Beckenham

Pollert, A (1981) *Girls, Wives, Factory Lives*, Croom Helm, Beckenham

Rabinbach, A (1990) *The Human Motor*, California University Press, Berkeley, CA

Ranciere, J (1991) *The Ignorant School Master*, Stanford University Press, Stanford, CA

Rattansi, A and Donald, H J (eds) (1991) *Race, Culture, Difference*, Sage, London

Rogoff, B (1990) *Apprenticeship in Thinking*, Oxford University Press, New York

Rule, J (1980) *The Experience of Labour*, Croom Helm, Beckenham

Salmon, P (1998) *Life at School*, Constable, London

Scott, J and Tilly, L (1978) *Women, Work and Family*, Cambridge University Press, Cambridge

Sohn-Rethel, A (1978) *Intellectual and Manual Labour*, Macmillan, Basingstoke

Thompson, P and Samuel, R (eds) (1993) *Myths We Live By*, Routledge, London

Vygotsky, L (1978) *Mind in Society*, Cambridge University Press, Cambridge

Winnicott, D W (1990) *The Maturational Process and the Facilitating Environment*, Karnac, London

Part 4
Modern Apprenticeship:
A Renaissance of
Work-based Learning?

10

A Sense of Belonging: The Relationship Between Community and Apprenticeship

Alison Fuller and Lorna Unwin

Introduction

In this chapter we want to share our formative ideas about the relationship between apprenticeship and a four-dimensional concept of community. In doing so, we will explore the extent to which community is still relevant to contemporary forms of apprenticeship, most notably the Modern Apprenticeship in the UK. We will argue that, given the increasingly fractured nature of social and occupational relationships, it is necessary to intervene and actively reconstruct some semblance of those communal experiences from which apprentices benefited in the past. The attempt to construct and implement a modern model of apprenticeship under contemporary economic, social and cultural conditions presents, we believe, a considerable challenge for policy-makers, employers and vocational education and training (VET) practitioners. This chapter is written in the light of data published by the Department for Education and Employment in the UK which shows that significant numbers of young people are leaving the Modern Apprenticeship before completing the programme (see DfEE, 1998a), and against a background of continued concern that too many UK employers are unwilling to make a substantial investment in improving the skills of their workforces (see Keep and Mayhew, 1995, 1996). We will discuss some of the ways in which both early leaver rates and employer ambivalence mean there is a strong case for intervention in the Modern Apprenticeship to build substantial learning and support infrastructures which recreate the positive aspects of past communal structures.

Apprenticeship and community

By launching the Modern Apprenticeship in 1994, the UK government acknowledged that as a vehicle for the development and transference of occupational skills, knowledge and understanding, apprenticeship has proved to be effective over several centuries and across many countries and cultures. The development of a social theory of learning by Lave and Wenger (1991) and Lave (1995) suggests that young people's motivation to learn is triggered and sustained by the creation of relationships between 'newcomers' and experienced practitioners, and between what is learned, its application and the development of adult identities. These relationships are likely to occur most fruitfully when the individual becomes what Lave and Wenger conceptualize as a 'legitimate participant' in their chosen occupational field. Here, learning is taken to be a naturally occurring process that happens when individuals participate first peripherally but gradually more fully in what Lave and Wenger have called 'communities of practice'. The use of the term 'legitimate' refers to the way in which the community of practice operates within a regulatory structure. At the same time the term is applied to the individual who, having been accepted into a regulated community, is formerly recognized as a member, with membership conferring both rights and responsibilities. Lave and Wenger use case studies to illustrate how their theorization of learning draws on the practice of apprenticeship in diverse cultural and occupational settings.

A central feature of apprenticeship is the placing of the apprentice in a community of more experienced workers (community of practice) with whom the apprentice interacts and learns from in a variety of ways. The apprentice's motivation to learn is stimulated by recognition of the gap between themselves and their more knowledgeable and skilful colleagues and through awareness that increased learning brings benefits in terms of the development of adult identity associated with occupational status. In this chapter we are focusing on the learning that occurs through 'formal' apprenticeships that are associated with industrialized countries such as the UK. These are 'based on a set of reciprocal rights and obligations between employer and trainee which are set out in an agreement or contract' (Gospel and Fuller, 1998: 5). Communities of practice in this context are likely to centre on the workplace and the off-the-job training location.

Building on Lave and Wenger's concept of community, we would argue that there are four interrelated ways in which this concept can be applied to apprenticeship, and which provide criteria against which the success of programmes can be analysed:

1. Pedagogical – a social theory of learning (explicitly drawing on Lave and Wenger's work) in which young learners (newcomers) are conceptualized as 'legitimate peripheral participants' who learn by participating first

peripherally and gradually more fully in communities of practitioners (communities of practice).

2. Occupational – the second dimension follows from the approach elaborated by Lave and Wenger: apprenticeship functions to initiate the individual into an occupational community, defined by the solidarity formed around shared knowledge, competence and skills, values, customs and habits.

To these we add a 'locational' and a 'social' dimension which we would argue are relevant to, and help to characterize the relationship between the practice of apprenticeship in countries such as the UK and the community:

3. Locational – where apprenticeships are made available to significant numbers of young people by local employers, apprenticeship becomes part of the life of the wider community.
4. Social – the perceived success/reputation of the employer influences the extent to which the local community sees those apprenticeships as an important element of the community's infrastructure and social relations.

We would argue that in the 'heyday' of apprenticeship following World War II and prior to the collapse of manufacturing industry in Britain in the mid to late 1970s, there was a strong relationship between apprenticeship and the four-dimensional model of community described above. Many towns and cities in the UK included one or more traditional apprenticeship providers who gave opportunities to young people (albeit largely to males) to acquire skilled status and long-term job security. At one site of Courtaulds Chemicals in Derby, for example, a minimum of 25 to 30 apprentices were recruited annually from the early 1960s to 1981 (see Unwin, 1996). The apprenticeship programme involved the development of knowledge and skills through a combination of learning in the workplace, off-the-job sessions in the company training school and day release at the local college of further education. Commitment to apprenticeship within the community was bolstered through parental and local support for the apprentice and by a paternalistic approach from both employers and colleges who undertook long-term responsibility for the development of the young person both socially as well as occupationally. Thus the apprentice progressed from partial to full participation (as a skilled worker and adult citizen) in the relevant communities of practice.

As Lane notes in her historical study of apprenticeship in England, despite the widespread abuses and sometimes impoverished standards of training which masqueraded under the term apprenticeship:

> Apprenticeship has retained a high place in the esteem of many and continued to thrive into the present century, for in the ancient trading cities its influence has always been considerable. Even today former apprentices

declare at which particular engineering works they served their time, with a sense of pride and belonging that their 18th century equivalents would have recognized and found entirely appropriate.

(1996: 239)

The socio-economic conditions associated with this long-standing, and we recognize somewhat idealized picture have, however, been undermined over the past 25 years or so. The occupational and employment map of the UK has changed. Demarcations between trades and occupations are no longer so rigid; some occupations have largely died out and new ones have emerged. The major employing industries of the post-war era have contracted, leading to the closure or take-over of companies and the loss of workers with highly specialized skills (Marsden and Ryan, 1991). Communities which were built around the employment (and apprenticeship) opportunities provided by 'sunset' industries have in some cases been devastated (eg, mining towns and villages) and in others have changed as new 'sunrise' industries have moved in. In addition, the growth of employment opportunities in alternative and new sectors such as business administration, information technology, tourism and leisure have provided young people with different career options to their parents. Changing social attitudes and the questioning of traditions in domestic and economic life mean that there is less tolerance towards the exclusive provision of opportunities to white males, while options for girls and those from ethnic minority backgrounds are being extended. In short, the communities within which apprenticeship is situated are no longer the same.

Community fragmentation and youth training schemes

The introduction of various government-sponsored training schemes from the late 1970s onwards led to a reduction of status for VET in general as the schemes became associated with cheap labour, social engineering and the massaging of unemployment statistics (see Dale, 1985; Finn, 1987; Unwin, 1997). Raffe (1988) developed a typology of youth training schemes which can still be applied in the late 1990s and which succinctly captures the fragility of the ties which bind young people to any substantive form of community of practice. Raffe's typology divides schemes into four sectors:

1. *the sponsorship sector* (trainee recruited by employer, given substantive training and kept on at end of scheme);
2. *the contest sector* (trainee recruited by employer who uses the scheme to sift young people);
3. *the credentialling sector* (trainee recruited by employer who will provide substantive training allowing the trainee to gain a qualification but with whom there is little chance of a permanent job);

4. *the detached sector* (agency-led with employers acting as placement providers).

We take the Modern Apprenticeship to be an example of a programme which falls into the 'sponsorship sector' and the Youth Training Scheme/Youth Training (YTS/YT) as schemes which broadly fall into the 'detached sector'. In this chapter we are interested in the differences between Raffe's first (sponsorship) and last (detached) sector types and the extent to which they fulfil the four dimensions of community outlined above.

Under the YTS from 1983, and YT since 1990, the UK has seen a significant shift from an employer-led training provision (sponsorship sector) to an agency-led provision (detached sector). We would argue that this has contributed to a fracturing of the relationship between communities and their training traditions and, in particular, to an undermining of pedagogical, occupational, locational and social aspects of the community in which apprenticeship is implemented. From the locational and social perspectives, large companies either stopped employing school-leavers or became involved, on a much smaller scale, with YTS. Previously, they had recruited large numbers of young people on an annual basis and had often had their own in-house training schools. Into this vacuum stepped a new type of VET organization, the training (or managing) agent (located in both the public and private sectors) who recruited young people and found them training 'placements' across a range of occupational sectors, often in very small businesses. For many YTS (and subsequently YT) trainees, the training agent rather than any one employer was the most important focal point for their period on the scheme. The agent was the 'home' to which trainees returned, from where they received their state-funded weekly training allowance and off-the-job training, met other trainees and bided their time if they were waiting to find a suitable placement or were looking for a new one.

Many YTS and YT agents were 'umbrella' agents organizing work placements in a range of occupational sectors and often with small businesses. Young people would be recruited from a wide area and be placed in ones and twos with employers. Placement switching was common, drop-out high and the majority of trainees failed to emerge from the schemes with a recognized vocational qualification. DfEE figures for 1997 show that only 53 per cent of YT trainees manage to graduate with a complete qualification at NVQ level 2 or above (DfEE, 1998a).

The low status image which YT inherited from YTS has been well documented (see, *inter alia*, Ainley, 1988; Evans *et al*, 1997). Research has shown that young people are not happy with having to tell people in their local communities that they are on a scheme (see, for example, Unwin, 1992). Those in the 'detached sector' find that they are doubly disadvantaged for not only are they labelled as being on a low-level scheme but they are also not attached to an employer which the community considers to be reputable or which is recognized for the quality of its workforce. Thus, the

locational and social dimensions of community were and still are significantly lacking on these schemes.

It follows that the detached sector approach is also likely to be weak in
terms of pedagogical and occupational aspects of community. While the
agent provides trainees with work placements and a site for off-the-job
training, this does not amount to providing a strong pedagogical dimension
to their experience. First, young people who are not employed by a firm are
less likely than employed trainees to be considered as 'legitimate' participants in a community of practitioners. Second, they are less likely to be
given the opportunity to complete the transition from peripheral to 'full'
participants as this would require a longer-term commitment to their
employment by the company. Relatedly, the agency-led approach does not
usually provide an occupational community of practice. Although, in some
instances, agents concentrate exclusively on one occupational sector such as
hairdressing or motor vehicle maintenance, it is more usual for them to
cover a range of occupational sectors. Their focus is usually on managing
and administering the scheme and its 'clients' and not on providing an occupational community. In this regard, the occupational dimension of trainees'
experience is effectively 'contracted out' to employers participating in the
scheme. We would argue, therefore, that systematic deficiencies in YTS and
YT as a whole have diluted their potential to provide the strong pedagogical
and occupational dimensions which we suggest underpin the most effective
apprenticeship experiences. It should be acknowledged, of course, that at
their best, 'sponsorship sector' YTS and YT schemes have replicated traditional apprenticeships and provided young people with effective communities of practice (Unwin, 1997).

Another contributory factor to the low status of YTS/YT has been the
short-term approach to the funding of the training agents whose often
impoverished premises and equipment and low-paid staff do little to relieve
young people's perceptions that they have entered the least glamorous
post-compulsory route (see Evans *et al*, 1997; Hodkinson and Unwin,
1997). Colleges of further education have also acted in the role of training
agents. As traditional apprenticeships and part-time vocational students
declined, colleges refilled their classrooms and workshops in response to the
state's 'guarantee' of a training place for all 16–19-year-olds. As vocational
and academic communities of practice, colleges have a long and admirable
history, responding to the needs of local employers and citizens. They were
key players in traditional apprenticeships and some colleges emerged in the
last century to provide vocational education and training for specific industries, notably mining, engineering and hotel and catering. Colleges were also
embedded in their local communities by being under the control of local
education authorities until, in 1993, they were turned into corporate institutions by the Further and Higher Education Act. Although still central to
the lives of their local communities, incorporation has forced colleges to
develop courses of study which attract the most favourable funding rather

than, necessarily, maintain a vocational profile that reflects the needs of local people and employers. This fracturing of the colleges' community relationships is a further factor in the changing landscape of VET provision which separates traditional apprenticeship from the youth training schemes of the past 20 or so years.

We will now turn to the introduction of the Modern Apprenticeship to explore the extent to which it might recreate the communities of practice which we suggest underpinned the most successful apprenticeships of the past.

The Modern Apprenticeship

In the 1990s, changing requirements of work and production have led to calls for a more highly educated and skilled workforce capable of adapting to new circumstances, and keen to continue learning throughout working life (see, *inter alia,* DfEE, 1998b; IPPR, 1997; Keep and Mayhew, 1995). The Modern Apprenticeship is expected to respond to those changes by creating a contemporary model of vocational learning that overcomes the shortcomings of traditional apprenticeships while at the same time providing a rigorous, high-quality vehicle to deliver intermediate skills across some 70 occupational sectors, many of which have no experience of substantive initial training accredited through recognized qualifications.

Fuller (1996) notes that in terms of qualification outcomes, the design of the Modern Apprenticeship is such as to differentiate it from other youth training schemes. Hence, modern apprentices will study to a minimum NVQ level 3, whereas for YT level 2 was the norm. (The new National Traineeships also have level 2 as their goal.) In addition, successful completion of the Modern Apprenticeship requires the attainment of key skills units in 'application of number', 'communication' and 'information technology'. From the contractual perspective, the Modern Apprenticeship is similar to 'traditional' apprenticeships in that during the training period, the apprentice is employed on a relatively low wage (Gospel and Fuller, 1998). An agreement is signed by employer and apprentice committing both parties to the requirements of the apprenticeship.

However, the feature that differentiates the Modern Apprenticeship more than any other is that each programme is designed and 'owned' by a specific occupational sector whose National Training Organization (NTO) is responsible for its sector's Modern Apprenticeship framework. Government rhetoric regarding a number of VET initiatives from the late 1980s (eg, YT, the introduction of NVQs, and the establishment of Training and Enterprise Councils – TECs) has stressed that they were 'employer-led' when, in reality, only a minority of leading employers and certain employer organizations have had some involvement in their development. Rather than employers, the key players in these earlier developments have been, in the words of

Field (1995: 80) 'a small coalition of modernizing civil servants and highly placed training professionals'. Here we can envisage a major test of the Modern Apprenticeship's potential for recreating three of the four community dimensions we identified at the start of this chapter: the occupational, the locational and the social dimensions. If the Modern Apprenticeship is truly employer-led and genuinely owned by the NTOs, then the ties which bound apprentices, employers and communities together in the past may be established again. However, when we look at early leaver rates for the Modern Apprenticeship, we see that there is substantial variation between sectors. Overall, traditional apprenticeship sectors such as engineering manufacture and electrical installation engineering have a below-average proportion of early leavers, whereas sectors such as retailing and health and social care which did not offer apprenticeships before the introduction of the MA have higher than average figures.

Early leaving on the Modern Apprenticeship

Data on early leaving are available by Modern Apprenticeship sector and by TEC area (DfEE Modern Apprenticeship database quarterly reports). A recent Modern Apprenticeship report for England (DfEE, 1998a) indicates that a third of those who start the Modern Apprenticeship are leaving early. The total number of Modern Apprenticeship starts is 160,882 across over 70 sectors, and the total number of leavers is 53,429. The database reports provide the numbers of starts and leavers but they do not offer any information on the leavers' destinations. In addition, the reports do not indicate the gender, ethnic and demographic characteristics of leavers. Although the data on leavers are limited we would suggest that they can be used to provide some insights into the strength of the inter-institutional relationships underpinning the communities of practice in which modern apprentices find themselves.

Focusing only on sectors which implemented the Modern Apprenticeship either in its first or second year of operation (1994 and 1995) and which have had more than 1,000 starts, we found that of the sectors with between 1,000 and 10,000 starts, the lowest leaver rates were for electrical installation engineering and the highest for health and social care (DfEE, Modern Apprenticeship database report, No 9, April 1998). In the electrical installation sector there have been 6,964 starts and 990 leavers (14 per cent) and in the health and social care sector there have been 8,496 starts and 3,569 leavers (42 per cent). In sectors which have had more than 10,000 starts, we noted that engineering manufacture had the lowest leaver rate (21 per cent) with 19,636 starts and 4,083 leavers, while retailing had the highest leaver rate (47 per cent), with 16,450 starts and 7,747 leavers (DfEE, ibid). The occupational areas with the lowest leaver rates (electrical installation engineering and engineering manufacture) are sectors which have a long tradition of providing apprenticeship training. In contrast, those with the highest leaver rates (health and social care and retailing) are sectors which have no tradition of apprenticeship training.

Gospel and Fuller (1998) conducted case studies of the Modern Apprenticeship in three sectors (engineering manufacture, construction and information technology) with contrasting inheritances in terms of apprenticeship. Engineering manufacture has a long tradition of apprenticeship, construction had a tradition of apprenticeship but such provision has largely died out in recent years, and information technology is a newcomer to this form of training. The researchers were particularly interested to investigate the range and structure of institutions (employers, employee representative bodies, industry training organizations, training providers and TECs) participating in the design and development of the programme. They were also concerned to assess the quality of the inter-institutional relations and their effect on the operation of the Modern Apprenticeship. Gospel and Fuller concluded that the institutional supports necessary for the successful operation of the programme were weak in construction and information technology. Both sectors have early leaver rates of 36 per cent (DfEE, ibid). In addition they found that only the engineering manufacture Modern Apprenticeship framework was designed and developed in a participative manner, and that there was clear evidence of the strong relationships which have been fostered between relevant institutions in this sector. Principal among these relationships were high-level ties between the Confederation of Shipbuilding and Engineering Unions, the Engineering Employers' Federation and the Engineering and Marine Training Authority. At the local level, there was evidence of long-standing and close relations between employers and colleges of further education (Huddleston, 1998). For purposes of comparison the research also referred to the electrical installation engineering sector, noting that:

> One of the main reasons why the quantity and quality of apprentice training have remained stronger in this sub-sector would seem to be the degree of collective regulation by the employers' organization and the trade union and the depth of institutional supports which they have jointly established.

> (Gospel and Fuller, 1998: 14)

This brief focus on early leaver rates in sectors which contrast in terms of their apprenticeship provision and traditions confirms that there seems to be a link between employers' and industries' previous commitment to apprenticeship and the re-establishment of the ties between apprentices, employers and the wider community which we have suggested characterized past best practice. Although further research into the leaver statistics and into what lies behind them is required, the data included here suggest that it would be foolish to underestimate the challenge of creating the sort of institutional supports and relationships associated with strong occupational, locational and social aspects of apprenticeship communities – particularly in occupational sectors that are new to apprenticeship. A different concern is that figures on the gender and ethnic characteristics of modern apprentices indicate that few inroads have been made into altering the stereotypical gender and ethnic profiles of traditional apprenticeship sectors under the Modern Apprenticeship. For example, while sectors such as electrical installation engineering are successful in recruiting and retaining trainees, this has not been achieved at the same time as widening participation from young women and those from ethnic minorities. Currently under 2 per cent of modern apprentices in this sector are female and under 2 per cent are from ethnic minorities.

Pedagogical concerns and the Modern Apprenticeship

We stated earlier in the chapter that aspects of the design of the Modern Apprenticeship framework differentiate it from other government-sponsored training initiatives. In this section we briefly consider the Modern Apprenticeship in relation to pedagogical issues. From the perspective of design we would argue that the Modern Apprenticeship has the potential to forge strong pedagogical communities of practice with the capacity to facilitate apprentices' development from legitimate peripheral participants to full participants. Of particular relevance in this regard is the Modern Apprenticeship framework's requirement that apprentices experience a combination of on- and off-the-job learning. On the other hand, we are concerned that inconsistencies in the interpretation of design requirements and in the quality of NVQ qualifications and key skill unit specifications may weaken the pedagogical experience for many modern apprentices, particularly in terms of their opportunity to benefit from a broad or 'holistic' approach to learning.

Fuller (1996) has suggested that the design requirements of the Modern Apprenticeship allow for the implementation of weaker and stronger interpretations of 'breadth' within the programme. A weak interpretation would include the minimum mandatory components required by the Modern Apprenticeship framework: these are an NVQ level 3 and key skills. In this interpretation the potential for the key skills to add breadth to the narrow occupational focus of the NVQ is limited by integrating the delivery and assessment of key skills with the NVQ. The Modern Apprenticeship framework in construction provides an example of this approach (Gospel and Fuller, 1998). As Fuller (1996) points out, the possibility of this type of implementation providing breadth is highly dependent on the scope of the standards included in the NVQ. In this regard, research on the content of NVQs has tended to highlight their narrowness (see for example Steedman, 1998; Steedman and Hawkins, 1994; Stewart and Sambrook, 1995).

Alternatively, the Modern Apprenticeship framework allows for the inclusion of optional components which can be used to extend apprentices' learning beyond the minimum mandatory specification. Fuller suggests that a programme which is designed to serve a range of goals through providing learners with the opportunity to pursue multiple qualifications, each of which is designed to fulfil a specific purpose, can be conceptualized as 'holistic'. The engineering manufacture Modern Apprenticeship framework has been found to provide an example of this approach (Gospel and Fuller, 1998). This programme exceeds government minimum requirements for the Modern Apprenticeship in two significant ways. First, by including as mandatory a conventional vocational education qualification such as a BTEC National Diploma and second, by separately assessing the key skills units at pre-specified levels (level 3 for communication and application of number, and level 2 for IT). In addition, the framework strongly promotes progression to level 4 qualifications.

Conclusions

Within the scope of this chapter we have been able briefly to consider the potential of the Modern Apprenticeship to develop the pedagogical, occupational, locational and social criteria which, we would argue, underpin successful apprenticeship programmes. We have suggested that the challenge is considerable, particularly in relation to the forging of the inter-institutional supports and social relationships necessary to embed apprenticeships within occupational and local communities. In terms of pedagogical concerns, we have argued elsewhere that the Modern Apprenticeship has some positive features such as employed status for the young person; recognition that the development of skills should take place in a structured manner over time; and the resources to ensure that modern apprentices receive both on- and off-the-job training (Fuller and Unwin, 1998). The requirement of NVQ level 3 and key skills as mandatory is also seen as an advance on previous government sponsored schemes (ibid). However, as we have outlined, the design of the framework's components allows sectors to adopt different interpretations of what should count as a Modern Apprenticeship. This has operational and experiential implications for all the participants in the programme as well as for how participants and others in the wider community perceive the Modern Apprenticeship's value. In this regard we would argue that under contemporary social, cultural and economic conditions it is not enough that modern apprentices are participants in occupational communities of practice. Employers, training providers and policy-makers need to recognize the ways in which the structures that support the Modern Apprenticeship promote or undermine 'legitimate participation'. Modern apprentices should have the opportunity to acquire the range of competences and depth of understanding that will enable them not only to belong to the relevant community of practice but also to shape it in the light of rapidly changing technological and organizational requirements.

We would argue that apprenticeship can be reconstructed to provide effective vocational preparation for the contemporary economic and occupational climate, although there are concerns about the variability and level of employer demand across sectors (Gospel and Fuller, 1998). There are already examples of good practice emerging, particularly in sectors which have an apprenticeship tradition, strong inter-institutional support networks and established links with the wider community. A challenge for traditional apprenticeship sectors engaged in reconstructing their approach is to widen participation to incorporate previously excluded groups such as young women and those from ethnic minority backgrounds. Overall much more effort has to be put into identifying and developing the pedagogical, occupational, locational and social criteria that can strengthen the relationship between apprenticeship and community. This is particularly the case in sectors with no previous experience of offering apprenticeships. Otherwise the Modern Apprenticeship may struggle to overcome the tendency of previous work-based VET initiatives to become fragmented, downgraded and marginalized.

References

Ainley, P (1988) *From School to YTS*, Open University Press, Buckingham

Dale, R (1985) *Education Training and Employment: Towards a new vocationalism?*, Pergamon Press, Oxford

Department for Education and Employment (DfEE) (1998a) *Statistical Press Notice, 270.98*, Department of Education and Employment, London

DfEE (1998b) *The Learning Age: A renaissance for a new Britain*, Department of Education and Employment, London

Evans, K, Hodkinson, P, Keep, E, Maguire, M, Raffe, D, Rainbird, H, Senker, P and Unwin, L (1997) *Working to learn: A work-based route to learning for young people*, Institute of Personnel Management, London

Field, J (1995) Reality testing in the workplace: are NVQs 'employment-led'?, in *The Challenge of Competence*, ed P Hodkinson and M Issitt, Cassell, London

Finn, D (1987) *Training without Jobs*, Macmillan, Basingstoke

Fuller, A (1996) Modern Apprenticeship, process and learning: some emerging issues, *Journal of Vocational Education and Training*, **48** (3), pp 229–48

Fuller, A and Unwin, L (1998) Reconceptualizing apprenticeship: exploring the relationship between work and learning, *Journal of Vocational Education and Training*, **50** (2), 153–72

Gospel, H and Fuller, A (1998) The Modern Apprenticeship: new wine in old bottles?, *Human Resource Management Journal*, **8** (1), pp 5–22

Hodkinson, P and Unwin, L (1997) Private training providers; out of the shadows, paper presented to the British Educational Research Association Conference, York University, September

Huddleston, P (1998) Modern apprentices in college: 'something old something new', *Journal of Vocational Education and Training*, **50** (2), pp 277–88

IPPR (1997) *Promoting Prosperity: A business agenda for Britain*, Vintage Books/Institute for Public Policy Research, London

Keep, E and Mayhew, K (1995) Training policy for competitiveness: time for a new perspective, in *Future Skill Demand and Supply*, ed H Metcalf, Policy Studies Institute, London

Keep, E and Mayhew, K (1996) Evaluating the assumptions that underlie training policy, in *Acquiring Skills: Market failures, their symptoms and policy responses*, ed A L Booth and D J Snower, Cambridge University Press, Cambridge

Lane, J (1996) *Apprenticeship in England, 1600–1914*, UCL Press, London

Lave, J (1995) Teaching as learning, in practice, Sylvia Scribner Award Lecture, American Educational Research Association, San Francisco, CA

Lave, J and Wenger, E (1991) *Situated Learning: Legitimate peripheral participation*, Cambridge University Press, Cambridge

Marsden, D and Ryan, P (eds) (1991) *International Comparisons of Vocational Education and Training for Intermediate Skills*, Falmer Press, London

Raffe, D (1988) The context of the Youth Training Scheme: an analysis of its strategy and development, in *Training and its Alternatives*, ed D Gleeson, Open University Press, Buckingham

Steedman, H (1998) A decade of skill formation in Britain and Germany, *Journal of Education and Work*, **11** (1), pp 77–94

Steedman, H and Hawkins, J (1994) Shifting foundations: the impact of NVQs on youth training for the building trades, *National Institute Economic Review*, pp 246–71

Stewart, J and Sambrook, S (1995) The role of functional analysis in National Vocational Qualifications: a critical appraisal, *British Journal of Education and Work*, **8** (2), pp 93–106

Unwin, L (1992) *Young People's Attitudes to Youth Training*, North and Mid-Cheshire Training and Enterprise Council, Winsford

Unwin, L (1996) Employer-led realities: apprenticeship past and present, *Journal of Vocational Education and Training*, **48** (1), pp 57–68

Unwin, L (1997) Reforming the work-based route: problems and potential for change, in *Dearing and Beyond: 14–19 qualifications, frameworks and systems*, ed A Hodgson and K Spours, Kogan Page, London

11

Modern Apprenticeships: Just in Time, or Far Too Late?

Malcolm Maguire

The introduction of Modern Apprenticeships in prototype form in 1994, and in a fully-fledged version in 1995, can be seen as representing a revitalization of the work-based route into employment for young people, and as a wholly appropriate response to employers' skill needs. As will be indicated, the take-up of the initiative by employers has been encouraging, and studies have pointed to considerable 'success' being achieved, from the perspectives of both employers and young people. But will it last, or could it be that a range of external factors and competing policy initiatives are effectively conspiring to inhibit the capacity of Modern Apprenticeships to fulfil their potential – at the very time when widespread concerns about skill shortages at the intermediate level are being voiced?

Background

In order to assess the potential significance of Modern Apprenticeships, it is important to understand the context in which they were introduced, particularly in terms of shifts in labour market demand for certain types of skills and, especially, for young people. It is now well established that the recession of the early 1980s and the wide-ranging changes to the occupational structure which have occurred since then, have profoundly affected the youth labour market. As a consequence, the demand for youth labour underwent a fundamental change, as exemplified by the dramatic shifts which occurred in the patterns of post-school destinations of 16-year-olds. Thus, the number of 16–17-year-olds who entered the labour market had fallen from 608,000 in 1984/5 to 276,000 in 1992/3. As a proportion of the age cohort, those 16-year-olds entering employment fell from 62 per cent in 1975 to 49 per cent in 1979, declined rapidly to 22 per cent in 1983, remained relatively constant to 1990, when it was 18 per cent, but then dropped dramatically to only 9 per cent in 1992. The 1997 Careers Service

Activity Survey shows that in autumn 1997, 8.4 per cent of those who completed Year 11 in that year were in 'employment outside Government supported training' (DfEE, 1998b).

This fundamental restructuring of the youth labour market could be attributed to shifts in, *inter alia,* industrial sectors, with the continuing decline of manufacturing and a burgeoning service sector; the distribution of occupations; employers' product market strategies; the employment relationship; organizational structures; and employers' skill requirements. The result has been a transformation of the opportunities available for school-leavers, with a significant reduction in the demand for the labour of relatively unqualified 16-year-olds. While fluctuations in the demand for youth labour had traditionally been explained by referring to the state of the economy, with employers reducing their demand for youth labour during recession and increasing it during the upturn, other processes of change were found to be causing this decline in demand throughout the 1980s, notably the decline of labour-intensive industries; the impact of new technology; increased business competition; and a process of increasing industrial concentration.

The effect on traditional work-based routes into employment for young people, and particularly the apprenticeship, has been dramatic. Roberts asserted that:

> The decline of manufacturing jobs has meant that school- and college-leavers have become less likely to find employment at all levels in manufacturing, and more likely to obtain jobs in services. It may be vital for Britain's economic future that manufacturers obtain the supplies of appropriately qualified labour that they need but it remains the case that young people's chances of obtaining such employment have declined, and, in all probability, will continue to do so.

(1995: 37–38)

Gospel has charted the decline of apprenticeships during this period and states that 'the most precipitous falls in apprentice ratios were in the late 1960s and early 1970s, in the early and mid-1980s, and again, most dramatically, in the early and mid-1990s' (1998: 439–40).

Much of our thinking in relation to employers' future demand for youth labour is predicated on the assumption that an ever-increasing majority of jobs will require high levels of skill which have been formally accredited. That such broad trends are in train, and will continue to generate a demand for more qualified and skilled entrants to the labour market, is undeniable. None the less, some commentators are more sceptical about the all-embracing nature of these forces. Keep and Mayhew (1994) contend that the level of skills demanded by employers may not be rising as quickly as has been suggested. Part of their argument is supported by Institute for Employment Research projections which show that the fastest growth rate for any occupational area will be among personal and protective service occupations, which include catering, travel, childcare and beauty occupations, as well as health service workers such as nursing auxiliaries, hospital orderlies and ambulance staff (IER, 1997). These occupations cannot be said to be at the leading edge in terms of high-level skills. Furthermore, Keep and Mayhew point to evidence from studies carried out by the National Institute for Economic and Social Research which have repeatedly shown that significant proportions of British employers effectively choose to adopt strategies which are based on low-quality, low-skill, price-based competition.

Having said this, it should be emphasized that not all firms operate in this way, but a large proportion do so in a manner which requires only low-level skills and places few demands on the workforce.

Clearly there has been a fundamental transformation of the youth labour market over the last decade and projections about occupational trends and the future demand for labour would suggest that there will be an ever-dwindling number of opportunities for young people (or any job-seekers, for that matter) who lack the higher-level skills which are increasingly being recognized and demanded. As a consequence, the once traditional route into the labour market for large numbers of young people, incorporating an emphasis on work-based learning programmes, has come to be regarded as offering 'low status and marginality' (Evans *et al*, 1997: 17).

The introduction of Modern Apprenticeships

The introduction of Modern Apprenticeships in 1993 was an attempt to address the acknowledged deficiencies of the British labour force at intermediate and technician level, by revitalizing the notion of apprenticeship training on the basis of competence-based NVQs and core skills attainment rather than time-serving. It was also viewed as a means of enhancing progress towards the higher level National Targets for Education and Training (NTETs). Prototype schemes were launched in 14 industrial sectors, led by their respective Industry Training Organization (ITO). From September 1995, Modern Apprenticeships became fully operational in over 50 industrial sectors. The initiative was developed jointly through the TEC/LEC network and ITOs and National Training Organizations (NTOs), with each sector having a nationally agreed framework for training provision. NVQ and equivalent qualifications to levels 3 and 4 are available, as well as coverage of core skills in information technology, numeracy and communication. An apprenticeship plan is drawn up between the trainee and the provider to form a contractual basis for agreement on factors such as attendance requirements, qualifications aimed for and overall career objectives. In essence, this epitomizes one of the great strengths of the Modern Apprenticeship, which is its appeal to employers' perceptions of what had been, for centuries, the bedrock of the system of skill acquisition, especially for craft skills – the apprenticeship. By evoking nostalgia for an institution which had immense credibility in the eyes of employers, the intention was, in part, to kick-start a process whereby work-based vocational training was accorded a level of esteem which had been absent since the introduction of YOP and YTS (YT).

A key component of the initiative was that it would introduce the idea of apprenticeship to occupations and industrial sectors which had no previous tradition of apprenticeship. Thus, in keeping with the fundamental shifts which had occurred in the distribution of occupations, areas such as business administration and information technology were flagged up as coming within the scope of Modern Apprenticeships.

Concerns expressed

The ability and willingness of industrial sectors which had little tradition of apprenticeship training was highlighted by Maclagan (1996) as posing potentially serious problems for the initiative. She hypothesized that industrial sectors such as engineering, with a long tradition of apprenticeship, would have little trouble in introducing and sustaining Modern Apprenticeships, and would, in effect, amend existing training provision to satisfy the requirements. In contrast, other sectors such as childcare would have greater difficulty in implementing them effectively, due to a lack of experience and appropriate mechanisms.

Maclagan also warned of the possibility of Modern Apprenticeships becoming elitist, and pointed to different responses by TECs to their introduction:

> TECs face a very significant dilemma in how they market Modern Apprenticeships. Some are emphasizing the difference between them and their YT provision, in order to attract high achievers, while others are drawing the distinction less clearly, so as not to devalue their remaining YT. The predicament goes to the heart of the problem of the Modern Apprenticeship initiative: that it offers some young people higher quality opportunities by implicitly devaluing or marginalizing what is available to the less favoured.

> (1996: 15)

Maclagan's concern was that Modern Apprenticeships are symptomatic of a lack of coherence in youth policy by targeting high-quality provision on those who are most able and most well motivated, at the expense of the 'residual group', whose members possess few skills or qualifications, and whose only opportunity is to gain access to 'poor quality YTS'. None the less, the evidence to date would seem to augur well for the future of Modern Apprenticeships. However, other developments in the policy arena may soon give rise to concerns about the ability of Modern Apprenticeships to

grow in terms of the numbers of both young people and employers participating, and of the initiative's status as an acknowledged route to the acquisition of higher-level skills.

Prototypes – early indications

Early findings from the research on the prototype Modern Apprenticeships
set up in 1994 (Everett and Leman, 1995) suggested that their introduction
had generated an increase in the number of employers training to NVQ level
3 or its equivalent. It was also found that the majority of young people participating in Modern Apprenticeships were convinced that they would benefit from their involvement. As far as employers' responses were concerned,
this had initially been favourable, with over 90 per cent of those involved in
the prototype expressing a preparedness to recommend that Modern
Apprenticeships should be adopted by other employers in their industrial
sector (Everett et al, 1996). Moreover, it was found that in comparison to
the type of training which has previously been provided, more training
places offering a route to the attainment of NVQ level 3 qualifications were
being made available. Over 90 per cent of the young people taking part in
the apprenticeships expressed satisfaction with them. However, it was indicated that there was an under-representation of females and ethnic minorities. The imbalance in the gender distribution at this time reflected the fact
that the prototype Modern Apprenticeships were predominantly in sectors
which had traditionally taken on male craft apprentices, although one study
found that Modern Apprenticeships were attracting considerable numbers
of employers who had not been involved in previous government training
initiatives (IDS, 1995). The need to be aware of implementing good equal
opportunity practice was highlighted in another commentary (ENTRA,
1996). Additionally, concerns were expressed about the applicability of the
scheme for certain industrial sectors, and the need for improved provision
of careers guidance for young people.

Some areas of concern were raised by other commentators. For example,
Adams (1996) pointed to:

- the difficulties of obtaining up-to-date information about current levels
  and types of Modern Apprenticeship take-up, due to the devolving of
  responsibility for their administration to the TECs;
- 'mumblings of discontent' from employers about differences between
  sectors and between TECs' approaches to Modern Apprenticeships, particularly in terms of funding arrangements;
- problems of sectors with high proportions of part-time employees;
- concerns over the funding mechanism, principally in relation to the need
  for annual negotiations and the variability in levels of subsidy between
  TECs;

- variations in the extent to which Modern Apprenticeship funding is channelled through training providers;
- problems associated with eliciting the participation of significant numbers of small and medium-sized enterprises (SMEs);
- concerns over equal opportunities, with relatively low early participation from females, ethnic minorities and the disabled.

None the less, she also confirmed that employers were responding positively and enthusiastically, to the extent of there being an element of 'additionality' brought to intermediate level skills training by Modern Apprenticeships, and suggested that evidence was emerging of Modern Apprenticeships making significant inroads into some occupational areas in the service sector.

A subsequent report from Incomes Data Services (IDS, 1997) indicated that, as of September 1996, there were 51,4000 Modern Apprenticeships in Great Britain. Given that this was just 12 months after they were launched, it suggested that the stated targets for 1996–97 and thereafter of 60,000 starts per year were achievable. Indeed, in March 1997, James Paice (then Education and Employment Minister) asserted that 'apprenticeships are being undertaken by more than 70,000 trainees – 6 per cent above the government's target for the scheme' (*The Financial Times,* 24 March 1997). IDS reported that in September 1996 alone there had been 8,800 new starts, representing the highest monthly intake up to that date. From the company case studies conducted for the IDS report, it was found that Modern Apprenticeships were being well received by employers because they provided good quality training; were relevant to the needs of the business and to the occupations to which they were related; and had the advantage of being susceptible to tailoring and adaptation to the company's needs. The majority of apprentices had employed status and were paid the rate for the job. Furthermore, it was understood that the majority would be offered a permanent job on completion of their apprenticeship.

An interesting development, given long-standing concerns about the rigidity in terms of age of entry of the traditional British apprenticeship system, was the low take-up of Accelerated Modern Apprenticeships, in both the prototype and fully operational phases. This apparent lack of interest resulted in the merging of the Modern Apprenticeships and Accelerated Modern Apprenticeships from April 1996 (Adams, 1996).

The evaluation of the prototype scheme found that they had been implemented most successfully in industrial sectors which had a tradition and history of offering apprenticeships; an ITO with wide coverage and support within the sector; experience of promoting and accepting NVQs and GNVQs; and strong existing support for apprenticeship training from employers (Everett and Leman, 1995).

Employer response

Following the evaluations of the prototype scheme, the initial impact of the fully-fledged Modern Apprenticeships was assessed. The IER undertook a study of the response of participating employers to Modern Apprenticeships (see Hasluck *et al*, 1997). Although the sample of 500 establishments differed from the national picture in being skewed towards establishments with a relatively high proportion of manual workers, it provided a reasonable representation of the distribution of employers participating in Modern Apprenticeships in the early stages.

An interesting finding from the study, given the somewhat premature demise of Accelerated Modern Apprenticeships, was that over half the employers in the sample had recruited apprentices who were aged 17 or over. A third had recruited 17-year-olds, 11 per cent had recruited 18-year-olds and 7 per cent had recruited 19-year-olds. There were also instances of 21- and 22-year-olds being recruited. This propensity to target older recruits was notably prevalent in business services, which do not have a long-standing tradition of apprenticeship, but do have a tradition of recruiting people after they have obtained some other form of qualification, often from college. Overall, there was some evidence of a shift to greater flexibility in the age at which apprentices would be recruited.

In terms of the selection criteria operating in the recruitment of modern apprentices, over 40 per cent of respondents stated that they did not stipulate specific qualifications as requirements for entry. Instead, as has been customary with employers over many years, qualification attainment was used in conjunction with other qualities when assessing candidates. Furthermore, even where minimum entry qualifications were stipulated, significant proportions of employers stated that they had recruited apprentices who did not satisfy these basic criteria. This may point to the fact that, even at this early stage of the initiative, some industrial sectors were experiencing difficulties in attracting suitable candidates.

The qualities most often sought in candidates were enthusiasm (mentioned by 81 per cent of respondents), the 'right attitude' (77 per cent), and common sense (72 per cent). More specific skills such as numeracy were mentioned less frequently, although they were still clearly regarded as important. Forty-six per cent of respondents mentioned numeracy as a desirable quality, while 52 per cent mentioned literacy and 60 per cent cited the ability to communicate.

Overall, employers appeared to be satisfied with the calibre of applicants, with two-thirds stating that applicants were fairly satisfactory or very satisfactory, and only 16 per cent expressing dissatisfaction. Those responsible for recruitment were particularly impressed by the applicants' ability and keenness and the quality of the programme being offered. Those who were dissatisfied were far less happy about the candidates' quality and attitude. These issues of quality and attitude of applicants were also apparent in responses to questions about whether it had been difficult to recruit modern apprentices. A significant minority, comprising a quarter of the sample, stated that they had experienced some difficulty when recruiting. In addition to 'poor applicants' and 'poor attitude of applicants', a shortage of applicants and recruiting applicants from among those who were not interested in work, were each cited by 6 per cent of the total sample as producing difficulties.

The indications from this study were that the availability of Modern Apprenticeships had affected recruitment practices, especially in SMEs. In total, one in seven of the respondents stated that this had occurred, with the proportions being higher among establishments employing over 500 people (20 per cent) and among establishments employing fewer than 25 people which were part of a larger organization (25 per cent). The main reasons given for practices being changed were the ability to be more selective and the creation of specific opportunities to take someone on. Representatives of sectoral bodies, notably ITOs or NTOs, confirmed that they would expect the impact of Modern Apprenticeships on recruitment practices to be greatest among smaller firms, which had tended to be less flexible and adaptable than larger organizations in their targeting of recruits. At this time it was felt that Modern Apprenticeships would benefit smaller firms by making them more attractive to school-leavers, who may previously have tended to target larger organizations with more formalized and structured training opportunities.

Another important finding from the study was that, even allowing for the fact that there has been an acknowledged steady increase in training activity across most industrial sectors in recent years, and that the firms included in the sample had tended to have experienced growth, both in terms of business volume and training activity, the introduction of Modern Apprenticeships appeared to have generated an increase in the number of training places at intermediate skill level. It was estimated that this shift amounted to a 16 per cent increase. Indeed, 12 per cent of respondents claimed that they would not have recruited trainees at this level if Modern Apprenticeships had not been available. It was also the case that those occupational areas which had no tradition of apprenticeships, such as personal services and business services, reported relatively high levels of additional training places.

Overall, then, the findings of the study suggested that Modern Apprenticeships had generated an increase in training activity at intermediate skill level across a range of industrial sectors, and especially among those with little previous tradition of apprenticeship. There was also evidence of increased participation in training by small firms and of enhanced take-up of NVQs. In addition, Modern Apprenticeships had brought about changes in training content and practice, an improvement in general skills training and a raising of the standard of training, with a greater proportion of training activity leading to a qualification, notably NVQs. Aspects of Modern

Apprenticeships which were highlighted were the scope, flexibility and certification of training, the balance between on- and off-the-job training and the support provided by government and by TECs. A minority of respondents voiced criticisms of the process of implementation (20 per cent), of the delivery (15 per cent) and of the content (20 per cent). Concerns were also expressed about the bureaucracy involved although, again, this was very much a minority view.

Crucially, an overwhelming majority (87 per cent) stated that they would continue to participate in the future, reflecting high levels of satisfaction concerning the quality of applicants, content of training and the administrative mechanisms.

Progress to date

These initial indications that employers were responding positively to the availability of Modern Apprenticeships appear to have been accurate, as the numbers participating have risen rapidly since their introduction. Thus, between March 1996 and March 1998, the number of young people following this route grew from 27,800 to 118,200 (DfEE, 1998b). In addition, the penetration of Modern Apprenticeships into more industrial sectors can be seen by the steady growth in the number of frameworks available, for example, from 62 (in England and Wales) in September 1996 (IDS, 1997) to 72 in March 1997 (*Financial Times*). Notwithstanding this growth, the most popular frameworks continue to be engineering manufacturing, business administration and construction. In the early months of the introduction of Modern Apprenticeships (up to December 1995) these three frameworks accounted for over a half of all starts, with engineering manufacturing accounting for 28.1 per cent, business administration for 12.6 per cent and construction for 10.2 per cent (Adams, 1996).

Significant change also occurred in the gender distribution of Modern Apprenticeships between Adams' study and the IDS report. Whereas in December 1995 only 28.3 per cent of modern apprentices were female (Adams, 1996), this proportion had risen to 42 per cent by September 1996. This again is indicative of the spreading of Modern Apprenticeships into 'non-traditional' occupational sectors.

Changing external context

The foregoing research evidence and increasing participation rates point to the Modern Apprenticeship initiative having been launched successfully and offering the prospect of that success being sustained in the future. However, other developments in the policy arena may soon give rise to concerns about the ability of Modern Apprenticeships to sustain their recent growth, of both young people and employers participating, and to become firmly established as the acknowledged route to the acquisition of intermediate level skills. A number of factors may contribute to this.

First, reservations were expressed in the early stages about the potential for Modern Apprenticeships becoming elitist and being regarded as a 'fast track' among the work-based training opportunities available to young people (Maclagan, 1996). This appeared to be borne out by the aggressive marketing of the initiative by many TECs, with emphasis being placed on the difference between them and YT provision, which was perceived to lead to a lower qualification and was less likely to confer employee status. The essential problem within Modern Apprenticeships was thus seen to be that, while providing a high-quality, work-based training route for some young people, they implicitly devalue what is available for the less favoured on other schemes. Certainly it has been the case that the growing number of enrolments on Modern Apprenticeships has been accompanied by a decline in the numbers on YT. As a consequence, high-quality provision has increasingly become targeted at the most able and best motivated young people, while those with few skills or qualifications have been relegated to what is perceived as the poorer quality YT route. Since that time, the thrust of policy, with the introduction of National Traineeships and the New Deal, may not only make competing claims on employers' commitment to training and to young people, but may result in Modern Apprenticeships becoming marginalized rather than elitist.

Secondly, some evidence is emerging of a potentially critical mismatch between the supply of young people seeking Modern Apprenticeships and employers' perceptions of what constitutes a young person of 'the right calibre' to be offered an apprenticeship. In part, this situation can be attributed to the 'success' that has been achieved in the drive to increase staying-on rates among 16-year-olds. During the latter half of the 1980s, a significant increase in the proportion of young people participating in post-compulsory education was widely advocated as an essential requirement of enhancing the skills base of the British workforce, in both higher-level and intermediate skills. Allied to growing concerns about Britain's lack of competitiveness (CBI, 1989; Hutton, 1995; Porter, 1990; Steedman and Wagner, 1987), a consensus emerged that salvation lay in creating conditions, in terms of both available places and young people's motivation, whereby higher proportions of the 16-year-old annual cohort would remain within the education system. This was to be the principle means of ensuring the development of a more highly skilled and highly qualified workforce. As we are now well aware, this transformation in staying-on rates has been achieved in a remarkably short period. Thus, for 16-year-olds, the participation rate rose from 48 per cent in 1987 to 72 per cent in 1994/95, before falling slightly to 68 per cent in 1997 (DfEE, 1998a). The rate for 17-year-olds rose from 39 per cent in 1989/90 to 59 per cent in 1994/95 (DfEE, 1998b).

A variety of factors have contributed to this increase (see Maguire and

Maguire, 1997). What is apparent, however, is that it has not, of itself, effected any sort of instant solution, either to the skills deficiencies of the British workforce, or to difficulties encountered by young people in entering appropriate employment. Indeed, concerns have been expressed about some of the facets of this participation, notably: increases in achievement lagging a long way behind increases in participation; lack of progression; high drop-out and failure rates; participation having peaked and now being in decline; increasing popularity of the work-based route; unemployment and under-employment among graduates; and large numbers of young people becoming employed in temporary or part-time jobs.

While that increase has occurred, evidence from recent and ongoing research focusing on employers' recruitment and training policies and practices points to employers experiencing considerable difficulties in attracting 'suitable' young people to Modern Apprenticeships, despite strenuous and innovative attempts to extol the virtues of the apprenticeship route. Certainly, in industries such as construction, textiles and other parts of manufacturing, where there is a tradition of apprenticeship, employers voice their anxieties about attracting young people. Maguire (1998) contends that 'the introduction of Modern Apprenticeships, with the offer of higher level training packages to young people, has done little to eradicate the problem'. In echoes of complaints about the inadequacies of the education system which have been symptomatic of many employers' perceptions over the years, there is a belief that schools actively discourage young people from entering these 'declining' industries. This is occurring at a time when they are aware of potential problems emanating from the need to replenish skills being lost through the ageing of the workforce, as well as from the existence of skill shortages. Crucially, those responsible for recruitment, who continue to target their efforts almost exclusively at 16-year-olds, have a very clear idea of the qualities and qualifications they are seeking in their recruitment of modern apprentices. Their inability to satisfy their immediate recruitment requirements and, more importantly, their long-term skill needs, is largely attributed to the fact that the young people who would formerly have applied and been deemed suitable for these opportunities, are now more likely to remain within the education system, with encouragement from schools, colleges and parents. At the same time, the need for recruits to Modern Apprenticeships to be capable of achieving NVQ level 3 (and funding being dependent on that achievement) means that, if anything, they are seeking more able and better qualified 16-year-olds than had previously been the case. There is, thus, growing disquiet among employers about the ability of Modern Apprenticeships to contribute to the future supply of employees with intermediate-level skills.

The recent assertion by Baroness Blackstone, Minister for Education in the Lords, that 'there is scope for many 16- and 17-year-olds to follow a broader and more demanding curriculum', with its echoes of support for Sir Ron Dearing's report which advocated an increase in the proportion of the less academically able staying on in post-compulsory education, would suggest that many employers may, in future, experience even greater difficulty in attracting young people to Modern Apprenticeships. Before Modern Apprenticeships disappear into a black hole created by a collision of competing policy options, it would seem appropriate to assess their efficacy in offering worthwhile career opportunities for young people, their potential role in satisfying the skill needs of employers and the threats posed by other trends. Few, if any, training policy initiatives introduced in the last 20 years have achieved such high 'approval' ratings from all sides – trainees, employers, trade unions – as Modern Apprenticeships. It may be perceived as a case of wilful neglect if such an opportunity to make a significant contribution to addressing acknowledged current and future skill deficiencies were to be missed.

References

Adams, K (1996) Modern Apprenticeships: the long haul to quality training, *Employee Development Bulletin*, August, pp 4–10

CBI (1989) *Towards a Skills Revolution: Report of the Vocational Education and Training Task Force*, Confederation of British Industry, London

Department for Education and Employment (DfEE) (1998a) *Moving On: Pathways taken by young people beyond 16. The Careers Service Activity Survey 1997*, DfEE, London

DfEE (1998b) *Labour Market and Skill Trends 1996/1997*, DfEE, London

ENTRA (1996) *The Modern Apprenticeship for Engineering*, 3, Engineering Training Authority, Watford

Evans, K, Hodkinson, P, Keep, E, Maguire, M, Raffe, D, Rainbird, H, Senker, P and Unwin, L (1997) *Working to learn: A work-based route to learning for young people*, Institute of Personnel and Development, London

Everett, M and Leman, S (1995) Modern Apprenticeships: the experience so far, *Employment Gazette*, June, pp 263–67

Everett, M, Leman, S, Unwin, L and Wellington, J (1996) Modern Apprenticeships: further lessons from the prototypes, *Labour Market Trends*, **104** (2), pp 55–61

Financial Times, 24 March 1997

Gospel, H (1998) The revival of apprenticeship training in Britain?, *British Journal of Industrial Relations*, **36** (3), pp 435–57

Hasluck, C, Hogarth, T, Maguire, M and Pitcher, J (1997) *Modern Apprenticeships: A survey of employers, Research Studies RS53*, DfEE, London

Hutton, W (1995) *The State We're In*, Vintage, London

IDS (1995) *Modern Apprenticeships, Study 592*, Incomes Data Services, London

IDS (1997) *Modern Apprenticeships, Study 620*, Incomes Data Services, London

IER (1997) *Review of the Economy and Employment 1997*, Institute for Employment Research, University of Warwick

Keep, E and Mayhew, K (1994) UK training policy – assumptions and reality, in *The Skills Gap and Economic Activity*, ed A Booth and D J Snower, Cambridge University Press, Cambridge

Maclagan, I (1996) How successful are Modern Apprenticeships?, *Working Brief*, March, **72**, pp 14–16

Maguire, M and Maguire, S (1997) Young people and the labour market, in *Youth, the 'Underclass' and Social Exclusion*, ed R MacDonald, Routledge, London

Maguire, S (1998) *The Youth Labour Market Revisited*, unpublished draft, Warwick Business School, University of Warwick

Porter, M (1990) *The Competitive Advantage of Nations*, Macmillan, Basingstoke

Roberts, K (1995) *Youth and Employment in Modern Britain*, Oxford University Press, Oxford

Steedman, H and Wagner, K (1987) A second look at productivity, machinery and skills in Britain and Germany, *National Institute Economic Review*, **128**

12

Modern Apprentices in College. So What's New?

Prue Huddleston

Apprentices in colleges: a long history

There is nothing new about the relationship between apprentice training and further education (FE) colleges; indeed the provision of off-the-job training for craft and technician apprentices is at the heart of the history of FE. The Mechanics' Institutes of the 19th century were established for the purpose of providing training, on a part-time basis, for those employed across the range of manufacturing industries seeking to gain qualifications. The central purpose of these institutions was to provide technical education, especially in engineering, for working men. As the century progressed, the numbers of such institutions grew in order to provide for the training needs of those employed within the rapidly growing industrial sector. The absence of a system of technical education, such as those in place in Germany and the USA, was also seen to be one of the causes of Britain's relative decline *vis-à-vis* its competitors in terms of its manufacturing output. By 1900, Great Britain had been surpassed by Germany and the USA in the production of steel; it had already been overtaken by the USA in the production of coal.

The technical schools and colleges in competitor nations were more numerous, reputedly more progressive and more prestigious than anything this country had to offer. The British response was a piecemeal development of technical education, including a system of day-continuation schools which youths between the ages of 14 and 16 could be compelled to attend for at least one day a week. These, however, fell victim to the economic reforms of 1921–22, the so-called 'Geddes' Axe', named after the chairman of the committee recommending the cuts, Sir Eric Geddes. Subsequently, the growth of the technical colleges was very much dependent upon the demands of local employers and local people for vocational training. Most students attended on a part-time basis, either through day release from the employer, or by attendance at evening classes. Sometimes this required up to five or more years' attendance in order to progress through the various levels of craft and technician training, eventually perhaps emerging with a Higher National Certificate qualification.

Most of these day release students were male, apprenticed to manufacturing employers and working within manual trades. They worked towards recognized and well-established qualifications, such as those offered by the City & Guilds of London Institute (CGLI), or for sector or occupationally specific qualifications, for example, the Institute of Meat. These courses and their students were the 'bread and butter' of FE college provision. There remained a fairly stable clientele which annually presented itself at enrolment and progressed through the various course levels until apprenticeship and qualifications were completed. 'By 1957, more than 400,000 employees were being released from work for part-time training in college' (Hall, 1990: 4). The college provision was characterized by a lack of flexibility, students having to attend when courses were offered and for prescribed lengths of time. Course content changed little from one year to the next, syllabi being tightly prescribed by the awarding and examining bodies. There was a nodding recognition to occupational relevance and to employers' needs through such structures as 'industrial liaison groups', 'employers' panels' and similar bodies.

By the early 1970s there had been a steady growth in other areas of provision within the FE sector. Full-time student numbers began to increase as colleges extended their range of provision to include GCE A- and O-level programmes and full-time vocational courses. Engineering courses declined as full-time business and commercial courses grew. As the economic recession bit, the numbers of apprentices began to decline and this soon impacted upon the FE sector. The TUC estimates that during the period 1978 to 1994 apprenticeships fell by 66 per cent. In the manufacturing sector it suggests that between 1979 and 1990 the cutback was as much as 60 per cent, ' a cut far greater then the decline of jobs in the sector' (TUC, 1995: 1).

Colleges were now faced with the challenge of attracting new clients: 'they could no longer rely upon a steady flow of apprentices year on year to fill the college workshops and classrooms' (Huddleston, 1998: 277). Some of the new students were going to come through the series of government schemes and initiatives designed to address the problems of youth and adult unemployment. This placed colleges in new relationships with both local and central government, through such agencies as the Manpower Services Commission (MSC), the Department of Employment and, in the early 1990s, through the new Training and Enterprise Councils (TECs). It is through the TECs that the Modern Apprenticeships are delivered and colleges have had to forge relationships with them and with other partners in order to ensure that they can contribute to the vocational education and training of this new generation of apprentices.

Modern Apprenticeships

In September 1994, prototype Modern Apprenticeships were introduced with the intention of providing young people with a route to achieve National Vocational Qualifications (NVQs) to level 3 or above, with the opportunity of progression into higher education (HE). This was to be achieved through a partnership between Industry Training Organizations (ITOs), TECs, employers and training providers. It was always assumed that the FE sector, as a leading provider of vocational education and training, would have an important role to play in the delivery of the off-the-job component of Modern Apprenticeships (Huddleston, 1998).

The qualification frameworks were designed by the relevant ITO and designated lead TECs. The frameworks were approved by a steering group of ITO and TEC representatives convened by the DfEE (Everett *et al*, 1996). Employers were then encouraged, with the aid of government funding, to participate in the scheme. The Careers Services were charged with the responsibility of marketing the scheme as an attractive option to young people who might otherwise be considering remaining in full-time education post-16. The early marketing of the scheme was criticized for its lack of focus (DfEE, 1997). This study emphasized the need for Careers Service providers to work in conjunction with schools to 'ensure that MAs are impartially presented as a viable option to 16/17 year olds, emphasizing "Employment with Training" and associated NVQs' (p 8).

Since each occupational sector made a different response to the design of its Modern Apprenticeship there was, unsurprisingly, a significant variation in design across different Modern Apprenticeships. In addition to the relevant NVQs for the sector, different ITOs included full, or units of, General National Vocational Qualifications (GNVQ) and key skills. One leading motor manufacturer, for example, includes foreign languages units as well.

When the prototypes were launched in September 1994, 14 industry sectors were represented; by July 1998, 73 industry frameworks were available. According to the DfEE Modern Apprenticeship database (31 July 1998) there were 84,911 modern apprentice starts in 1997–98, of whom 44,249 were male and 40,662 were female. The age on entry ranged from 16 to 25 with 18.5 per cent entering at 16; 18.9 per cent at 17; and 31.8 per cent between the ages of 20 and 25. Thirty-one per cent of the young people had previously been on a Youth Training scheme; 97.9 per cent had employed status; 2.9 per cent had disabilities; and 4.5 per cent were drawn from ethnic minority groups (DfEE Modern Apprenticeship Database, July 1998).

Modern Apprenticeships cover an extremely wide range of occupations including those sectors which have traditionally offered apprenticeships, for example engineering, and those which have no tradition of apprenticeship, for example retailing and child care. The numbers on such programmes also vary enormously according to the occupational area, local labour market conditions, competing post-16 options, the attitude of local employers and the general level of awareness of Modern Apprenticeships and their potential benefits (DfEE, 1997).

In introducing Modern Apprenticeships, the then Head of Youth and Education policy at the Employment Department, Valerie Bayliss, stated that: 'Modern Apprenticeships combine work-based qualifications and learning methods with the best features of traditional apprenticeship' (Bayliss, 1994: 23). In short, they are intended to provide high-quality training in technical skills leading to an NVQ level 3 qualification and employment. They include an undertaking on the part of the employer to provide worthwhile training which is drawn up in the form of an individual training plan and signed by all parties, thus agreeing to see the training through to its conclusion. In some regions the local TEC cements this relationship by inviting apprentices, their parents and employers to an induction evening, thus providing a symbolic reminder, perhaps, of the 'golden age' of apprenticeship.

There is no limit on the amount of time required to gain the full qualification, although it is expected that in most cases the training would be completed within two-and-a-half to three years. I have seen a variation of six months in the time taken to complete by different young persons on the same scheme. Learners are, therefore, able to proceed at the most appropriate pace to their learning needs.

In drawing up the training plans, consideration has to be given to the appropriate balance of on- and off-the-job training and the appropriateness of the training providers. FE as an established, indeed, the largest provider of vocational education and training should be well placed to fulfil a role within the delivery of Modern Apprenticeships. The next section will attempt to examine the nature of that role within the context of a number of colleges situated in the West Midlands.

Modern colleges, Modern Apprenticeships?

Of the 2.4 million students enrolled on 1 November 1997 at colleges in the FE sector in England (FEFC, 1998) it is impossible to say how many were modern apprentices: 'Since MAs have employed status, their learning programmes will not normally attract FEFC funding, except where additional education and training is provided' (Armstrong, 1996). Their numbers are more likely to be included in the 0.4 million students enrolled on provision not funded by the Council (FEFC, 1998), although distinctions are not always that clear cut. Armstrong (1996) suggests that colleges do not see Modern Apprenticeships as a way of making money; nevertheless, there appear to be a number of ways in which colleges can contribute to the development of programmes.

Linkages with local employers and with the local TEC appear to be critical in ensuring FE involvement in Modern Apprenticeship schemes. Colleges are in competition with other training providers and with in-company training and, therefore, have to prove that they can deliver a cost-effective service which reflects current industry needs and standards. The FEFC Chief Inspector's report draws attention to the need for colleges to forge greater links with employers and 'to sharpen the relevance of their curriculum to industrial needs' (FEFC, 1997: 3).

In a survey[1] I conducted in two Midlands colleges delivering parts of a Modern Apprenticeship Engineering Manufacture programme (see Huddleston, 1998), college staff had undertaken company placements and developed joint teaching assignments in collaboration with company staff. This had proved a significant motivator to all staff involved and had provided college staff with much-needed experience of current practice. Nevertheless, the exercise was extremely time-consuming and was dependent upon the goodwill and commitment of both company and college personnel.

Colleges can access local employers through the Modern Apprenticeship networks and use the opportunity to market other areas of college provision. For example, colleges are already major providers of assessor training; if Modern Apprenticeships are to be increasingly assessed in the workplace then this implies a significant demand for the training of workplace assessors. Several companies visited during the survey found the lack of trained workplace assessors a significant barrier to the implementation of their Modern Apprenticeships. Some colleges have been able to work creatively and to deliver training and assessment on company premises; one college recognized for its work within the hotel and catering sector was able to successfully market its services to small hotels and boarding houses which had accepted modern apprentices.

A defining feature of the provision which colleges can offer the Modern Apprenticeship will be the size of the cohort. A large employer, with a significant number of modern apprentices, will be able to access a programme specially designed for company needs. In the colleges visited, groups of students, usually about 15 in number, were being taught on programmes designed jointly by company and college staff, using equipment provided by the company. In other programmes a heterogeneous mix of students was observed 'in-filling' on courses which bore little resemblance to their normal workplace experience. Some young people were unsure of the programme they were following. The wide diversity of schemes available within the Modern Apprenticeship, designed to provide a closer alignment with the realities of workplaces in differing sectors, has made it difficult, in some cases, for colleges to provide individually tailored programmes: they are simply too costly. In other cases, there are simply too few students following that pathway.

Each individual modern apprentice's training plan will include: formal vocational training; work-based skills development; and appropriate vocational education. The local FE college may be able to provide some or all of these. If part of the programme involves training using up-to-date industry-standard equipment, some colleges may have difficulty in providing adequate experience. The Chief Inspector's Report 1996–97 draws attention to the fact that: 'Although heavy equipment in areas such as engineering is satisfactory for students to work with, much of it now fails to meet industry standards and very few colleges have plans for its replacement' (FEFC, 1997: 9). However, in areas such as hotel and catering and hairdressing, links between colleges and industry were described as 'generally good'.

The colleges visited in the course of the study had benefited greatly from the injection of new equipment which the employer had provided. This allowed apprentices to work on the same standard of equipment as that which they would find in the workplace; it was regularly replaced and updated, and it enabled staff to keep abreast of current developments in design and technology. In contrast, a group of retail trainees did not have access within the college to an industry-standard till.

Colleges should be well placed to provide the key skills elements within the individual training plans. This is something which employers interviewed during the course of the study found difficult to comprehend. It should be said that the lack of comprehension extended to the apprentices themselves, and sometimes even to college staff. In some cases key skills were taught as separate subjects; I observed a series of dull and uninspiring series of mathematics classes supposedly covering the numeracy key skill. In other examples use was made of the vocational education components to identify key skills, and teamwork and problem solving were addressed through a residential outward-bound experience. Such findings are not restricted to Modern Apprenticeship programmes but reflect a general concern expressed by a recent FEFC report:

> Many of the difficulties facing teachers and students in developing and assessing core skills (now Key Skills) arose from the language used to describe the criteria, the variety of levels available, the problems associated with making core skills an integrated part of assignments and the burden of recording achievement.
>
> (1995: 22)

Although employers' complaints about the lack of young people's skills and attitudes abound (Keep and Huddleston, 1998) it is often these very components of the training for which the employer is unwilling to pay. The research indicated that where college and company staff had worked closely together on the design of assignments and had identified opportunities for key skill development, then the accreditation of key skills was far more easily achieved.

The construction of a portfolio of evidence is an integral part of both the NVQ and the GNVQ assessment process. Colleges are well placed to assist modern apprentices in portfolio development and to work with workplace assessors on portfolio building and verification. In the colleges visited, the construction of portfolios was one of the most common problems and grievances aired by apprentices. Complaints were made about the excessive paperwork and jargon entailed in their compilation.

If colleges are to play a role in the delivery of Modern Apprenticeships, particularly against a background of increasing competition from other training providers, then they have to ensure that college staff are adequately qualified and experienced in the programme areas which they seek to deliver. FEFC (1995: 23) concludes that currently: 'The industrial and professional experience of many staff is outdated and few colleges have schemes to rectify this.' The integration of the on- and off-the-job components of the Modern Apprenticeship programme and the exchange of staff between the two may help to provide the necessary staff development and professional updating. Unless colleges are able to achieve this then their offering may compare unfavourably with that offered by private training providers.

Apprentices or students?

Old apprenticeships were closely aligned with the company in which they were taking place. Thus, young people described themselves as a 'Rolls Royce apprentice' or a 'British Leyland apprentice', for example. This was usually accompanied by a certain amount of pride, dependent, of course, upon the company involved. Apprenticeships were eagerly sought not just for the formal training they provided but for the opportunities they afforded young people to become part of the recognized, local social and occupational structure. They enabled the young people, in other words, to become part of what Lave and Wenger (1991) have described as the 'community of practice'. Through their associations with those already recognized as skilled craftspeople, among whose number were frequently to be found relatives and friends, the young apprentices were initiated into the roles and responsibilities expected of the trained craftsperson. These often extended to areas beyond simple workplace competence.

What has been described here reflects an apprenticeship system essentially male-dominated and chiefly associated with blue-collar manufacturing employment. There were, of course, a few other apprenticeships which did not quite fit this model. Hairdressing, for example, has had a long history of apprenticeship but is different in many ways from the manufacturing apprenticeships: the industry is characterized by female employment and most employers are small businesses.

FE colleges were often heavily involved in the training of traditional apprentices. Some colleges were established for the sole purpose of providing vocational education and training for a specific occupational sector, for example, Barnsley College was established to provide training for the local mining industry and Lowestoft College for the local fishing industry (Huddleston and Unwin, 1997). There were, of course, companies which did not use colleges but which provided their own off-the-job training through their own training schools.

FE's role in the delivery of traditional apprenticeships was often remote from the reality of the shopfloor. The reasons for this lay in the syllabus content of many of the examining boards, which bore little resemblance to existing practice, and in the lack of recent and relevant experience of college teaching staff. For example, a City & Guilds syllabus for hairdressing in the 1980s still contained techniques which had been current in the 1930s and which would only be required by those employed within theatre or television. Similarly, the syllabus for confectionery included skills which, outside the college, could rarely be practised except in an Austrian or Swiss patisserie and which did not reflect the reality of plant bakeries.

Nevertheless, there was a sense in which progression through the college programme, albeit a lengthy one, was seen as a 'rite of passage' to the achievement of full craftsperson status since it provided the necessary credentials for entry into the craft, or technician, occupation. The qualifications were well recognized and well understood by those within the industries concerned. There was a clear view of what an apprenticeship was.

The rationale of Modern Apprenticeships is different in several ways from the traditional apprenticeship, for example, in the opportunity it provides for progression from the craft to technician and, potentially, to graduate level. As one training and development manager, based within the design function of the motor manufacturing company in our survey, put it: 'A 16-year-old has the possibility of developing into the engineer of tomorrow – there's no limit and no pigeon-holing as was the case with YT.' Although this may be regarded as a desirable opportunity for the apprentices themselves, there was a clear distinction in the views expressed by the apprentices interviewed between those following an NVQ level 3 route and those following an NVQ level 4 route. Apprentices on the NVQ 3 pathway often saw themselves as essentially practical people; some of them appeared to resent the amount of time spent on what they described as 'writing and assessment'. They felt that the workload was too heavily biased towards written work, in particular the completion of the NVQ and GNVQ portfolios. One young man suggested that: 'Time should be spent on the most relevant areas of work... subjects should be prioritized so that we don't do irrelevant stuff'.

Another apprentice complained about the time he spent 'sorting paper'. Referring to the compilation of his portfolio, he continued: 'It was a total nightmare to start with; we had sheets and sheets we did not know what to do with.' He said he had applied for the apprenticeship because he thought it would enable him to practise and develop practical skills; he saw himself essentially as a 'practical person'.

Some of these views were shared by shopfloor supervisors interviewed during the course of the research, particularly those working within production and maintenance areas. They were concerned that an over-emphasis on the possibility of progression would lose good 'craft' people from the shopfloor. One supervisor remarked: 'We don't want graduates, we want practical people.' Others felt that the off-the-job training element could have been better provided by the company, 'as it always used to be', than by colleges. It is important to recognize, however, that some of the respondents were former company trainers and were unhappy about relinquishing control of the training, and to some extent the apprentices, to the colleges.

Unwin suggests that one of the perceived attractions of apprenticeships was that they provided opportunities for a 'job with an employer who would take you under his/her wing and teach you all you needed to know' (1996: 57). Responses varied among those interviewed in this study as to how much they felt part of their company. In the sample from the large motor manufacturer, company loyalty appeared strong, to the extent that all apprentices wore company workwear in college. This extended to the college staff who were teaching on the programmes. There was even some healthy rivalry with apprentices from another motor manufacturer who also wore their company's workwear and were taught by different staff, again wearing the corporate uniform.

To this extent it appears that these apprentices saw themselves very much as company people, not as students. The college workshops in which they were training had been refurbished and equipped by the companies, and they involved themselves very little in other aspects of college life. When asked if they made use of the college's Learning Resources Centre, some apprentices answered: 'What Learning Resources Centre?'; others said: 'The staff in there aren't helpful'. However, the majority of them were satisfied with the level of resources provided and with the willingness of staff to help them with assignments.

Unsurprisingly, apprentices who were attending on a day release basis found it more difficult to integrate into college life, whereas those attending for a six-month block-release found it easier. Even so, company identity and loyalty were strong. The in-company experience had been extended into the college through the dedicated workshops, the company-loaned equipment, the corporate uniforms and, perhaps most significantly, the development of work-based assignments. The college experience had become part of what Lave and Wenger (1991) describe as 'legitimate peripheral participation'. For individual apprentices coming from smaller employers the experience appeared quite different: some had no real image of themselves either as students or apprentices.

College work or real work?

In describing traditional apprenticeships, Venables (1974) suggests that the training provided by FE colleges could be something of a 'hit and miss' affair in terms of the relationship between the content of college programmes and workplace practice. Earlier in this chapter reference was made to FEFC concerns about the current workplace relevance of some college provision and of the experience of college staff. During the course of this research the relationship between college programmes and workplace experience was investigated. Some striking differences emerged. The alignment between college and workplace was usually closer where companies had been able to negotiate bespoke programmes for their apprentices; otherwise, apprentices had simply to fit in with what was on offer. This does not necessarily imply that the offering was inappropriate, or irrelevant – it suggests that the linkage may be harder for the learner to make.

Traditionally, learning within classrooms and learning within workplaces have been seen as two rather different things, the former relying heavily upon a transmission pedagogy and concerned essentially with the transfer of knowledge with little reference to context, whereas the latter is heavily context-dependent and involves 'learning by doing' and 'learning by watching', with a 'master' acting as both role model and mentor. (For a fuller discussion see Guile and Young, Chapter 8 in this book.) There is a sense in which FE colleges inhabit a world at the juncture of these two models since their *raison d'être* is to provide realistic and relevant vocational education and training. This implies that knowledge must be contextualized and that learners must be encouraged to draw out learning from their work-based experience in the same way in which they need to apply knowledge learned in classrooms to workplace contexts and, most importantly, to see the relationship between the two.

This requires both those in companies and those in colleges to see Modern Apprenticeships as a holistic model which involves integrated on- and off-the-job training. Two of the colleges visited during the course of this study had undertaken an extensive mapping exercise in conjunction with company personnel in order to identify placement opportunities and associated potential learning outcomes. Assignments had been designed as a result of the exercise and the apprentices were expected to complete these with the assistance of both college staff and workplace supervisors. The fact that some workplace supervisors still saw these work-based assignments as 'college work' – 'Isn't that college work, you shouldn't be doing that here' (line manager, talking about a work-based assignment) – suggests that there is still some distance to go before the integrated rationale of Modern Apprenticeships is fully appreciated and accepted by those used to the traditional apprenticeship model. Underlying this are much deeper historical and cultural perceptions about the nature of apprenticeship.

There were marked differences in perceptions held in different business units of the motor manufacturing company about the appropriateness of this new model of apprenticeship. Concerns were raised by those within production and maintenance areas that the new model gave insufficient attention to 'craft' training. As one training manager said:

> This type of programme needs a big commitment from staff. Some of the staff cannot see the benefits of the new scheme, particularly Pathway 3 [the old 'craft route']. Older employees appear to prefer the old scheme. But this course is better suited to business needs. The GNVQ units meet business needs.

Another company training officer drew attention to the need for staff development for workplace supervisors in order to understand and cope with the assessment regime associated with NVQ and GNVQ:

> There needs to be some skills development for our own people in order for them to understand and carry out workplace assessment, particularly for those dealing with the Pathway 3 apprentices. Some of these apprentices will not be adequately trained for the job, they will need extra units, for example in pneumatics and hydraulics. These will have to be taught on site. The college course is basic rather than specialist, this reflects the differences across different business units.

The Modern Apprenticeship is designed to be an integrated programme of vocational education and training which will allow progression from craft to technician, and possibly to graduate, levels. This is markedly different from the way in which old apprenticeships were perceived by those working in traditional 'craft' areas. It is here that resistance to the new model appeared most marked. A training manager responsible for Modern Apprenticeships within a maintenance area indicated some of the potential problems which he saw as inherent in the new model:

> Line managers need educating about Modern Apprenticeships and about NVQ in general, the system is bureaucratic and administrative. Modern Apprenticeship requires written and verbal skills which are not needed for NVQ 3.

Key skills, including communication, form an integral part of all Modern Apprenticeship frameworks. This suggests that there is some distance to go in transmitting the rationale of Modern Apprenticeships to those involved in shopfloor delivery of the programme and in gaining their acceptance. Interviews held with apprentices from the same business unit suggested that this view was shared by them; how much of it had been internalized from remarks made by supervisors was, of course, impossible to determine. The response of those working within the design function was markedly different, company personnel describing the FE contribution as 'Good practical education which incorporates workplace experience'.

The role of the 'master' was clearly central to the rationale of traditional apprenticeships. In the Modern Apprenticeship model this role may not be clearly defined and may, in some cases, not exist. The modern apprentices within the car manufacturing company were provided with a range of role models and a company mentor to support them through the programme. Nevertheless, this support was patchy and it was clear that there would need to be further encouragement of line managers to take a more active role, particularly in workplace assessment. The programme design often requires apprentices to move from department to department throughout the training; it is therefore difficult to build relationships with particular 'masters'. Where the mentorship programme was fully developed the young people responded very positively to the support which mentors provided, reporting: 'My mentor's brilliant', 'He's like a really big wheel in the company, but I can call him with any problems', 'He helps me with my assignments'.

The role of college tutors as 'quasi masters' would merit further investigation. Among some of the college staff interviewed were those who, by constant association with the company involved, acted as if they were company personnel. In fact, it became clear that their job security might indeed depend upon the company's continued use of the college for apprenticeship training. They had certainly benefited from considerable staff development and professional updating as a result of their involvement. They were eager to retain the apprenticeship training contract within the college and confirmed that they would have been unable to undertake the workshop refurbishment without the company's support, both in cash and kind. It was clear that staff wished my research to reflect the colleges in a favourable light.

So what's new?

Fuller and Unwin (1998: 164) have pointed out that:

> There is an explicit intention in the MA to promote learning on- and off-the-job... There is also an attempt to develop an inclusive approach to delivery... No mechanism is suggested for ensuring that workplace and college-based colleagues collaborate in developing a curriculum, planning its delivery and evaluating the quality of provision. This allows the possibility that on- and off-the-job learning remains unintegrated, with providers both at work and college working to discharge narrowly conceived roles and responsibilities.

This research has attempted to assess the extent to which a small number of Midlands colleges have been able to develop integrated Modern Apprenticeship programmes for client companies. Conclusions, at this stage, are tentative since the college sample was small and the range of companies limited; nevertheless, one company is a major Midlands-based employer and has a long history of apprenticeship training. It is, therefore, possible to highlight some similarities to and differences from the traditional model.

Colleges were often heavily involved in the off-the-job training elements of traditional apprenticeships; the extent to which this was integrated into the on-the-job components is a matter for conjecture (Venables, 1974). The integration of the on- and off-the-job components within Modern Apprenticeships appears to be patchy, responses in this sample ranging from, 'I have never used anything I've learned at college' to, 'Everything was realistic, relevant and in context'.

From the interviews with college staff, it appears that significant efforts are being made, certainly within the engineering manufacture framework, to integrate the on- and off-the-job components, but that integration is not fully complete. The exercise was time-consuming and required the commitment of a large number of company personnel across different locations and business units. This commitment appears variable because, as one production supervisor put it: 'Young person development does not stop the track'. In the design and development area a complete mapping exercise had been jointly undertaken by company and college staff and 22 work-based assignments identified. These were eventually jointly assessed.

All those apprentices interviewed from the large car manufacturer felt that most college staff were familiar with current company practice. Where apprentices were coming from smaller manufacturers then lecturers' specific company knowledge appeared less secure, and was more general in nature. This supports the view that colleges can only really provide a fully integrated programme that is company-specific when a company is large enough and has sufficient resources to contract a specially designed programme. Some colleges, however, identified the potential risks involved in 'putting all the college's eggs into one Modern Apprenticeship basket' since this could result in financial loss should that company decide to withdraw.

A distinctive feature of the Modern Apprenticeship is the integration of key skills units within its design. This has clearly proved problematic in its conceptualization and delivery, the worst manifestations appearing as isolated, decontextualized maths and English classes. In the best integrated schemes key skill development opportunities had been identified in workplace contexts. This in turn allows the possibility 'to provide young entrants with a broader and more flexible range of skills' (Ernst and Young, 1995: 10). It is clear that this message needs to be transmitted to shopfloor supervisors and line managers who do not always appreciate the importance of what Fuller and Unwin describe as 'expansive learning' (1998).

Old apprenticeships tended to be male dominated. Although early Modern Apprenticeship entrants were predominantly male, the balance has now, to some extent, been redressed, with 44,249 male and 40,662 female starts in 1997–98 (DfEE Modern Apprenticeship Database, July 1998). The gender balance is skewed towards specific occupational sectors, however. In engineering manufacture entrants are still predominantly male. The female representation is strongest in areas such as child care and health;

here there is no tradition of apprenticeship and, therefore, programmes are being designed without reference to any progenitors. They do not have what Guile and Young (1998) describe as the 'institution of apprenticeship', in other words the combination of both formal and informal learning experiences, usually under the guidance and supervision of an established 'master', which provide the necessary pre-conditions for entry into the 'community of practice'.

Colleges have a great deal of experience in providing vocational education and training for a diverse range of clients and they should, therefore, be well placed to design and deliver effective Modern Apprenticeship programmes. Much will depend upon the relationships colleges are able to forge with their local TECs and with employers. Funding may also be an important factor in determining whether or not colleges wish to become involved. Armstrong (1996) suggests that there may be some indirect benefits to colleges from their involvement with Modern Apprenticeships, for example, through improved industry links which may in turn lead to further work.

Colleges can help companies with the training of workplace assessors; this was identified as a priority during the course of the research. If companies are to increasingly take on the responsibility of assessing not only apprentices but all company personnel, then they will require help in building that capacity. This can be undertaken by college staff on company premises, and some were already doing this. It also helps to forge a closer relationship between colleges and industrial partners and gives recognition to the fact that learning occurs in a range of different contexts.

The integration of the college and company components of Modern Apprenticeship programmes will be crucial to ensuring that colleges become part of the extended 'community of practice'. The research suggests that some colleges are already doing this, moving towards more flexible models of delivery and ensuring that their provision is relevant to current industrial needs. Others had decided that Modern Apprenticeships were not for them or, if they were, then the apprentices would have to fit in with the provision already offered.

Armstrong suggests that 'modern apprenticeships are intended to be industry-driven and employer-led. As such they are like traditional apprenticeships to which FE could respond' (1996: 4). It appears that FE could also have a role to play in the delivery of the Modern Apprenticeship. Armstrong outlines three possible models for college involvement:

1. as 'partners' – this was certainly the case in the car manufacturing company;
2. as 'suppliers', with colleges providing a range of finite services, such as assessor training or additional NVQ units – this was found in the case of the college working with the hospitality industry; or
3. as 'enablers' actively promoting Modern Apprenticeships to employers – none of this type was found within the sample investigated.

Note

1. The research, sponsored by a leading motor manufacturer with sites around the Midlands, involved large-scale quantitative and qualitative analysis of responses from modern apprentices, college staff, company training and development personnel and workplace supervisors to the engineering manufacture Modern Apprenticeship. The company has apprentices placed around three separate sites and within five different business units.

References

Armstrong, P (1996) Back to the future, *FEDA Bulletin*, **1** (2)

Bayliss, V (1994) Employers hold the key, *Training Tomorrow*, October, pp 23–24

Department for Education and Employment (DfEE) (1997) *Modern Apprenticeships: Emerging good practice*, QPID Study Report 61, DfEE, London

DfEE (1998) *Modern Apprenticeship Database*, July, DfEE, London

Ernst and Young (1995) *The Evaluation of the Modern Apprenticeship Prototypes*, Final Report, October, DfEE, London

Everett, M *et al* (1996) Modern Apprenticeships: further lessons from the prototypes, *Labour Market Trends*, **104** (2), pp 55–61

FEFC (1995) *General National Vocational Qualifications in the Further Education Sector in England*, FEFC, Coventry

FEFC (1997) *Quality and Standards in Further Education in England: The Chief Inspector's Report*, FEFC, Coventry

FEFC (1998) *FEFC Annual Report*, FEFC, Coventry

Fuller, A and Unwin, L (1998) Reconceptualizing apprenticeship: exploring the relationship between work and learning, *Journal of Vocational Education and Training*, **50** (2), pp 153–73

Guile, D and Young, M (1998) Apprenticeship as a conceptual basis for a social theory of learning, *Journal of Vocational Education and Training*, **50** (2), pp 173–93

Hall, V (1990) *Maintained Further Education in the United Kingdom*, Further Education Staff College, Bristol

Huddleston, P (1998) Modern Apprentices in college: something old, something new, *Journal of Vocational Education and Training*, **50** (2), pp 277–89

Huddleston, P and Unwin, L (1997) *Teaching and Learning in Further Education: Change and diversity*, Routledge, London

Keep, E and Huddleston, P (1998) What do employers want? Questions more easily asked than answered, paper presented at the International Partnership conference, Trondheim, Norway, July

Lave, J and Wenger, E (1991) *Situated Learning: Legitimate peripheral participation*, Cambridge University Press, Cambridge

TUC (1995) *Modern Apprenticeships: A negotiator's guide*, TUC, London

Unwin, L (1996) Employer-led realities: apprenticeship past and present, *Journal of Vocational Education and Training*, **48**, pp 57–60

Venables, E (1974) *Apprentices Out of Their Time*, Faber & Faber, London

13

Working To Learn: An Holistic Approach to Young People's Education and Training

*Peter Senker, Helen Rainbird, Karen Evans, Phil Hodkinson, Ewart Keep,
Malcolm Maguire, David Raffe and Lorna Unwin*

Introduction

How should the government improve the system of education and training of young people who finish their full-time education between the ages of 16 and 19, to make it better for the young people involved, better for the economy and better for society as a whole? This was the question we addressed in our 'Working to Learn' report (Evans *et al*, 1997).

We believed that there were serious deficiencies in government policy, and that it was important for the views of employers, young people, training providers and others concerned, which have been assembled in numerous research studies, to be marshalled and brought to the attention of policy-makers. The 'Working to Learn' report summarized in this chapter analyses deficiencies of current policies and makes out a strong case for fundamental reform.

The Conservative Government's approach seemed to be based on the assumption that we were making gradual progress in the right direction. From this perspective, further fine-tuning was all that was needed. The Labour Government has so far adopted a similar attitude. It is, indeed, introducing several major new initiatives, such as the New Deal, the University for Industry and Individual Learning Accounts. A significant development has been the establishment of a statutory right to time off for paid educational leave for 16- and 17-year-olds. Recently, the Local Government Association, the Further Education Funding Council and Training and Enterprise Councils agreed to give a right to three years' free education to everyone under 25 (Bright, 1998). These measures include some steps in the right direction. However, these piecemeal initiatives do not represent a coherent strategy to tackle the fundamental problems afflicting work-based learning. We believe that such a strategy is needed, and present our case in this chapter.

We begin by outlining the reasons why we think that new proposals are needed, from the point of view both of individual young people and the national economy. Despite numerous attempts at reform, the pattern of provision remains incoherent, and international comparisons show that the quality of much of what is on offer to young entrants to the workforce in this country is inferior. Next we consider some of the major changes within the economy and the youth labour market which the development of policy has so lamentably failed to match. Many initiatives have suffered because they were predicated on too simplistic a notion of the problems requiring solution. The ineffectiveness of policy has also partly been a consequence of conflicting visions of economic development underlying policy and resulting in confusion – one view stressing the value of a skilled workforce as the sole source of sustainable long-term competition, the other seeking the benefits for enterprise which could flow from the availability of deregulated, flexible and casualized labour.

The long-standing government commitment to voluntarism which is at the root of many problems is then discussed. While employers have extremely important roles in relation to every aspect of employment and training, voluntarism fails to take account of the legitimate and substantial interests of other stakeholders. For example, the wider public interest requires that young people be given broader and better education and training than most employers are ever likely to provide in view of their own relatively short-term private interests.

After outlining the case for an holistic approach to the development of a high quality work-based route, the 'Working to Learn' proposals are presented in outline. Admittedly, the direct costs of meeting young people's needs for broader education and training would be significantly higher than at present. However, reducing the massive and excessive administrative costs in the present system could release funds to be used for these purposes. In contrast, the economic and social costs of continuing on the present path are likely to be substantial.

In conclusion, we suggest that reform of the system of work-based learning to provide high quality opportunities for those young people not in full-time education is a priority because young people need the opportunity to continue to learn beyond the period of compulsory education; and also because without a high-quality system of work-based learning, the foundations necessary for their lifelong learning will be absent.

Background

From a national economic point of view, skills are an important determinant of economic advantage. From the point of view of individual young people, the transition they make from education into employment shapes their attitudes to learning throughout their lives. We wrote the 'Working to Learn' report because research evidence points towards deep reasons for serious past policy failures in this area. Many initiatives have suffered because they were predicated on too simplistic a notion of the underlying problems that have to be solved. There is also a worrying trend of increasing narrowness of policy focus, with the possible exception of parts of the Modern Apprenticeship scheme. Several times what were originally broad-based policy aims have become narrowed down. Sometimes, as with the New Training Initiative, economic recession and the associated growth of youth unemployment resulted in a dramatic shortage of training places. The subsequent concentration on finding sufficient places inevitably undermined broader intentions. On other occasions, narrowing has been built in to policy design. For example, the development of NVQs has restricted the content and scope of training programmes, and led to an over-emphasis on qualifications. Yet research evidence has shown that the achievement of a qualification does not guarantee valuable learning, and that the learning context, the learning process and the expertise of those providing education and training are at least as important as qualification structures in determining scheme success.

In 1989, the CBI identified a set of minimum foundation training standards that it claimed would allow the British workforce to become competitive, concluding that:

> there is inadequate and insufficient education and training of young people to meet skill needs and the current situation is unsustainable... employers believe that there must be a quantum leap in the education and training of young people both to meet the needs of the British economy and to face the competition on even terms.
>
> (1989: 13)

None of the CBI standards has yet been met. Despite the expectations raised by the introduction of the Youth Training Scheme, the majority of the trainees left the scheme before completing their training and failed to achieve a full qualification; and in 1996 14 per cent or more of all school-leavers were not in full- or part-time post-compulsory education, nor receiving benefits, nor on YT.

Even now in the late 1990s, young people can still effectively end their participation in formalized learning when they leave school at 16. We doubt whether current approaches to young people's vocational education and training based on voluntarism can meet either the needs of young people themselves, or those of the economy. And we suggest that the potential of work-based learning to both motivate young people and develop their latent talents is woefully undervalued.

Many young people leave the education system disillusioned with formal learning: they have low expectations of what they can achieve and are little motivated by the quality of vocational provision. The economic and social costs of this continuing failure are very high. Unless initial foundation education and training is accessible to the whole young workforce, costs of subsequent training will be excessive and much will have to be remedial. If many young people are effectively excluded from education and training, or what they are given is unsuitable or of low quality, then they will have poor employment prospects and their ability to become participative citizens will be gravely impaired. Despite current concern about the role of education in creating a more civilized society, the lack of education for social citizenship remains a serious deficiency. Work-based learning for young people needs to address broad issues of social justice, and should do all that is possible to redress disadvantages of gender, ethnicity, social class, geographical location or sexual orientation.

A persistent problem faced by work-based learning programmes for young people in Britain is their low status. In recent years, as staying-on rates in full-time education have increased and participation in training schemes has correspondingly diminished, this problem may well have intensified. With the possible exception of the Modern Apprenticeship, these are schemes for other people's children, and for lower-skilled, lower-status and insecure jobs.

Yet work-based learning programmes will continue to play an important part in the lives of at least one in five of British young people, and of far more in certain areas and in certain groups. They must, therefore, be good enough for anyone to enter. They have a role to play in underpinning the upskilling of the British workforce and the progress towards a learning society. They have a place in extending social justice and in addressing problems of youth alienation which sometimes lead to crime – although improving work-based learning for young people could not achieve such ends on its own.

Employment needs and changes in the youth labour market

Shifts in policy for work-based training for young people have been accompanied by tremendous changes within the economy and the youth labour market. Changes include the massive and continuing shift of employment out of manufacturing and into the service sector; the decline in skilled and unskilled, often male, manual employment; the growing casualization of employment; increases in demand for female labour; a sharp rise in staying-on rates in post-compulsory education, and an overall reduction in the size of the youth labour market.

An increasing proportion of young people are being employed in part-time and temporary jobs, and youth unemployment is becoming increasingly concentrated among lowly qualified males. At the same time, the withdrawal of unemployment benefit for 16- and 17-year-olds, combined with the perceived low status of much YT provision among its potential clients, has led to a growing number of young people disappearing from the official statistics.[1] The existence of this 'unknown' group of significant proportions confirms the inadequacy of current provision for the age group, as well as underlining the weaknesses of existing mechanisms for monitoring the transition from school to work.

The potential client group for a future work-based learning route is likely to be significantly smaller than the mass provision envisaged for the original YTS, but it is not going to disappear. This smaller client group is volatile and varied in nature. Many will be among the least academically successful school pupils, although the Modern Apprenticeship pilots have shown that others with high ability will continue to choose the work-based route, perhaps especially at 17-plus. Some young people will move into and out of work-based learning, as their circumstances and career ambitions change during their transition to adulthood.

The progress of work-based learning for the 16–19 age group cannot easily be separated out from wider problems in the acquisition and usage of skills within the British labour market. The demand for more and better skills is patchy, and the remnants of the youth labour market are one of the areas where such demand may be weakest. Problems in demand stem, in part, from the product market strategies adopted by many companies, and associated systems of work organization and job design that offer limited opportunities for higher levels of skill to be deployed. If firms' demand for skills is to be increased, and the skills that are created are to be put to productive use, policy needs to address ways in which organizations across the economy can be encouraged to 'de-Taylorize' work, and better integrate skills into their competitive strategies. Policies that assume that the demand exists, and that all that is needed is institutional reconfiguration of the supply of skills, are doomed to failure. Many employers have shown little interest in upskilling their young workers. They withdraw many trainees from training before it is complete, and allow them to leave schemes without qualifications.

Prior to its defeat in the general election, the Conservative Government was offering two conflicting visions of economic development. One stressed the value of a skilled workforce as the sole source of sustainable long-term competitive advantage. The other told firms that the low labour costs that stem from a highly deregulated, flexible and casualized labour market would create the 'enterprise economy' of Europe. The latter strategy not merely offers an alternative to the former, but its pursuit tends to produce structural conditions within the labour market that make it increasingly difficult to develop a national workforce capable of sustaining a high-skill, high-commitment, high-quality competitive strategy (Keep and Mayhew, 1996). We need to be clear as a nation which vision we want to pursue, and why.

The need for a more highly skilled workforce is often asserted by a general consensus. If it is to be taken seriously, then there is a need to foster conditions and incentives that would encourage firms towards competitive strategies based on the delivery of high specification, high value-added goods and services needing a highly skilled workforce. Such strategies exist in many other developed countries. They have been absent in Britain, where it has been believed that market forces alone will produce the desired results.

Success is more likely to attend a work-based learning programme that forms part of a wider range of policies aimed at increasing demand for skills. Without a greater demand for higher skills among young employees and their current and future employers, it is harder to create the incentives that would underpin a successful scheme, and there is the danger that the skills being created would be ineffectively used in the absence of product market and competitive strategies that emphasize the delivery of goods and services of high quality.

If any form of work-based learning is to warrant even the levels of government expenditure now incurred, longer-term national employment needs must be reasserted, with a recognition that society as a whole, not just employers, has a legitimate interest in this being done. This means other stakeholders, such as the trade unions, representing employees' interests, should be involved in regulatory structures.

State-supported work-based learning programmes should be more widely targeted even than at national employment needs, important though they are. Such programmes also have a role to play in helping young people make the transition into being adult citizens and in addressing questions of social justice. Work-based programmes have enormous potential to widen young people's opportunity for learning. This broader objective is in the interests of the young people themselves and of society as a whole. It requires a general educational component to the programmes, to broaden the abilities and perspectives of young people in their transition from school to adulthood and work. This should be the case for all abilities, whereas in the Dearing proposals (1996), a limited notion of breadth seems to be reserved for the more able.

Many young people between the ages of 16 and 19 are cut off from education and training. Some are in insecure jobs where no training is provided. Others, sometimes referred to as 'status 0', have dropped out of official records, being absent from employment, education or training. In the current English and Welsh social and economic climate, a significant number of these young people see no incentives to join the official systems, preferring the attractions of informal labour market activity and crime (Istance *et al*, 1994). We need to offer such young people opportunities for learning that are accessible and of value, whether or not they are able to get a regular job. It is unreasonable to expect employers to shoulder the full responsibility for these broader aspects of a work-based learning programme.

The problems of voluntarism

Voluntarism for employers takes different forms. Employers are free to choose whether or not to involve themselves in youth training programmes. They are free to choose whether or not to train young people whom they employ. They are free to terminate any employment and/or training placement, subject to employment law, and they are being given increasing freedom to determine the nature of training a young person placed with them receives. But it is against the national interest for employers to provide full-time jobs without training to young people under the age of 19. There is a need for legislation to make it illegal to employ young people for more than the equivalent of three days per week, except as part of an approved training programme. Supplementary training should be provided for those employed part-time. This would ensure a level playing field for all employers, and reinforce the existing trend towards fewer jobs without training for 16–19-year-olds in Britain.

It would be unfair and unworkable to remove from employers the right to terminate employment or a training placement. However, young people should be protected from situations in which they are unable to continue training through no fault of their own. Every 16–19-year-old should, therefore, have an entitlement to an on-going learning programme which should continue regardless of contextual changes.

It would be unrealistic to expect employers to provide the breadth required in such a system on an entirely voluntary basis. There is need for government stimulation of the capacity of small and medium-sized firms – which account for a very large proportion of employment – to offer more and better work-based learning opportunities. There should be public funding of the broader educational elements, and the entitlements of learners to job-specific, occupational and general education need to be secured through nationally agreed frameworks, backed by legislation. For example, learning for citizenship and the wider employment agenda require all young people to have access to off-the-job learning, which very few small and medium-sized employers could possibly provide themselves. Further, many young people placed with small employers would require a second placement to give them greater breadth of experience. Although employer goodwill could provide such opportunities for some young people, it could not guarantee them for all. A voluntarist system involves the danger that those employers facilitating breadth and flexibility are disadvantaged if their training costs are higher than those of rivals who train more cheaply or do not train at all. Legislation could ensure the entitlement of young people, and give involved employers a level playing field.

So structures should be put in place to allow employers to determine the level of their involvement, with mechanisms for that to be supplemented where necessary. The right to choose the level of involvement should be balanced by an acceptance of nationally and locally agreed programme standards, so that the interests of young people, employers in general and the state as a whole could be safeguarded. This would require the replacement of employer control over training with partnership structures where employers have a key role and a strong voice, as should others such as education representatives and the trade unions.

Group Training Schemes could have a greater role in stimulating the training capacity of small and medium-sized firms. They expanded rapidly in the late 1960s, stimulated by Industry Training Boards – especially by the Engineering Industry Training Board. Their primary role was not to provide training, but to act as training departments for small firms which could not afford their own. This involved them helping small firms recruit and select trainees and devising training programmes for them (see Senker, 1992). In recent years, Group Training Schemes have been transformed into private training providers. Many still provide 'training department' services for small companies on a commercial basis. For example, they help small firms to secure TEC financial support for training and assessment to NVQ standards by dealing on their behalf with the paperwork, and also by training and providing assessors and external verifiers. However, the emphasis for many years has been on them competing in the training market.

To meet the wider social need for youth trainees which we identify, such organizations need to be encouraged and supported in devoting resources to partnership with employers to help stimulate and meet the need for many more young trainees. In addition, support needs to be made available to encourage and stimulate the creation and development of many more such organizations. They are still concentrated in specific sectors, particularly engineering, and such services need to be far more widely available to stimulate demand for trainees. The present availability of these services reflects market demand, but does not reflect adequately the important roles these organizations could play for the wider benefit of society.

There are continuing problems of finding work placements in areas of low employment and for those who need special support and/or a sheltered work environment. In these cases, the social costs of not making special provision outweigh the costs of providing alternative placements through appropriate forms of community activity, sports and recreational activity with a work dimension. The voluntary sector is a major potential provider both of training and work placements.

The need for an holistic approach

Motivation for the development of a high-quality work-based route derives from recognizing that the workplace can be a creative and motivating site for learning; and that this requires an integrated and holistic approach to enabling young people to combine on- and off-the-job learning experiences.

The concept of a 'community of practice' provides a useful model for considering how the different partners who come together on the work-based route might complement each other (Lave, 1991). At the centre of the community are the young people who combine theoretical and practical knowledge with skills to transform their practice. Both the workplace and the off-the-job learning must, therefore, be organized in such a way as to ensure the young people can demonstrate as well as acquire new skills and knowledge and, hence, their true potential as both employees and trainees. Because a high-quality work-based route should transcend the boundaries of both the traditional classroom and shopfloor/office, we would advocate the development of new pedagogical approaches. These might comprise a pedagogy of work (Fuller and Unwin, 1996) practised in such a way as to create meaningful links between learning, production and work organization. An expansive approach to learning would be adopted so that young people would be encouraged to question workplace practices.

The 'Working to Learn' proposals are intended to provide young people with a broad, work-based learning experience to prepare them for a future of uncertain change, and to help them to grow and develop as people. New forms of work-based learning for young people are most likely to be effective in the context of a new style and direction of policy-making at national level. A broad, holistic model of work-based learning needs to be underpinned by legislative authority. Such a programme should be built around partnerships at local and national levels, in which the sometimes conflicting but legitimate interests of various stakeholders can be expressed and considered. In addition to young people and employers, stakeholders with a legitimate interest in work-based education include trade unions, the state and professional providers of training and guidance.

At national level, delivery of work-based education and training would be through partnership between sectoral and/or occupational groupings and locally approved training providers. Occupational groupings would be particularly important where skills are cross-sectoral (for example, secretarial skills), and there would be the need for a national consortium of partners with a remit to look across sectors and help to minimize duplication of effort and provision. Sectors and/or occupations could create sectoral templates for the scheme in partnership with other interested parties. In the case of sectors with many small employers, NTOs could be encouraged to establish group training provision to deliver schemes.

Partnership is also important at the level of individual young people and employers, and the structure should reflect the legitimate needs of the different partners. In this context, the concept of entitlement is central. 'Working to Learn' would centre on the development of job-specific competence within the workplace, in ways similar to current youth training schemes and the Modern Apprenticeship. However, it should go much further. Young people studying for the 'Working to Learn' qualifications would receive a variety of learning experiences – a balance of on-, near- and off-the-job learning. Determining that balance would involve considering the needs of the different stakeholders and the availability of local facilities. Off-the-job experience and learning might be on the employer's premises, or elsewhere.

Each trainee would work in at least two different placements to ensure sufficient breadth in their learning experience. In many larger firms, this might mean spending time in more than one department. In other circumstances, a temporary move to a second employer might be necessary. In recognizing that young people change, that their original choices of training placement might cease to be appropriate, and that a key aim of 'Working to Learn' would be to nourish the growth of the person, the scheme would build in the opportunity to change occupation at least once, with no penalty to the young person, the employer or a training provider. Furthermore, all young people would be entitled to a period of work sampling if appropriate.

Educational breadth is essential to contribute to personal growth and as preparation for future changes in career and work. It should embrace communications and numeracy skills, but go well beyond them. Trainees might usefully learn about business organization and the role of trade unions. There should also be scope for trainees to follow studies of their choice.

Mechanisms would need to be provided for allocating the trainees to particular training providers and establishing that training and workplace arrangements are satisfactory. This function could be carried out by the Careers Service. A flexible form of development plan for an individual training programme should play a central role. This would differ from the action plans which have constrained developmental work and have tended to become bureaucratic and 'paper-driven' in their operation. It would focus on the evaluation of past and present experiences and on self-managed learning in order to anticipate future actions. A mentor would give the young person guidance and support, and where necessary would take the young person's part, for example by acting as sponsor or advocate and making arrangements. Mentors should have powers to intervene if either the young person was being inadequately trained or an employer or other training provider was not getting reasonable behaviour from a trainee.

A key part of learning for an occupation is to acquire extended experience in that occupation. For this reason, and to make possible the greater breadth advocated, full-time training should be a minimum of two years, with the possibility of extending this to three years where necessary. Those who learn fast should be stretched by developing their skills, knowledge and understanding further, not by early completion.

Broad frameworks would be developed nationally, but the details of the individual programmes will be worked out locally. We envisage the creation of sector-specific local partnerships between employers and other training providers, with the balance depending upon the ability and willingness of the individual employers to provide a high-quality, broad-based programme. Many employers, especially small ones, cannot cope with the complexities even of current narrowly focused training approaches, let alone programmes with the wider objectives advocated here. Their role is and should remain central, but there is a need for structures to support and enhance the contribution which such employers can reasonably make.

At local level, local learning co-ordination units (LLCUs) would have the prime responsibility for balancing the needs of the various partners involved in a training programme, while giving the legitimate needs of the young trainee primacy. Financial and regulatory functions would be operated at local level through the LLCUs. We envisage four kinds of training provider relating to the LLCU: employers, an extended network of group training schemes working in co-operation with smaller employers, private training organizations and Further Education (FE) colleges. The last three would all need to establish liaison arrangements with the trainee's employer through the LLCU. Providers would allocate an appropriately qualified mentor to each trainee.

Regulation would take place through sectoral or occupational boards which would establish standards for training courses and job placements within their remit. This would include stipulations about courses and placements leading to recognized qualifications, and in the case of employers acting as training providers, this might include the existence of structured work placement programmes, the employment of a recognized trainers and/or achievement of standards such as Investors in People.

Funding distortions: how resources could be used more effectively

Our proposals outlined above would cost significantly more than present arrangements in terms of the direct costs of the education and training provided. However, the complexity, inefficiency and ineffectiveness of present arrangements for administration are excessive to the extent that it is probable that our proposals could be delivered at little or no extra net cost to the public purse.

Funding methodologies for the UK's system of post-16 education and training are far too complex. The government funds education and training for 16–19-year-olds via four main systems:

1. Local Education Authority (LEA) school sixth forms receive funds through their LEA's Local Management of Schools (LMS) system.
2. Grant maintained school sixth forms receive funds from the Funding Agency for Schools.
3. FE and sixth-form colleges receive funds from the Further Education Funding Council (FEFC).
4. Work-based training providers receive funds from their local Training and Enterprise Councils (TECs).

Each of these systems operates in a unique way, even though some of the courses and qualifications they deliver may be the same. FE colleges and private training providers participate in an annual battle to secure adequate funding from a steadily reducing allocation granted by the DfEE. This annual scramble for funds has contributed to short-term planning and has acted against the development of a robust infrastructure to support the work-based route. Moreover, outcome-related funding has promoted financial priorities above concern for the quality of the learning process and the quality of learner achievement.

One of the main consequences of annual funding allocation and budget cuts is that providers cannot afford to invest in the capital equipment required for vocational subjects such as engineering and construction. Providers are forced to deliver courses which require little in the way of resources and can be taught largely in the classroom. Outcome-related funding also biases providers towards courses that are risk-free in terms of ensuring students will achieve the necessary passes and which take the minimum amount of time. In the current competitive climate, it is easier for training providers to increase profitability by cutting costs than by improving the quality of their programmes and their relevance to local labour market needs. Therefore, the pedagogical, occupational, locational and social aspects of the community of practice, identified by Fuller and Unwin in Chapter 10 in this book, are weak. The main controls on the quality of training provision are the achievement of specified qualifications and the attraction of customers. NVQs are inadequate to protect programme standards, and young people and many employers do not choose a training programme because of its quality or lack of it (Steedman and Hawkins, 1994). These factors combine to cause major distortions of funding priorities away from meeting the needs of local economies and providing young people with a meaningful occupational identity and status.

For the purposes of this chapter, the two most relevant funding systems are those administered by the FEFC and the TECs, as both provide resources for the work-based route. A key difference between TECs and colleges is in the level of funding freedom they enjoy to operate as individual organizations. All colleges have to comply with the FEFC's national funding methodology, whereas each TEC negotiates its own funding arrangements with its Government Regional Office (GRO).

Although they operate under different funding arrangements, colleges and TECs have to co-operate at local level to deliver the work-based route. Colleges, for example, may act as managing agents for YT and all colleges provide off-the-job training for both YT and Modern Apprenticeship. TECs control a national pot of some £20 million which colleges can draw on in their efforts to meet the needs of local labour markets. TECs and colleges may also collaborate on bids to the Single Regeneration Budget and to the European Social Fund.

The current system is manifestly inefficient, involving the waste of large funds in cumbersome administration. We estimated that there could be enough money in the present system to allow every 16-year-old in an annual cohort to study to NVQ level 3, based on an average cost per programme of £6,500. To liberate that amount of funding, however, requires a considerable alteration of the existing arrangements. Structural reform of the system could yield savings which could make major contributions to funding the additional costs inherent in some of our proposals.

Furthermore, the current funding regime ensures that much training effort is ineffective from an economic point of view, being deployed to create competencies which are relatively inexpensive to produce, rather than creating those competencies in demand and needed to enhance the productivity of the economy.

It is also relevant to take broader considerations of social cost and benefit into account. The Prince's Trust estimated that the average cost to the public purse of a crime committed by a young person (aged 10 to 20) was £2,620 in 1994. Given that 44 per cent of all crime is committed by young people, the bill for 1994 came to £5,500 million. By helping more young people to participate in interesting education and training directed at meeting the economy's needs, and by helping even slightly to reduce youth crime and its enormous costs, the work-based route outlined above could represent a first-class investment of public funds.

Conclusions

Central to the development of a high-quality work-based route is a recognition that the workplace can be a creative and motivating site for learning and that an integrated and holistic approach is required which enables young people to combine on- and off-the-job learning experiences. There are a number of deep-seated inter-related factors that have contributed to this country's inability to deliver a coherent, comprehensive, high-quality work-based education and training route for the young. These include an education system that in some cases produces young people who want nothing more to do with formalized learning; a society that has low expectations of what many young people can achieve; an implicit belief that many are destined for unemployment or a life of low-skill work that requires little in the way of formal preparation; cynicism (often well-founded) about the quality of provision on government training schemes aimed at the unemployed; the continued existence of employment opportunities for the young that offer little or no training; and little demand from UK employers for a general upskilling of the workforce. The result has been work-based learning for the young that has, in effect, been aimed largely at the lower achievers from the schools system. Many youngsters, especially from the most disadvantaged groups, have fallen through the gaps in the system and do nothing.

Reforming our system of work-based learning so as to provide high quality opportunities for those young people not in full-time education is a priority both because all young people need the opportunity to continue to learn beyond the period of compulsory education, and also because without a high-quality system of work-based learning for the young, the foundations necessary for an effective system of lifelong learning will be missing.

If there were a simple solution to these issues, it would have been discovered and adopted long ago. All aspects of the problem of youth training are complex, and some are intractable. Furthermore, economic and political circumstances, combined with recent institutional and political history, significantly constrain the avenues that are available for policy development. The legacy of earlier failed attempts to solve this problem tends to colour perceptions of what is possible, and the effort invested in the creation of institutional mechanisms and modes of delivery that have subsequently been discarded has led to disillusionment and cynicism about any future developments.

Unless we are willing to face up to these issues, and to tackle them in a broader and more co-ordinated fashion than hitherto, significant progress is unlikely in creating and extending what Guile and Young called the 'institution of apprenticeship' in Chapter 8 of this book. While it is important to build on the strengths of the work-based learning route embodied in the apprenticeship tradition, simply tinkering with the institutional mechanisms is not a sufficient response. Failure to attempt more far-reaching reform, based upon higher expectations, notions of entitlement and active partnership between all those involved in the provision of learning opportunities for the young, will mean that 10 years from now we will still be bemoaning the inadequacy of provision for young entrants to the labour force.

Note

1. These youngsters are not legally employed, not in receipt of benefit and not in any form of education or training. Research in South Wales (Istance *et al*, 1994) found that, rather than being the 1.5 to 4.5 per cent of the age group that official government estimates suggested, in South Glamorgan this group accounted for between 16 and 23 per cent of the age cohort at any one time. Research in other areas of the country has replicated these results and confirmed the scale and depth of the problem posed by these 'drop-out' youngsters (Wilkinson, 1995).

References

Bright, M (1998) Free lessons will stretch youth education further, *The Observer*, 17 May

CBI (1989) *Towards a Skills Revolution – A youth charter*, CBI, London

Dearing, R (1996) *Review of Qualifications for 16–19-year-olds*, London, SCAA

Evans, K, Hodkinson, P, Keep, E, Maguire, M, Raffe, D, Rainbird, H, Senker, P and Unwin, L (1997) *Working to Learn: A work-based route to learning for young people*, Institute of Personnel Development, London

Fuller, A and Unwin, L (1996) Reconceptualizing the work-based route: the potential of the Modern Apprenticeship, paper presented to the inaugural conference of the Work and Learning Network, Division of Education, University of Sheffield, 14 November

Istance, D, Rees, G and Williamson, H (1994) *Young People Not in Education, Training or Employment in South Glamorgan*, South Glamorgan Training and Enterprise Council, Cardiff

Keep, E and Mayhew K (1996) Evaluating the assumptions that underlie training policy, in *Acquiring Skills*, ed A Booth and D J Snower, Cambridge University Press, Cambridge

Lave, J (1991) Situated learning in communities of practice, in *Perspectives on Socially Shared Cognition*, ed L Resnick, J Levine and S Behrend, American Psychological Association, Washington DC

Senker, P (1992) *Industrial Training in a Cold Climate: An assessment of Britain's training policies*, Avebury Press, Aldershot

Steedman, H and Hawkins, J (1994) Shifting foundations: the impact of NVQs on Youth Training for the building trades, *National Institute Economic Review*, August, pp 93–102

Wilkinson, C (1995) *The Drop-out Society: Young people on the margin*, Youth Work Press, Leicester

Index

References in *italic* indicate figures or tables

Index

Visit Kogan Page on-line

Comprehensive information on
Kogan Page titles

Features include

- complete catalogue listings,
  including book reviews and
  descriptions

- special monthly promotions

- information on NEW titles and
  BESTSELLING titles

- a secure shopping basket facility
  for on-line ordering

PLUS everything you need to know
about KOGAN PAGE

http://www.kogan-page.co.uk